WORSHIP
AS
THEOLOGY

WORSHIP
AS
THEOLOGY
FORETASTE OF
GLORY DIVINE

Don E. Saliers

ABINGDON PRESS

Nashville

WORSHIP AS THEOLOGY
FORETASTE OF GLORY DIVINE

Copyright © 1994 by Abingdon Press

Scripture quotations noted NRSV are from the New Revised Standard Version Bible, Copyright © 1989 by the Division of Christian Education of the National Council of the Churches
of Christ in the USA. Used by permission.

Library of Congress Cataloging-in-Publication Data

Saliers, Don E., 1937–
    Worship as theology: foretaste of glory divine/Don E. Saliers.
        p. cm.
    Includes bibliographical references and index.
    ISBN 0-687-14693-3
    1. Public Worship.   2. Liturgics.   3. God—Worship and love.
    I. Title
    BV15.S25   1994
    264'.001—dc20   94-17519

The poetry on page 171 is from T. S. Eliot's "Choruses from *The Rock*" from *Collected
Poems, 1909–1962;* by permission of Harcourt Brace Jovanovich and Faber and Faber Ltd.

The excerpt on page 184 is from "All Who Love and Serve Your City" by Erik Routley ©
1969 Stainer & Bell Ltd. Reproduced from *New Songs for the Church* Book 1.

The quotation on page 199 is from "When In Our Music God Is Glorified," words by Fred
Pratt Green. Words copyright © by Hope Publishing Company, Carol Stream, Illinois 60188.
All rights reserved. Used by permission.

The excerpt on the dedication page and on page 202 is from, "Arise, Shine Out, Your Light
Has Come" by Brian Wren. Words copyright © 1989 by Hope Publishing Company, Carol
Stream, Illinois 60188. All rights reserved. Used by permission.

The hymn "Toda la Tierra" (All Earth Is Waiting) on page 224, English translation © 1989
United Methodist Publishing House. Reprinted from *The United Methodist Hymnal* with
permission.

The hymn "Sleepers Wake" on page 247, was written by Carl P. Daw, Jr., and © 1982 by
Hope Publishing Company, Carol Stream, Illinois 60188. All rights reserved. Used by
permission.

04 05 06 07 08 09 10 — 18 17 16 15 14 13 12 11 10

In memory of
Fr. Michael Marx, Order of Saint Benedict
who lived and taught me the meaning of
ora et labora

The dancing air shall glow with light,
and sun and moon give up their place,
when love shines out of every face,
our good, our glory, and delight.

CONTENTS

PREFACE

Every book is a result of sustained conversation. The pages that follow are especially so, joining a growing range of discourse known as liturgical theology. Its origins are not in academic circles, but in the travail of Christian churches I know and in which I have worshiped. Thus it is a book originating in Western, ecumenically-informed Protestant circles.

How does one worship God in an age of confusion and suspicion about the very traditions which provide the means of prayer and liturgy we have? Is the vision of human life and the world which is actually being celebrated in our churches faithful to the revelation of God in Jesus? Can Christian liturgy actually address the situation of our time and place—in an age some have called an age of abandonment by God? Or, in specifically North American terms, can Christian worship survive a consumerist culture of exaggeration and forgetfulness?

This book proposes to rethink worship as an eschatological art. On one level it may be read as a series of investigations aimed at elucidating the meaning and point of what we do in worshiping God. That is, we will be thinking *about* liturgy. But it must also be read as thinking *with* the primary acts of common worship. This is more at the heart of my concern: to trace the contours of particular modes of prayer, symbol, and ritual actions which constitute Christian liturgy. I desire to show how the praying, the common meal, or the singing *is* theological, and more particularly, is *eschatological.* All this, a unique art.

I am indebted to my students at Emory University, and to those in summers at Notre Dame and St. John's University, who have listened me into speech, helped me ask the questions, and provided valuable critique when my ideas were quite rough and incomplete. To my colleagues in the North American Academy of Liturgy, who will recognize my Berakah Award response in these pages, I am deeply indebted for their sustaining me and continuing the conversation, especially within the liturgical theology study group.

Several hospitable occasions to explore in public some of the present themes and turns of inquiry were afforded me by lectureships at Bangor Theological Seminary (the William French Stearns Lectures), Brite Divinity School at TCU (the Oreon Scott Lectures), and most immediately, the Valparaiso Liturgy and Music Institute Lectures in 1992. The Valparaiso Lectures produced early drafts of what are now chapters 1, 2, and 13. For hospitality and encouragement, I wish especially to thank Walter Dickhaut, Jr., George and Deborah van Deusen Hunsinger at Bangor, and David Truemper at Valparaiso.

Certain chapters have incorporated sections of earlier articles. Parts of chapter 5 are taken from "Liturgy Teaching Us to Pray," an address given at Notre Dame and published in *Liturgy in Context,* edited by Eleanor Bernstein, C.S.J. (Collegeville: The Liturgical Press, 1990), pp. 62-82. Chapter 11 is a reworked version of "Liturgy and Ethics: Some New Beginnings," first published in the *Journal of Religious Ethics,* vol. 7, no. 2 (Fall 1979), pp. 173-190. Parts of chapter 13 incorporate material from "Liturgical Aesthetics" in *The New Dictionary of Sacramental Worship,* ed. Peter Fink, S.J. (Collegeville: A Michael Glazier Book, The Liturgical Press, 1990). Chapter 4 evolved from a lecture given to a conference on Karl Barth sponsored by the Christic Institute at Stony Point, New York.

Persons who have been directly helpful in reading portions of the manuscript include Bruce Morrill, S.J., who assisted with several bibliographical footnotes, and my treasured colleague, Fred B. Craddock, whose appreciative critique came at the right time (just like his preaching). Gordon Lathrop, whose work in liturgical theology has influenced my own thinking, encouraged me from the beginning of the project. I am deeply indebted to the Reverend Dr. John A. Berntsen for key insights into Barth, and certain phrasings of those insights, especially in the section "acknowledgment," stimulated by work leading to his provocative dissertation on liturgical themes in Barth. To these, and to my other colleagues at Emory University, I am deeply grateful.

Special thanks goes to Barbara Thompson, whose theologically alert mind complemented her tireless secretarial skills in preparing the manuscript. To Janet Gary's gracious response to my printing needs and to Marilyn Horrisberger for ridding the computer of that nasty virus, my gratitude. I wish to thank the Lilly Endowment for a grant to carry out hymnal and liturgical research in local congregations and for enabling me to spend time away from the classrooms for the writing of these pages.

Finally, gratitude must be expressed to those communities with whom I have been privileged to worship during the catechumenate leading to this book: the University Worship Community at Cannon Chapel, Emory University; the thirteen United Methodist churches in my hymnal research project; and St. John's Abbey Church, whose praying community has formed me more deeply than words can say.

INTRODUCTION

This book stands at the intersection of three pathways of reflection: liturgical studies, theological aesthetics, and eschatology. Their crossing is less familiar to us because we rarely stop there. I attempt in these pages to linger where these disciplines converge in order to trace the lay of the land. In one sense this book is a kind of topographical map, asking "what can be seen from this vantage point?" In another sense this book is a series of investigations asking "who lives and what may grow there?" Both questions come together in the domain of liturgical theology.

Over a period of time I have become increasingly convinced that prayer and the liturgical life of the church are indispensable to Christian theological reflection. Encouraged and taught by a number of theologians who are also persuaded that this is true, I offer this extended essay as investigations in liturgical theology. The fountainhead for many of us working on relations between Christian liturgy and theology remains Alexander Schmemann, the American Russian Orthodox theologian, whose book *Introduction to Liturgical Theology* opened up a new theological world to me and many others.[1]

These investigations traverse territory familiar to those who have read Romano Guardini, Aidan Kavanagh, Robert Taft, Mary Collins, Geoffrey Wainwright, David Power, or Mary Douglas. The eschatological nature of liturgy is well established, as is the fundamental understanding that liturgy is enacted, and is always embedded and embodied in particular cultural forms. At the same time, many pastors and churchgoers engaged in the actual practices of worship (planning, leading, and participating) are not familiar with the ecumenical scholarly discussion over the past twenty-five years. Such readers deserve to know and to develop new insights concerning Christian worship and the relationships between liturgy, art, and human life. I hope to have put some recently established ways of approaching Christian liturgy together in a new and illuminating way.

The central thesis of this book is simple: Christian liturgy as rite and as prayer is thoroughly eschatological. How this is so is the burden of my investigations. Can the study of liturgy contribute to the renewal of church and theology in our age? This is a time of dissatisfaction with inherited forms. Many suspect liturgy to be a means of suppression or social imperialism of one kind or another. Yet ours is also a time of extraordinary ecumenical ferment and retrieval. One way in which the study of liturgy can contribute to the renewal of theology is precisely by exploring the particular manner in which authentic Christian worship is theological, and specifically eschatological.

During the writing of these pages I have also spent a year studying a dozen or so diverse local congregations—worshiping, listening, observing, singing, and praying with them. My aim was initially to find out how these particular United Methodist churches were receiving a new denominational hymnal in its first years of life. What actually occurs to worshipers when new hymns, ritual patterns, and prayer texts are introduced and used? What impact has this hymnal had on the singing practices and the "sung theology" of these congregations? How have people adapted to and resisted such changes and why? These were the questions addressed to particular congregations. What I now see is how observing them at song, prayer, and celebration directed my own attention to questions of aesthetics and eschatology in this book.

Out of hundreds of hours of group and individual interviews, four comments struck home with me. These are the nontechnical, anecdotal access to what lies behind much of the reflection in this book. One layman, unhappy with the new hymnal, quipped, "This can't be much of a Christian songbook; it's got all those foreign languages in it!" He was the same person who said that he finds few hymns not connected with his childhood very singable— the "languages" of liturgy, indeed. A slightly xenophobic remark opens up questions that go well beyond the appearance of Spanish or Latin or Lakota in a hymnal.

A second instance came as a disarming remark by an eight-year-old member of a children's choir who, when asked why she liked a particular new hymn they had learned, replied, "Cause the words taste so good"—aesthetics, indeed.

The third comment occurred in the sacristy following a well-celebrated baptismal renewal involving the whole congregation. "Was that a sacrament or a revival we just had?" she asked with tears of joy, instead of, "I couldn't tell the difference!" — liturgical prayer and human emotion, indeed.

The fourth comment came in a sobering letter sent after one of my weekends at a particular church. A person wrote, "With all the changes in worship and the new songs in the hymnal, where's the hope?" Indeed, where's the hope? This is a question about Christian liturgy and the pathos of contemporary life. It is the question that haunts my inquiry. It is a question about eschatology and the worship we offer God. It is a question about what the Christian community has to offer the world.

The phrase "worship as theology" may seem odd to some readers. To those who are used to a clear distinction between "doing theology" and worship or prayer, this may seem an unhelpful blurring of important differences. After all, is not theology critical thinking, well-ordered, which argues and interprets ideas about God? And is not prayer and participation in the public liturgy of the church a matter of "experience" and social practices, or at least of uncritical habit? This book seeks to show that this way of dividing theological thinking and liturgical participation simply fails. By contrast, I argue that the continuing worship of God in the assembly *is* a form of theology. In fact, it is "primary theology." Worship in all its social-cultural idioms is a *theological* act.

To other readers, knowledgeable in recent developments in the field of liturgical theology, the phrase may seem to ignore the differences between a general concept of worship (which includes devotional prayer and individual adoration of God) and liturgical worship that refers to public rites with specific histories. If we follow a line first drawn by Alexander Schmemann's *Introduction to Liturgical Theology* through works by Kavanagh and others, we will contrast "liturgical theology" proper from a "theology of worship" and a "theology oriented to worship"—a systematic example of which is found in Geoffrey Wainwright's magisterial *Doxology*.[2] A recent study, *What Is Liturgical Theology?*, has drawn such categories with some precision.[3]

This book does, in fact, concentrate on the liturgical assembly of the church. But rather than *liturgy* I choose the term *worship* since the latter suggests a vital activity that is a whole form of life. "Liturgy" can, though it need not, be taken to refer narrowly to what is on paper in the books, or simply to the historically received and authorized rites. My interest is with the *performed liturgy*, the actual "lived" liturgy that throws together our lives and what we do in the assembly. It is the worship of God in cultic enactment *and* service of God in life that constitutes the "primary theology." This is the foundation of all critical reflective theology. It may be helpful to distinguish the theology realized in the liturgical act from theological reflection that follows from it. As we shall see, the very attempt to "state" what is prayed in the act of worship already is a kind of "secondary liturgical theology."[4]

At the same time, these investigations also show how reflective and critical theology enters into the liturgical texts and hence in the church at prayer. In this light one may view the inclusion of a conversation with Karl Barth (chapter 4) on worship and prayer as necessary to theology. This is basic to my own account of the reciprocity between worship and theology.

In Part 1 the complex set of relationships between liturgy as an act of assembled believers and theology as knowledge of God and the world is explored. From the outset the anthropological (human) and theological (divine) features are taken together, beginning with human suffering and the divine involvement, and the reciprocity of doxology and doctrine in chapters 1 and 2. The initial characterization of Christian liturgy as radically eschatological follows in chapter 3 concluding with a more formal consideration of the orientation to worship in Barth's theology in chapter 4.

In Part 2, I present an interpretation of four principle modes of liturgical prayer. Each, if examined carefully, is a source of theological insight into the relation between God and humankind in the context of creation and history. Each has something to do with the presence and absence of God. So praise and thanksgiving are viewed as a "school" for gratitude, and intercession a "school" for compassion. But neither praising God nor petitions to God are possible without invoking the name and Spirit of God. However, chapter 7 is the hinge. For in lamentation and in confessing human sin we find the test of truthfulness emerging. All these modes are found in the liturgy over time, and all are co-present in the eucharistic prayers, both in the texts and in the ritual action of the gathered assembly.

We turn in Part 3 to the human social and cultural contexts in which all Christian liturgy takes place, tracing how the words we use in worship depend radically upon the symbolic languages that constitute the deeper aspects of participation in the worship of God. Because liturgy is always culturally embedded and embodied, the task of theological elucidation of worship must always be accompanied by a "culture critique" as well. In these chapters I explore how the very means of cultural communication in worship can and do become the means of the prophetic critique of both liturgy and culture. Thus chapter 11 sketches one crucial way of conceiving the inner unity of liturgy and ethics, of prayer and service. This shows the problem and the limitations of Western, Protestant ways of seeing.

In the final chapters, I pose the question of how liturgy may be understood as an eschatological art. The "aesthetics" of the rites—both intrinsic and in the "performance" (enactment) of the texts and actions—are part of what makes them eschatological. For what is seen and what is heard in Word and sacrament over time reveals what is not yet fully seen or heard in human life. The final chapter takes some specific elements of Advent as a touchstone to the central claim that Christian liturgy is best understood as eschatological prayer and action.

PART ONE

Liturgy and Theology

1

HUMAN PATHOS AND DIVINE ETHOS

The American writer-contemplative Annie Dillard has taught many of us about prayer and worship. In her book *Holy the Firm*, she contrasts the compelling and fearsome mystery of life in nature with the timid and superficial behavior of those of us who gather in churchly assemblies to worship. She speaks about our surface meetings with God, referring to the "set pieces of liturgy as certain words which people have successfully addressed to God without getting killed."[1] Elsewhere Dillard challenges the cliches and commonplaces of our worship art: "on the whole," she quips:

> I do not find Christians, outside of the catacombs, sufficiently sensible, aware, of conditions. Does anyone have the foggiest idea what sort of power we so blindly invoke? Or, as I suspect, does no one believe a word of it? The churches are children, playing on the floor with their chemistry sets, mixing up a batch of TNT to kill a Sunday morning.[2]

We should be lashed to the pews because God just might awake and draw us out to new depths. Dillard is not rejecting the art of Christian worship or the arts we employ in worshiping God. Rather, she is calling attention to the fact that our *leitourgia*, our life of prayer and work with God and neighbor, is much more demanding than the habitual "this is the way we go to church" would ever lead us to believe. Indeed, the waking God may "draw

us out to where we can never return."[3] That is Easter and Pentecost. That is the threat of authentic liturgy. But that is also the
hope: this is why we assemble.

In such assemblies, to meet God is to meet our own human lives
in unexpected form, and to "pray without ceasing" is the stretch
of a whole lifetime—in season and out of season, in joy and in
pain, in fear and in hope, in great gratitude and in sorrow, in cries
for justice and healing, and in sheer ecstatic delight in the beauty
of God. This is the offer of our humanity restored and empowered.
Human pathos is drawn to the divine ethos of faithful worship.
By *pathos* I mean the human suffering of the world. Human
emotions and passions, despite vast differences in cultural patterns, provide access to what is counted real. By the divine *ethos*,
I mean the characteristic manner in which liturgy is a self-giving
of God to us, the encounter whereby grace and glory find human
form. Christian liturgy transforms and empowers when the vulnerability of human pathos is met by the ethos of God's vulnerability in word and sacrament.[4]

Such is the hopeful vision of what the Christian assembly may
be. Underneath Dillard's critique is a profound conviction about
the power of God to break in upon us. And yet the human
situation we face seems to go against such a confident hope.
Jacques Ellul, in *Hope in Time of Abandonment*, portrays a world
from which God seems to have withdrawn. The daily news
throws into our homes "a hundred disjointed and unpredictable
happenings."[5] Incoherence and the absence of God seems the
dominant pattern in our social and political experience. The world
is "incomprehensible, touchy, disquieting as ghosts' veils, a broken world, full of holes and full of the irrational. There is nothing
to be done about it."[6]

Ellul speaks boldly of such absence. Has God decided to abandon the world? He cites a French novelist, Monteilhet, who observes in *Policiers pour la forme*:

> There's a rare quality of silence surrounding certain atrocities, an end-of-
> the-world silence, more frightening even than instant justice. One has the
> impression that a presence has been withdrawn which could one day fill
> everything. That total absence of charity takes the form of the low-pressure
> areas which bring storms.[7]

In such an age we cry out to call God back to life; to move God to end our abandonment. So Ellul urges hope. Apart from such hope for God, "the only thing left is childish indignation, pompous proclamation, and fruitless agitation."[8] Ellul writes with dramatic extremity. But there is already extremity in biblical passages that cry out in the experience of abandonment, such as in Psalm 88: "You have caused my companions to shun me." Such observations force us to ask what can be said, if anything, about the presence of God which Christian liturgy promises.

Others have spoken of the banality of evil in our world. Regarded from the point of view that dwells on the enormity of human suffering, it is a terrifying world. When we try to comprehend the enormous suffering caused by an earthquake in which thousands are lost, much less the unthinkable human genocides haunting the twentieth century, the forces driving nature and human history are not benign, but malevolent. We can and do sort out natural evil that befalls human beings in earthquakes, fires, and floods, from the moral evil wittingly and unwittingly wrought by human beings upon one another and the created order. But such distinctions may hold little comfort for those who go to church. Little wonder that most who believe in God try to avoid thinking about the world in these ways. Yet traces are heard in every Sunday's gathering: "deliver us from evil"; "help, save, pity, and defend us."

Still, this is a beautiful world. The sheer wonderment of life, of moon rise or dawn, or of the luxurious variety of living things, is its own testimony. The face of the beloved, the play of children, persons of moral integrity, human creativity in music, painting, film, literature, and all folk arts from every society and culture—all these offer a glimpse of that which seems deeper than all ugliness and violence. Such are clues, perhaps, to something good and beautiful permeating human beings. Poets sing of this: "There lives the dearest freshness deep down things," as in Gerard Manley Hopkins' poem "God's Grandeur."[9]

No wonder persons who believe in God find confirming evidence in their consent to being, and in attending to the particularities of everyday life. Little wonder that religious gatherings for worship should turn and return to thanks and praise for such a world, both in the order of nature and in human relationships. The Hebrew Psalms speak such a language: "O LORD, our Sovereign, how majestic is your name in all the earth . . . When I look at your heavens" (Ps. 8:1*a*, 3*a*).

A beautiful world, a terrifying world. A world of intense presences, a world of absence and abandonment. Such a mixed texture of human consciousness is so great as to generate dualistic views of the whole world. Hence the "forces of good" forever against the "forces of evil"; light against the darkness; soul against the body; and the spiritual/intellectual warring against the physical world.

What does this seeming digression into questions of good and evil, the beauty and the horror, have to do with Christian worship in general, and Christian liturgy in particular? The short answer is: everything. For unless the forms, the language, and the style of our worship of God as a gathered community can confront and live honestly with these disparate features of our life-world, our liturgies become, sooner or later, a self-serving flight from what is real. More pointedly to the concerns of this book, when we ignore this mixed texture of the world, our liturgy ceases to be knowledge of God. For the human pathos implied in living with these contrasts is, as I shall try to show, a condition for authentic Christian liturgy, whether "high" or "low," in all circumstances. There is a theological as well as an anthropological reason for this that will unfold in our explorations of the act of liturgical assembly in the name of Jesus.

Where do we begin our explorations? Perhaps with the Psalms which, for Jewish and Christian liturgical traditions alike, have provided powerful juxtapositions of precisely these realities: the suffering, the sense of abandonment, the glory and the praise, the laments and the thanksgivings. Some, like Psalm 88, are left untouched by praise. Others fluctuate wildly between anxiety and hope:

Why are you cast down, O my soul, and why are you disquieted within me? Hope in God; for I shall again praise him, my help and my God. (Psalm 42:5)

24

But we could also begin with the intercession or prayer of the people. Many early texts of the intercessions for all sorts and conditions of human beings are set side-by-side with the most glorious praise of God. But so may a "free-church" contemporary liturgy throw together thanksgivings and excruciating cries of pain and calls for justice. Indeed, we find this juxtaposition in the very heart of the holy meal: blessing and thanking God for bread and wine, which contain the hurt and suffering of the world condensed into one human life: "my body given for you, my blood shed for you." Clearly, there are many places we might begin our exploration of the conjoining of human pathos with the liturgical ethos of God's promised self-giving. The strategy of this book is to begin with the Advent character of all Christian prayer and worship, with the pathos and ethos of remembering God in hope. In Parts 2 and 3, we move to a detailed study of praying and celebrating the Word and mystery of the gospel.

For now we turn to the human conditions that surround the theological act of gathering around the book, the font, and the table of the Lord. Christian liturgy is both God-attentive and thoroughly grounded in human life always found in specific social/cultural patterns. How these are related to liturgy as a unique art of God's ethos is to be discovered. I shall argue that this art is best understood as the art of receiving God's future for the world—that is, an eschatological art. Understanding Christian liturgy as an eschatological art requires, especially in our age, setting forth some conditions for understanding.

Initial Soundings: Liturgy and Pathos

Some essential reminders can set the framework for the chapters that follow. We have all been taught to rethink worship as communal action: response, dialogue, and communion with God. Communal worship is first and last blessing God, praising and giving thanks. Certainly the whole economy of the Christian liturgy is much more than praising, thanking, and blessing, but it is rooted and grounded in these. Such praise and thanksgiving is evident in our eucharistic prayers:

"It is right, and a good and joyful thing, always and everywhere to give thanks to you." If only we were to take that in with our lives over time, we could understand ourselves and our world so differently. The language of praise, the language of the vocative in addressing God is *enacted* by human beings in our speaking, listening, singing, eating, and drinking.[10]

When we come to the liturgy on the Lord's Day, "until the day of the Lord," we gather in that *deep pathos of memory* of God with us. Still deeper is the *pathos of hoping* for God's promises yet to be fulfilled. Without remembering that creation is a gift, without remembering that our lives are gifts, without remembering that the whole history of God with the earth points toward the liberation from bondage and death made real in Jesus, we can never begin to grasp the hope that is offered to us in the symbols, words, and the ritual actions of the Christian assembly. Without the desire and yearning for history to be different, memory becomes nostalgia or self-serving.[11] If we are to make any sense at all of God's offer of salvation, we must attend to the pathos of those memories and that hope. Born as response to God—who God is and what God has done—authentic liturgical life lifts up all that is human to the transforming power of communal life animated in the Spirit. The study of liturgy is everywhere and always the study of what real men and women do and suffer in their lives. Liturgy thus enacts that which devotional prayer alone cannot. The assembly of believers, the gathered body, comes out of the pathos of living and struggling, seeking God together with restless hearts. This itself is an intensification of social being before God. The very act of remembering who God is and what God has done confers dignity and honor and deepens the pathos of those who gather. "You have held us worthy to stand before you and [praise] you." Later we must ask how this corporate sense of our social being is possible in contemporary American life.

Liturgy is an intentionally gathered community in mutual dialogue with God's self-communication. We are to bring our *pathos* to the time and place, to the book and the table of living memory that is God speaking to us. In every generation, God calls forth a people in their time and circumstance to be a holy people. Therefore, liturgy is the art of acknowledging the Holy One who creates us, who loves us into freedom, and who knows the pathos of our lives.

Let us then consider some initial definitions of liturgy. Think first of the church gathered, as the ongoing prayer and word of Jesus Christ—and the ongoing self-giving of God in and through Christ's body in the world made alive by the Spirit. Christian liturgy is something prayed *and* something enacted, not something thought about or merely "experienced." Liturgy is a common art of the people of God in which the community brings the depth of emotion of our lives to the ethos of God. In these acts we discover who we are, but also and primarily, we discover who God is in this art. If understood fully, liturgy is doing God's will and work in the world while providing human beings with a time and a place for recalling who God is and who we are before God, and identifying the world to itself—what it is in God's eyes—the pathos of this terrifying and beautiful world. Therefore the ongoing prayer of Jesus, and the ongoing word and self-giving of Jesus, shapes our existence and brings *us* to expression. Worship that focuses primarily on self-expression fails to be worship in Spirit and in truth.

If this is so, that the art of joining Jesus in his liturgy is God's ongoing work, then the promise of real life is given and received. Here the essential connections between communal worship, devotional prayer, and work are found. The words, the texts, the songs, the actions, and the symbols of the liturgy, *wait* for us, just like the Holy Scriptures wait in each context for a fresh rereading. Symbols without the life experiences of the believers brought to the liturgy can indeed become empty. Individual faith without the symbols of liturgical action can remain blind and isolated. Joseph Gelineau, in *The Liturgy Today and Tomorrow*, reminds us of this connection by observing: "Only if we come to the liturgy without our hopes and fears, without our longings and our hungers, will the rite symbolize nothing and remain an indifferent or curious object."[12]

Our pathos, the reality of human life, our daily struggle to make sense of longings, hopes, fears, joys, provides an experiential link. In the language of the Second Vatican Council, "full, active, and conscious participation" in this art depends in the first instance upon our acquaintance with prayer and daily life over the whole range of our humanity. Put another way, participation in the liturgy requires our humanity at full stretch. Let us say that liturgical celebration is that place of convergence where our lives are brought together about the book, the font, and the table of the Lord in which the grace of God becomes audible, visible, palpable, kinetic.[13] In this way the ongoing prayer and work of Christ in the church must always and everywhere be *both* fully communal and deeply and profoundly personal. This reminds us of the central paradox of the Christian life itself. Christ, in and through the Spirit, prays for the world and for us in and through our prayers in his name. Hence, Christian liturgy both forms us in certain characteristic ways of being human, and brings these things to expression through the arts of worship.

The very act of gathering is a slow, inexorable dance by which we assemble in the name of and by invitation of Jesus. One can see this in the gathering of very ordinary people on an ordinary Sunday morning in a very ordinary church. When we least expected it, on the most "flat EKG" Sunday you can imagine, people gather and we may not have noticed the inexorable dance because it seems so habitual and so unremarkable. Then they make their way to the altar and with those rough hands that know the farmer's art or skill of the carpenter or that have cared for many a person by many a sickbed, stretch out and with trembling receive their own mystery back. Yes we have gathered, and this dance and song is real. Some traditions go on to sing the question, "Shall we gather at the river?" Suddenly the ordinary gathering becomes itself a metaphor for what is given in the invitation itself. The words and the dance mean *more* than we can speak.

A wonderful story out of my own ministry may help make this point about the pathos we bring. Several years ago, a former student of mine who had a parish in Florida invited me to come down shortly after the Christmas season and spend a day with him. After the Sunday service, he said, "We're going to see Myrtie." So I went with Gary to see Myrtie, driving out to one of those low, one-story buildings surrounded by the parking lot into which you enter and see the wheelchairs. And you smell the smells of a place of old age and dying. Being the Christmas season, there were many in their housecoats with small trinkets pinned here and there, and the Christmas carols softly reverberated on a Wurlitzer somewhere.

Down the hall and to the last of the doors at the end of this long hallway, we came to Myrtie's room. There she was, expecting us. Gary said, "Myrtie, this is Don; Don, this is Myrtie." And Myrtie looked at me and she said, "Oh boy." We sat down, and Gary said, "The children made some Christmas gifts for you this morning, Myrtie." She said, "Oh boy." One by one, the small gifts were unwrapped—a Christmas tree ornament, the small Christmas card made up by the children in the Sunday school, a little book, and a small candle. Each one she, with Gary's help, unwrapped with her one good hand. Then some conversation, mostly between Gary and me, and then Gary said, "I've brought the communion." "Oh boy," she said. And the piece of bread and the prayer and her receiving it, saying "Oh boy"; and the cup and the same. Then a few farewells and out we went down the hall, back past those smells, out the front door, and into the parking lot. But just as I was getting into the car, I glanced up and there she was at the window, her good hand having parted half of the curtain. She stood waving, and I could see her mouth shape "Oh boy."

A stroke, I learned from Gary, had reduced this remarkable woman to two words. That was her language. But, oh, what a language! In that short sequence of events that day, I was stunned by how the art of God is to take human pathos and give it an ethos for its flourishing—a place and a time. In this case, few gestures and few sounds; but, oh, what music. So I carry it as a living icon. When I'm in a great festival place, I bring Myrtie with me. When I hear great, great singing, I can hear echoing through it the *cantus firmus*: "Oh boy." A kind of hallelujah, Amen.

Now let me put the point in perhaps a less immediate way. Liturgy is the ongoing mutuality of God and the pathos of our human life. The liturgy exists, the classical definitions say, to glorify God and to proclaim the mystery of faith while sanctifying all that is human before God. Glorifying God, giving praise and thanks together, is a way of coming to know God and ourselves. Yet this is precisely how life comes to fullest truth and to the realization of what it is to exist in faith. To discover and to welcome the gift of creatureliness is to perceive the holiness in this divine art. This means that the cry of pain may comingle with our praise and our thanks. These are offered together in solidarity with the whole church so our daily life is not fully received or understood until it is conjoined with others in the art of praising God. T. S. Eliot expressed this well in "Choruses from *The Rock*":

> What life have you if you have not life together?
> There is no life that is not lived in community,
> And no community not lived in praise of GOD.[14]

Our current American cultural search for intimacy and our experience of so much laceration and fragmentation, so much privatization, so much loneliness stands out in bold relief. The liturgy waits patiently for us to bring this, and to bring it expectantly. No one who hears and sees the litany of human laceration night after night on the eleven o'clock news should abide Christian liturgy without our cry, our cry on behalf of others, our cry on behalf of this beautiful world so far from God. Not all of us who say the words in the liturgy participate fully or are fully formed, and not every Sunday can we bring it all; there's so much moral pain to bring and much diversion. Jesus' words still sting: "Not everyone who says to me, 'Lord, Lord,' will enter the kingdom" (Matt. 7:21). This is the very theological tension we face, the "already" of God's faithful word and the "not yet" of our pathos in time and place.

To remember God with the Scriptures, to remember God with the holy men and women in all times and places, to remember God with the angels and the archangels and all the company of heaven, those loved and lost and now in the communion of saints, means that we seek to be living reminders of these truths.[15] This leads us, as Annie Dillard reminds us, right back into a place far from home. We are taken by the living God to places we do not wish to go. I'd rather have a liturgy that was my language, my values, my self-congratulation, my "feeling good." But God will not have it this way, and certainly not among those of us belonging to this community of memory and witness. We are to nurture the ethos in which the Spirit of God may work to bring our pathos to God's saving mystery.

Modes of Prayer, Patterns of Experience

There's another way of looking at the pathos and ethos of Christian liturgy. By looking at four basic modes of prayer together with the liturgy, we discover how we may be formed in certain necessary human ways of being before God. When we bring our own suffering of the world, our own emotions and desires and longings to the liturgy, we find a language there in which they may be articulated. We are not always able to do so. Much of the time we are distracted or simply tired. Yet when we come ready to participate, we can perhaps see more clearly how certain patterns of human experience are brought to life in the assembly by word, song, and sign-act. The very modes of prayer found in the liturgy exist over time to form us in our own primary humanity before God.

The first mode of prayer is *the language of gratitude*, blessing, and thanking God: Blessed are you, ruler of all things, creator of all that is, for everything that we now name. Thus, liturgy is like a school for gratitude that takes time, allowing us to name every single thing. Some great liturgies in the past are like this, such as the eucharistic prayer in *Apostolic Constitutions*, Book VIII, which if ever used, of course, would have named everything![16] Or that final song of the psalter (Psalm 150) that just won't quit until it names everything breathlessly. In praising and thanking God we name all things in creation, but also all things in our lives.

> Blessed are you, O Lord our God, who have caused my ear to hear the first bird sing this morning; blessed are you, you have caused me to look upon the face of my friend; blessed are you, you have caused me to look upon the face of death. Bless the Lord, O my soul, give thanks to the Lord, let everything that breathes praise the Lord.[17]

Such ancient utterances given to us by God in liturgy shape and form us in another kind of pathos—a pathos of praise. Not *apathea* or indifference, but that praise which seeks to name and to be named by the God of all creation. We can find in the imagery and the literary forms of the ancient Jewish Berakah, this wonderful language that has come down to us and that is retrieved in the twentieth-century liturgical reforms. Think of the *Didache,* at the close of the first century or the beginning of the second, with regard to the prayer of thanksgiving:

> We thank you our Father for the holy vine of David and your servant which you have revealed to us through Jesus, your servant. Glory be yours through all ages. We thank you, our Father, for the life and knowledge you have revealed to us through Jesus your servant, your child, glory be to you.[18]

The utterance is not a statement of information, it is a *gesture* of blessing and thanking God in the context of the meal that allows us then to receive gratefully. Received in gratitude, the gifts and the giver provide a language whereby we unlock the secret consent to God's grace in our being, receiving ourselves and one another as gifts.

Such prayer is a gesture against all blind indifference, a school against forgetfulness. Learning this gratitude goes against all those things that curve us inward and against all those things that take us away from God. When the language of gratitude is spoken and it finds its beautiful object in the God who created all things and more magnificently redeemed all things, it teaches us who we are and who we are to be. Praising and thanking God is remarkable. In the eyes of the world, it is hopelessly naive. In the eyes of the unfaithful, it is wildly irrational. Yet it is most fitting that human beings should learn gratitude. The cynical notion that everything has a string attached to it is not essential to our finding out who we are. Christian liturgy, then, schools us in this art of speaking, this art of listening. God's name is revealed in thanks and praise. This has healing relevance to the deep human pathos of our ingratitude. Karl Barth once said that the fundamental sin was ingratitude. The world of the grateful person and the grateful community is very different from the world of the ungrateful.

Insofar as worship continually shapes us in naming God this way, then our daily lives are opened up to God's grace. But a caution! There is such a thing as perverting the language of grace and gratitude and thanks by thanking God *only* for the blessings God has bestowed on us. The language of gratitude rings false that ignores the complexity of social reality including the patholo-gies so destructively internalized in our time—anxiety, self-imposed guilt, fear of neighbors (xenophobia) everywhere, of the stranger; and the terrors of a loveless and capricious moral world. Johannes Metz has warned against our tendency to be overly positive in the liturgy because of an absence of suffering in the official language of prayer. He says, "We generally fail to notice what modern humanity loses with its gradual impoverishment of language of prayer."[19] He calls it a "eulogistic evasion of what really matters." Such evasion turns our praise to untruth.

Psalm 150:6 teaches us that the very same voice that says "let everything that breathes praise the Lord" can cry out with cracked voice in the face of death: "Where are you God now, why have you abandoned us?" We lose the only social language capable of expressing and sustaining our humanity in open love when we lose this kind of thanksgiving in the midst of the human situation. Only to appease the individual conscience is to deny the trajec-tory, if not the essence, of biblically formed prayer. Here I have in mind the demanding emotional range of the Psalms, which do not shrink from what really matters and yet bring those also to formed praise. To pray for and with and out of a suffering world—and I do not mean merely physical suffering—is to learn again the comingling of praising and blessing. To pray for and with and out of suffering forces the liturgy to yield its tremendous consolation and the depths of thanksgiving we should never know without it. For only here can we begin to discern and to acknowledge who this One is to whom we pray, the Lord who stretched out his arms on the cross to embrace us all and all our pathoi.

The first mode of prayer was *the language of gratitude,* the prayer or the language of prayer, praise, and thanks. The second, is of course, *the language of speaking the truth in love.* Liturgy is to be a school for our struggle to listen for, to hear, and to speak the truth in love. And this is not simply true of ourselves in the "moment" of confession and penance. It is part of our very life with one another. Why is it that the church that knows full well in its liturgy and language about speaking the truth to God, lives on so little of the capital? Why is it that the church can destroy itself in gossip and innuendo and xenophobia when it has in its very books and in its own sound, Sunday by Sunday, language addressed to the One who is the searcher of hearts? "Almighty God, unto whom all hearts are open, all desires known, and from whom no secrets are hid, cleanse the thoughts of our hearts by the inspiration of Thy Holy Spirit," runs the Collect for Purity, that we may speak the truth in love. The liturgy in this second way is a school for our common struggle to speak the truth in love. It of course has to do with confessing our sins, yes, but more than that it has to do with amendment of our life in the direction God's love looks.[20]

Therefore, Annie Dillard is right. God will take us way out to a place from which we can't return if we begin this process of speaking and loving. If our problem is with pride, we must name it before God. If our problem is self-hatred or no sense of self at all, that too must be uttered and named. We all know people who are involved with Alcoholics Anonymous or Twelve Step programs who offer more palpable truth-speaking, at least at the beginning, than many offer in the holy sanctuaries. The art of our liturgies will be a sin and an abomination unless our lives learn to speak the language we pray, unless our emotions and desires and longing for one another are empowered to speak truthfully and to be loving with one another. We cannot ignore our dark side, the fears, the fantasies, the ambivalences, and the doubts. But here too the language of the Psalms is clear. God *can* hear us out; nothing we can confess before God is so powerful or so ugly that God would be offended. Is not honesty with God and neighbor precisely what Jesus wishes us to do and to be? So the liturgy requires that we bring real life to the healing and the consoling and the reconciling and illuminating work of God.

The third mode of prayer is *liturgy as a school for remembering who God has promised to be*. Thus our confessed lives of forgetfulness of God and our capacities for love and justice are made real. By recalling who God has been for us, we then recall who God will be. As Luther kept saying, "I am baptized." This gesture speaks the whole gospel. We are baptized into God's future for us. In speaking of remembering God, Huub Oosterhuis, the Dutch priest-poet, observes: "The whole creation is listed and the whole of God's history with us is brought up again."[21]

So when we pray with the Scriptures, we appeal to creation and covenant, we call God to mind (and here is a new kind of wonderful Hebraic twist): *we remind God to be God!*[22] What God has done, what God used to mean for us in the past, is a promise of who God will be for us in the future. We are so polite with God. Why be so polite with one who knows us so well? If you struggle with that in your devotional life, think of how a whole community could just present its best side to God. I don't think that's what George Herbert, the seventeenth-century Anglican poet, meant when he said, "Heaven and ordinary man well dressed." No, not the polite and well-dressed side, but the real, actual human beings we are. We call God to mind and remind God who God has been for us so that we do indeed remember our future.

And finally, *the liturgy is a continuing prayer of intercession,* a cry on behalf of the whole world, in season and out of season. To pray to God and to remember our neighbor is in fact to recall that God wishes to remember us. And so to pray the intercessions with the church is to be in solidarity with those who are also victims of our complicity. A set of intercessions from the fifth-century liturgy of St. James speaks more eloquently to this point than I can:

> Remember, Lord, those in old age and infirmity, those who are sick, ill, or troubled by unclean spirits, for their speedy healing and salvation by you, their God . . . . Remember Lord, all men for good; on all have mercy, Master; reconcile us all, bring peace to the multitudes . . . disperse the scandals, abolish wars, end the divisions of the churches, speedily put down the uprisings of the heresies. . . . Grant us your peace and your love, God our saviour, the hope of all the ends of the earth.[23]

If for one moment we could truly let those words speak in and through our pathos, then we should know who it is that is praying in us, with us, through us, and sighing with prayers too deep for words, that the language of the liturgy can make audible for us. A community that prays with this range is open to the world's suffering, no doubt. But, oh, how it is also open to the grace of God. For to pray these words is to engage in the eschatological art that God gives us in the Christian liturgy of word and table. To pray with the people of God is to remember the world, to be in dialogue with God about the sufferings and yearnings of the whole inhabited world. And so we pray our praise and our blessing, we pray for truth and for love, confessing our sin and looking for healing and stretching hands to receive it. And we pray also, remembering all that God is and has promised to be, interceding in the name of Jesus even as he intercedes for us in this very act of gathering.

Ethos of Liturgy: God's Self-Giving

To speak of the ethos of authentic Christian liturgy is to speak about the time and place in which human energies and passions are transformed in light of the passion of God for the world. To remember God in prayer and in life requires a continual participation in what the liturgy promises but cannot guarantee. Human affections such as yearning for justice, love of God and neighbor, gratitude, and even anger over injustice and suffering are not alien to the ethos of God. If we are disposed to the paschal mystery celebrated every Lord's day in the gathered community, our daily lives receive a new illumination. Father Godfrey Diekmann, the salty and peripatetic monk from St. John's Abbey, puts the point this way:

> Holiness is not something I get in the morning at Mass and then which throughout the day leaks out of me, grows ever less so that I must recharge myself again the next morning or the next Sunday. Instead, our day, our day's meeting with other people, our work should itself become an unfolding, a development, a deepening renewal of the morning's mystery of love.[24]

We take our human suffering of the world—not only moral pain or individual struggle, but the condition of being human in its wide and wild stretch—before God. In that place and time where God's self-giving is figured in Word and sacrament, and in the embodied healing of becoming a human community there, we are empowered to unfold, as Diekmann observes, "the morning's mystery of love."

Pathos without God's ethos is tragic self-expression; God's ethos without human pathos figured in Jesus is opaque, that is, sovereign but not saving. As Augustine said long ago: "Without God we cannot. Without us, God will not." But we must not confuse the bringing of human desires and longing to the ethos of the divine self-giving in liturgy with experiencing highs and lows during the actual time of liturgical celebration. We live in a culture that finds it difficult to distinguish between immediacies of feeling and depth of emotion over time. Blatant consumerism obliterates this distinction.[25] This is a cultural problem for worship and the arts ingredient in liturgical celebration. Thus to speak of how modes of prayer form us in deep emotions such as thankfulness and trust in God, does not mean simply "feeling thankful" from time to time. Vital liturgy certainly may produce feeling states, but that is not the criterion for praise and thanksgiving to God.

The ethos of God as the transformative power of liturgy relocates our tendency to look for immediacies of feeling. Over time, authentic liturgy deepens our disposition to perceive the world as God's creation. Thus Christian gratitude is not so much "felt" or "produced" as it is elicited in season and out of season. Joy in the midst of tribulation, or speaking the truth in love, or coming to love as God loves takes time to unfold.

So, too, the matter of remembering God, for who among us can say that in one single instance he or she remembers all that God's grace has conferred? This is the problem with the instantaneous conversion approach and the pragmatic utilitarian spirit that takes a perfectly good religious affection and turns it into a commodity. Flash it on the screen, "feel it now," and everything's OK. No, it is not this way, for God takes the long way with our condition. It is God's passion for us and for the complexly fallen world that makes this so. While we can experience particular liturgical events in the immediacy of its engagement, the set of meanings that illuminate life can only unfold over time. Even immediacy of feeling, however intense, deals with something selected out of the rich and largely inchoate, concealed pattern present to our consciousness.

Consider, for example, the experience at a family reunion. We listen to Uncle Fred tell the old stories, we meet a new relative, and we eat foods often placed on the table in a highly ordered sequence with Grandma's cream fruit salad last because it is the ritual dessert now. Yet we only receive part of the significance of the gathering at the time. We go through an array of meeting, eating, talking, singing, stories, but not until much later, or next year, do we seem to have "taken in" our belonging. The deeper levels of symbolic presence necessarily go beyond immediacy toward shared memories, encoded in the actions becoming ritualized.

With respect to Christian liturgy, the following episode is typical.[26] A parishioner came to the Sunday liturgy vaguely aware of her father's illness. At several points during the rite she drifted into her sense of "a lot of pain in the world." She became very engaged in singing the "Gloria," she reported, and in specific moments in the liturgy. Then she observed, "But again, I think I was thinking about my dad." Later, during the eucharistic prayer she remarked, "I remember thinking about my husband's grandmother who passed away and an aunt of mine." Vivid episodes of consciousness were triggered by participation. But what we could not see in her report is how, over time, the ethos of God took that pain and fused it with the communion of saints.

There is no reason to deny that people have moving immediate experiences in the liturgy—perhaps especially prompted by music. But the transformative power of God's self-giving in and through liturgical action has to do with the shaping of perception, of knowing and of feeling over time. The true ethos of Christian liturgy is that web of grace through word, sacrament, and song, through eating and drinking together, and being remembered by God, whereby God's saving power in the flesh transforms and transmutes all human pathos. This is what eye has not yet fully seen, nor ear heard. God sees in our life patterns what we cannot yet see. Authentic liturgy lures us by grace into a new pathos, now directed to the passion of God at the heart of the gospel.

C H A P T E R

2

DOGMA AND DOXA

Joseph Sittler once asked whether there were some centers of theological concern emerging in the twentieth century that would have a bearing on the language and action of the liturgy.[1] He called these "constellations aforming." Out of a vast array, he named three of these constellations, or areas, that were beginning to reshape our style of approach to questions about Christian belief:

1) Nothingness and darkness or the ability to peer into the abyss of emptiness in all human striving (taking his cue from the dark-night-of-the-soul tradition);

2) Revolutions in our very way of knowing the world that are reopening ways of being acquainted with the created order, moving from empiricist ways of knowing, detached from community and the known, to the retrieval of aesthetic, moral, and religious ways of knowing; and

3) The recovery of eschatology in twentieth-century theology.

Sittler's existentialist analysis of nothingness and darkness sketches themes related to our discussion of pathos in the previous chapter. The recovery of aesthetic modes of knowing, and shifts in theories of knowledge coupled with the recovery of eschatology, are central to chapter 3 and to the work of liturgical

---

theology to be developed in Part 4. This book presupposes that ritual action, language, music, and symbol are ways of knowing, opening up the reality of God through liturgical celebration, and levels of human soul and society by virtue of liturgical participation.

Sittler concluded that address with a musical analogy:

> Dogma and Doxa—what we believe and what we pray, constitute a single music in contrapuntal form; the somber remembrances and fresh probings of faith as Doxa always illuminate the freshly unfolding intelligibility and power of the faith as Dogma, as truths believed. . . . The songs of praise the church sings are a lyrical way of disclosing what the faith knows and how we know.[2]

Liturgical theology proposes that we must become familiar with *doxa* and doxology if we are to understand what it is to know God and how we come to such a knowing. The indicative of theology will always be diminished when it ceases to be formed in the authentic praise of God.

Ortho-doxa means right praise to God. *Doxa*, of course, has the wonderful ambiguity of referring both to human belief and to something intrinsic to God: doxa as the divine glory. *Ortho-doxa* is the practice of right ascription of honor and praise and glory to the One to whom all such ascription is due. It is not simply believing arcane stuff before breakfast, nor is it getting one's theological system right, and then debating other claims. Aidan Kavanagh helpfully distinguishes between *orthodoxia* (right worship) and *orthopistis* (right believing) and *orthodidascalia* (right teaching).[3] *Ortho-doxy*, then, is not a rational system by which we can differentiate ourselves from all others who are faithless; rather, *ortho-doxy* is being lured and drawn by the ethos of the liturgy to know God's glory. As John of Damascus and those preceding him in the patristic period knew so well, we cannot understand who God is until we know the shared life of glory in God: the divine *perichoresis*, to cite the Greek theological term.[4] Intrinsic to the Christian concept of God is this mutuality of glory in the inner life of God. The inner life of the Trinity is that blessed community that shares glory and honor among the persons. *Ortho-doxy*, then, in the first instance, returns to the very font (or shall we say the very table, or shall we say the Word proceeding from silence?) of this God of glory. *Orthodoxy* is learning in the long, hard, joyous way to ascribe unto God the *doxa* due God's name.

But how is such glory known? *Doxa* is that permanent attribute or essential character of God that is shown in the *manifestation* of God also. The *shekinah*, the glory, reflected in the shining on the face of Moses, the manifestation of God's presence, is always associated with powerful illuminating light that emanates from the uncreated life of God. We find it in Exodus and in Isaiah; we sing it in Advent and Epiphany. We sing it in every "Gloria." It is the *cantus firmus* of Isaiah's vision: "Arise, shine; for your light has come, and the glory of the LORD has risen upon you" (Isa. 60:1). We echo the glory of God in the Sanctus, "Holy, holy, holy, Lord God of hosts, heaven and earth are full of your *doxa*." We sing it in Isaiah 40 and in Handel's *Messiah*, forever forging it for speakers of English: "And the glory of the Lord shall be revealed, and all flesh shall see it together."

Doxa begins as the intrinsic character of God, the shared glory in the blessed community that is God from before all time and in all time. It becomes the self-giving of God; therefore it becomes the means by which we perceive who God is. Those who gather around Jesus to listen to what he says and to participate in what he does in word and sacrament, come to say that the eternal, awe-inspiring, life-giving glory of God is now in flesh. John's prologue proclaims, "We have seen his glory" (John 1:14b). This dance around (*perichoresis*) of honor and blessing in the very heart of God will not rest content until it is also shared in brokenness and in the actualities of life. The sons and daughters will not be fully revealed until the final manifestation, but are nonetheless already participating in glory. How? By ascribing glory and honor and power, by learning the language of *doxa* in its entire range. All God's works, we say in hope and trust, will indeed glorify God. God's deepest yearning is that the whole creation will share in the liberty of the sons and daughters of God.

In the prayers of the Eucharist, in many hymns, in canticle and psalm, the glory still sounds. Thus the third stanza in the final hymn sung often at evening prayer: "Guard us waking, guard us sleeping, and when we die, may we in your mighty keeping all peaceful lie. When the last dread call shall wake us, then O Lord do not forsake us, but to reign in glory take us with you on high." Here is eschatology breaking out in the form of *doxa*. Precisely because we are so filled with pathos in a suffering world, we need the transforming *doxa* that comes from the very heart of God flowing forth to creation, taking our brokenness into the Word-made-flesh. When we sing with Christ, listen to him, walk with him, we are learning how to ascribe glory to God. Such ascription is not easy, nor without demand.

God's glory will not rest until it becomes paradoxically manifest in the situations of violent and ugly human events—the very violation of God's glory.[5] Theologians may formulate beautiful systems of doctrine, but if they do not signal the paradox of God's glory in the cross, such systems are totally inadequate. We cannot sing that song of glory without the cross, for the shared glory of God comes finally in the ultimate human form of the utterly unglorious cross; the violence against God's *doxa* shown paradoxically as the manifestation of God's love. Therefore, to participate doxologically, to learn the vocative of how prayer forms and shapes us in our being before God, is also to remember and confront our complicities.

One thinks of John Donne's remarkable transference of sacred rhetoric into the secular love poems. In "Twicknam Garden," he speaks of his self-traitor, whose "spider love that transubstantiates all, And can convert Manna into gall."[6] Sin might be regarded as transsubstantiating in reverse, turning God's glory into something pedestrian. It is as if we say, "I've turned the manna you give us out of the love of your heart, God, into this gall which, in the long run though it be immediately strong, will not satisfy."

Our task is to search for ways to let the *doxa* of God shape our actual doxological practices. Because only that way will the indicative art of our theology have enough resiliency and be rooted and grounded in its true object. Consequently all the affections—gratitude, hope, sorrow, moral pain, repentance, love, and compassion—all of those affections which the liturgy over time invites us to have transformed in the direction of God—will find their best being when the glory is shown in human flesh. In contrast, a theology focused solely on the glory and power of God will probably combine again, as it has in the twentieth century and in times past, with the powers of oppression to invoke God and the power and glory of God for the most inhuman ends. Only the theology of the cross can counterpoint that. But the theology of the cross is not a contradiction to the theology of glory when our worship is attuned to the whole Word of God, and to the whole story of Jesus Christ. What Jesus said, and did he *now*, in this ethos of present liturgy, wishes to say and to enact. He will continue to say and do these things until God's reign comes in fullness. That to my mind, simply put, is the foundation for thinking about word and sacrament in every Christian assembly seeking doxology to offer to God. What Jesus said and did, he now says and does and will say and do. By the Spirit's power, we join him in his liturgy to God. Such liturgy also takes time and effort and is a disciplined, obedient art. How this is so is the concern of later chapters.

It is useful to distinguish between doxology as a mode of liturgical prayer and our *becoming doxological* or prayerful. This is especially important in a consumer culture in which much spiritual renewal is warmed over, privatized pietism. Much worship is the rehearsal of our class value aspirations, sentimentalized with a dash of immediacy of feeling. We may begin by confessing complicity in the very culture that provides the modes of communication, music, and language employed in our liturgical celebrations.

A true theology of the cross and glory will explore ways to take our cultural modes and to hold them up to the *doxa* of God until their very fragilities and inadequacies are transformed. This means something practical. How can we sing "Out of the Depths" (Psalm 130) in G Major with happy melody and harmony? That is to say, we must seek those modes of communication, verbal and nonverbal—accoustical, kinetic, tactile, and olfactory—which preserve the permanent tension between us and the *doxa* of God. There are times, of course, when simple elements, a simple visual, or a simple strong pattern of textile will do this. Too many words may prevent us from seeing the glory of God. Think of Leontyne Price singing "This Little Light of Mine." All that artistic power concentrated in the simplest line was, for me, an icon of something that can shine through the most elaborate festival liturgy we can imagine. In the midst of a lengthy, elaborate Easter Vigil, as well as in a small rural church's ordinary Sunday morning service, this is possible. Every prayer, every sequence, and every unit of the liturgy must be shaped in light of the glory of God revealed in the cross and resurrection. This includes how best to signal our deepest sorrows in light of the *doxa* of God.

Here is precisely where the paradox of the cross comes in for us. Liturgical prayer is that ongoing living relationship and awareness between our humanity and the glory of God.[7] We cannot neglect the human arts and the dimensions of praying, but they must always be reoriented. Johannes Metz has a wonderful paraphrase of Ernst Bloch's comment about prayer: "Prayer is at times like the daydream of that home whose light shines in our childhood, yet a home where none of us has ever been."[8]

Communal prayer to God is at times like a dream, a vision of that home whose light shines before us. This, as we shall examine in some detail, is the eschatological character of all Christian prayer and wellspring of every Christian assembly.

Why is it that when a reading is so well read, the reader sounds the voice of Christ to us? Why is it that a homily so offered and poured out of a pastor's caring for a congregation, or the simple sound of a child's voice singing, or the most glorious brass fanfare—why is it that these things evoke our yearning for something more? That is the way of God's glory with us: taking us beyond the confines of what we say we believe toward participation in the reality of what is promised.

Consider a homely instance of another gathering that takes its cue from our Sunday worship. You gather with friends, eating, drinking, and talking into the evening. Little by little the stories unfold and the images of life emerge—images of loss and gain, of hurt and healing, of promises made and broken, and of years quickly sped in childhood dreams now seemingly so far behind, not turning out as you had expected. But toward the end of the evening someone remarks, "Wouldn't it be wonderful to be in a place where you could share everything and be able to live with all the others truthfully because you were at home?" No longer a stranger or a guest, but like a child at home.

Or, the news from the hospital was not good; you begin to gather in: your sister from Chicago, the brother from St. Louis, and the aunt and uncle from Florida. You have been keeping the lonely vigil at her bedside and now the gathering, crowded in the room, the last breath is taken, the circle forms, and out of that artless art some primordial impulses are articulated and you say as if with one voice, "Gather her home, O God, gather her home." You have been there in that liturgy or you will be. And it is only because we have been in another assembly that we can understand how that is being transformed. Only because we have had other songs to sing, explicitly and implicitly of the glory of God coming to us in human form, can we begin to take in, if we can take in at all, this holy moment, this liturgy in life.

Covering the Range of Glory

Christian liturgy is the ongoing prayer, act, and word flowing from the cross and empty tomb. We also say it is the humanly embodied arts that Christ prompts when we receive some sight and some sense of grace and glory. Christian liturgy ought always and everywhere to be our response to that glorious self-giving of God, in, with, and through our humanity in Christ. The community called into being to continue his prayer, continues to bring its hope on behalf of the whole world. Three inferences central to the remainder of this book can be made.

Glory in Human Form

First, all of our arts must be seen in light of the comprehensive glory of God, or congregations will be starved and become spiritually anorexic, if we do not cover the whole range of glory. This is the hidden glory of God to be praised in song and word and gesture and sight, as well as the revealed glory in Christ. No true worship is possible without the naming of the blessed Trinity, or without participation in the mystery of God. The hymn, paraphrasing 1 Timothy, declares this in addressing God: "Immortal, invisible, God only wise, in light inaccessible, hid from our eyes." There are those times when specific feasts and seasons speak of the immanent, intrinsic glory of God. All classical and recently reformed eucharistic prayers begin this way. But these are ordinary times and occasions to figure in speech, in song, in gesture, and in all the art of liturgy the conditions for God's grace to operate. We must find ways to reflect how God actually is manifest on the earth in the human condition. This requires being faithful to the whole sweep of biblical reality, not just to a personal "canon within the canon," but to the tensions within the great library of witness to God's manifestation in the earth.

Christian liturgy, authentically celebrated, does not avoid those areas that seem to create tremendous tensions between the suffering of human beings and the purposes of God. Yes, Psalm 88 is part of our vocabulary just as we move through Good Friday in which Psalm 22 is cried out by the one who bore the glory. Furthermore, authentic prayer and proclamation explores how the glory of God is also reflected in the human witness itself, in the lives of those who follow in trust and wonderment at the glory.[9] Liturgy must bear some form of witnessing to how Jesus Christ, as Gerard Manley Hopkins said, plays in myriad places,"lovely in limbs, and lovely in eyes not his/To the Father through the features of men's faces."[10] But can we experience this gathered community also as the domestic household in which we discern Christ in one another? In the new *United Methodist Hymnal* (1989) there is a wonderful Hispanic hymn, "Cuando El Pobre," which sings: "When the poor ones who have nothing share with strangers, . . . then we know that God still goes that road with us." The glory of Christ is given in the humility of earth, in those in seeming weakness who witness to us and are not merely the subject of our benign and benighted ministry. Honesty about the manifestations of God and the ambiguities of history is what I think Joe Sittler meant by "learning from darkness and nothingness." We see Christ in the flesh. Therefore, all flesh is available to the glory of God. Do we mean what we sing in Händel's Messiah: "and all flesh shall see it together"?

Gratitude as Attunement

A second inference concerns thankfulness. Gratitude to the divine for the gift of life and the giving of God's *benefits* is not a mysterious inner experience as much as it is a pervasive attunement by the church to the world in all of its beauty, terror, mystery. Therefore gratitude is not, as we noted in chapter 1, simply my personal gratitude for all these blessings God has given me; it is an opening to the human maturity in which we say this outpouring of God is the source of our life. Without gratitude, communal and personal, we cannot see. If we are to know God in any sense of the word, it will be because we have a heart that responds in gladness and gratitude in our complexity.

The person without gratitude rooted and grounded in God's self-giving sees the world differently from those who catch a glimpse of seeing the world anew in light of God's first gift (creation) and in light of God's ultimate gift (redemption). The deepening capacity for gratitude and thankfulness of the heart in the community leads to a greater sense of the truth of how things are. We should not be surprised that God has so arranged matters that if we learn gratitude grounded in God's self-giving and the *doxa* of God shown in Christ, will see more. We will also see more pain. One cannot have one without the other, for it will plunge us more deeply into the gap between the already and the not yet, between the manifestation of glory in the flesh seen in the face of Jesus Christ and in the eyes of the faces of pain in our neighbors. At the same time, thankfulness to God requires a reconfiguration of our natural desires because they find a new object. To this we return in chapter 4.

Full Participation

Third, there are three levels of our participation in *doxa*. These three levels of participation in liturgy are part of our work as pastors, as musicians, and as worshipers. The first is, as the Vatican Council said in the constitution on the liturgy, "full, active, conscious participation " in the rites. That means singing, listening, attending to one another, and bringing our lives to the symbols and actions. The second level of participation in these rites is *as church, as the Body of Christ.* Mere activity or lively participation in itself does not constitute faithful worship. In a culture of exaggeration and overly stimulated feeling, it is too easy to mistake active participation and self-expression for worship. When we come to Christian liturgy we participate *as* church, as a social body, wherein as one is honored, all are honored, where one suffers, all suffer. This must somehow shine through. It is the church at prayer and the church in solidarity with Jesus that is central to liturgical participation.

Third, this being the deepest mystery of all, worship is participation in God's very life. In the mystery of communion with God is where God seeks, not only to be glorious for us, but to allow us to be sons and daughters, bearing the hope that *all* shall share in the glory of a liberated creation. What more profound belief (dogma) than "all manner of things shall be well," and all manner of things shall be well in the glory of God.[11]

CHAPTER

3

THE ESCHATOLOGICAL CHARACTER OF WORSHIP

As this broken bread was scattered over the mountains, and when brought together became one, so let your Church be brought together from the ends of the earth into your kingdom. (*Didache*, chapter 9)

At the heart of all Christian prayer and worship is the cry for God's will and covenant promises in Jesus Christ to be made real. The Lord's Prayer, which from earliest times was both a liturgical and devotional prayer, begins with a plea for the rule and reign of God: "Thy kingdom come, Thy will be done on earth," concluding with a doxology ascribing to God everlasting rule and reign and glory. Asking that *in us* the will of God be done on earth—*in us* as the early writings on the prayer keep repeating—is both cry and a command. It emerges from our human distress, but it is also the promise of God upon which faith stands and hopes. The early Alexandrian theologians were fond of the phrase, "Ask for the great and spiritual gifts." So the prayer asks that God's reign be found growing in our actual life, that we receive and flourish in the promises of God, and that the final triumph of God's justice and righteousness be expected. This is a way of translating, "Seek first the kingdom of God." This prayer, echoing the Kaddish and the eschatological hope found in Jewish liturgical prayer, is one point of access to a prayed theology of promise.

The final prayer in the New Testament is *Maranatha!* This utterance may originally have been simply the urgent imperative: "Our Lord, come!" At the same time it may be understood as a kind of invocation as well: "The Lord has come and is present" in the assembly faithfully gathered. The force of this Aramaic expression, as Geoffrey Wainwright observes, is "an acclamation of the presence of the one who is still to come and yet who promised His presence to the two or three gathered in His name; The Lord is here!"[1] This magisterial study is a key sourcebook for the discussion during the past two decades of eschatology in Christian eucharistic worship.

One of the most distinctive features of twentieth-century theology has been the reorientation of Christian thinking to eschatology. Whereas traditionally the term has been used to refer to the "doctrine of last things"—final judgment, death, heaven, and hell—it has, in contemporary theology, come to be a principle of thought. That is, to posit any Christian claim about God and the world requires considering it from the standpoint of the future of God. Theologians as diverse as Jürgen Moltmann and Hans Urs von Balthasar and Dorothee Soelle have incorporated this basic insight.

The theological recovery of eschatology as a way of thinking began among New Testament scholars at the turn of the century. Albert Schweitzer's critique of liberal nineteenth-century views of Jesus focused upon his radical preaching of the kingdom of God. That Jesus proclaimed the immediate end of time, an expectation that was not fulfilled, created a crisis for the early Christian movement. Jesus' teaching and preaching were regarded by Schweitzer strictly from a viewpoint of Jewish apocalyptic. But the severity of this view generated a more existential interpretation, culminating in the work of New Testament theologian Rudolph Bultmann. The very notion of the imminent end of the world and the apocalyptic imagery in which it was cast in the New Testament was recast by Bultmann and his followers as mythical language that must be reinterpreted in the twentieth-century context. In light of Paul's Letters and John's Gospel, Bultmann translated "demythologized" eschatology from the goal of human history and the cosmos to a profound expression of the present life of faith among and within the believers. Thus emerged the concept of true eschatology as a radical openness toward the future.

Other strands in twentieth-century eschatological thinking took a "realized" form, especially with C. H. Dodd, and later with Ernst Käsemann. Out of the crisis of the primitive church, the Jewish apocalyptic expectation is reshaped to focus on the future promises of God already being made real. Human history is seen from the standpoint of the object of hope: namely, God's new covenant promises for the future of the world. The key point is found in the resurrection of Christ. In some way the eschaton has already occurred, but its final actualization among human beings is yet to take place. From this line of thinking comes the paradox of the "already" and the "not yet" of the kingdom of God. This is one of the characteristics of eschatological thought in contemporary theology. In the last chapter of this book we will return to a discussion of authentic liturgy and the "new creation." For now let it be noted that liberation theology has taken up this theme, pressing the idea that the promises of God are to be fulfilled, at least in part, in the course of concrete human social-political history. In this case the liturgy is regarded as empowering the oppressed to participate in movements and events that anticipate the goal of God's purposes for the whole world.

Such twentieth-century developments in biblical studies and in theology have indeed produced a critical reinterpretation of eschatology as a doctrine. However, the most significant impact on the life of Christian communities has been occurring in the liturgical reforms, especially since the Second Vatican Council. Every major liturgical reform among a wide range of Christian denominational traditions has attempted to recover the freshness of the eschatological hope of early Christian worship and prayer. These reforms have reoriented the prayer texts, the readings, the central symbols, and the pattern of the essential ritual sign-acts: hoping to renew the *ethos* of liturgical gathering.

A brief examination of the principal patterns of time, Baptism, Eucharist, and Christian funeral rites reveals how liturgy, now critically informed by historical, biblical and pastoral insight, is freshly capable of a praxis of eschatology.

Liturgical Praxis of Eschatology

Secondary theology as critical thought, is now once more attending to the formative and expressive power of the act of liturgy. In the "live" common action of liturgical life we find the true revolution in eschatology taking place. In looking at time, Christian initiation, the Lord's Supper and the funeral we can discern how Christian liturgy in the Western churches is once again becoming eschatological in its texts and structures. Eastern Christianity has retained more evident eschatology in its ethos.[2]

Time

The eschatological character of worship may be seen in relation to the essential act of gathering for the eucharistic assembly on Sunday. This is itself a primary "eschatological act" and a theme for reflection. The eschatological significance of Sunday is well known in the early church's practice and teaching. Three interrelated points make this clear. First, Sunday emerged from the witness of the women who found the empty tomb. On the first day of the week Jesus appeared to the disciples. So it is the "day of resurrection." The very name the "Lord's Day" found in Acts 20, in Revelation as elsewhere signified the reorientation of Jewish practice to the Christian practice of the assembly.[3] The connection between gathering to worship on Sunday and the gathering to greet the risen Lord is at the very beginning of Christian liturgy. Justin Martyr, writing in the mid-second century, perhaps reflecting a tradition going back to the very first generation of his church's practice, writes:

> And we all assemble together on Sun–day, because it is the first day, on which God, having transformed the darkness and matter, made the world; and Jesus Christ our Saviour rose from the dead the same day.[4]

Second, Sunday was known as the "eighth day," a day both in time of the week, but already participating in the future age to come. The first witness to this is found in *The Epistle of Barnabas*, a late first or early second-century letter:

> The present sabbaths are not acceptable to me, but that which I have made, in which I will give rest to all things and make the beginning of an eighth day, that is the beginning of another world. Wherefore we also celebrate with gladness the eighth day in which Jesus also rose from the dead, and was made manifest, and ascended into Heaven.[5]

We note also the association of Sunday with the ascension of Jesus. Thus the concept of an octave between Sunday and Sunday gathers into itself a rhythm of death/resurrection/ascension moving from Sunday to Sunday.[6]

A third point is closely related. Sunday, if conceived as the resurrection day, is readily associated in the mind of the early traditions with the final advent, the *parousia* itself. On the one hand the church took great care to avoid specifying the "Day of the Lord." The teaching of Jesus is clear: "You know not the hour." Yet there are evidences here and there that many Christian communities expected the judgment of Christ's appearance to the world would occur on the first day of the week.[7]

Thus the liturgical assembly, gathered for praise, reading and teaching, the prayers and the holy meal, was itself an eschatological sign. This is not so much a piece of doctrinal theology as it is implicit in the act of gathering. In this sense, the Sunday assembly is a primary theological act: the "eschatology" is in the assembling itself, not something first thought out then ritualized. Rather, the symbol of the assembly gave rise to the later critically elaborated thought about Sunday being an eschatological day.

How the Christian community keeps time is eschatological. That is, Christian worship inherited from Jewish liturgy the rhythm of feasts and seasons in which God's mighty acts and the covenant promises of God for the future were commemorated. The Passover was enacted not simply as a remembrance of things past, but a present encounter with the power and reality of God's liberating hand. At the foundations of the Christian Pascha, now celebrated as a passing from death to life in Christ, we find images pointing toward the realization of God's future-oriented promises. So the celebration of the Easter Vigil in the early church was a fully eschatological communal action. This is witnessed in all the early liturgies of which we have descriptions and, from the fourth century on, extensive prayer texts.

From the beginning, Christians gathered at set times, especially on Sunday. Daily prayer was offered in homes following Jewish custom at certain hours, especially morning and evening. But this "keeping time" was itself informed by the rhythm of commemoration and hope in the weekly and yearly cycles. The *Didache*, from the late first or early second century, admonishes the churches: "On the Lord's day of the Lord come together, break bread and hold Eucharist."[8] The days of the week thus became patterns of witnessing to Jesus Christ. So daily life was rendered holy, in prayer and in daily work. Each day took significance from the Lord's Day.

The year itself was patterned for commemorating Jesus Christ. In the New Testament literature, Paul brings the language of the Jewish feast of Passover (the Pascha) to bear upon the significance of Easter:

> Clean out the old yeast so that you may be a new batch, as you really are unleavened. For our paschal lamb, Christ, has been sacrificed. Therefore, let us celebrate the festival, not with the old yeast, the yeast of malice and evil, but with the unleavened bread of sincerity and truth. (1 Cor. 5:7-8)

This passage forms the basis of the liturgical acclamation found in many eucharistic rites today: "Christ our Passover is sacrificed for us; therefore let us keep the feast!"

As the church spread geographically and moved through historical time, the liturgical calendar expanded. The three original feasts—Easter, Pentecost, and Epiphany (especially in the Eastern churches)—were extended and surrounded by periods of preparation and elaboration. The season between the Christian Passover through the Day of Pentecost was itself originally called "the Pentecost," constituting fifty days of great joy. Here were fifty days emphasizing the reality of the eschaton begun in human history. Augustine refers to this:

> These days after the Lord's Resurrection form a period, not of labor, but of peace and joy. That is why there is no fasting and we pray standing,

which is a sign of resurrection. This practice is observed at the altar on all Sundays, and the Alleluia is sung, to indicate that our future occupation is to be no other than the praise of God.[9]

Beginning in the fourth century, especially in the churches in Jerusalem, Holy Week emerged as a complex and distinctive period. The Jerusalem practices eventually were spread throughout Christianity. While Holy Week rites focus on the narrative of the final days of Jesus' ministry, trial and death in Jerusalem, they are dependent upon being celebrated from the standpoint of the resurrection faith. Thus the memory of Christ's passion and death can be said to be eschatologically informed in the actual liturgical practice of the early church. Liturgy follows the New Testament biblical pattern: the remembrance of what Jesus said, did, and suffered was a function of the assembly gathered to praise, to pray, to baptize, and to celebrate the supper. So the "passion narratives" were at the heart of all that was to be remembered and brought together in the Gospels.

Touching briefly on the feast of the Epiphany, we have a sermon of John Chrysostom's, preached on December 20, 386:

For if Christ had not been born into flesh, He would not have been baptized, which is the Theophany [Epiphany], He would not have been crucified [some texts add: and would not have risen] which is the Pascha, He would not have sent down the Spirit, which is the Pentecost.[10]

Here is clear testimony to the theological understanding of how these feast days were related. But this understanding was itself a product of the practices, the prayers and readings and the ritual actions. The eschatological reality of what God had accomplished in Christ pervades the whole temporal pattern. It is this celebrated pattern of time known as the Christian year that itself bears witness to eschatological hope made present in the community's worship.

Of course there was not one single, univocal "theology" in the modern sense. Rather, the prayed and enacted signs carried the significance that was elaborated in various cultural and historical contexts. There can also be little doubt that the actual practices of the churches could obscure and even pervert this eschatological dimension.[11]

Baptism

An equally impressive and perhaps even more central way in which worship is eschatological is found in Christian baptism. In referring to baptism Paul declares, "Therefore we have been buried with him (Christ) by baptism into death, so that, just as Christ was raised from the dead by the glory of the Father, so we too might walk in newness of life" (Rom. 6:4). The central images of baptism show that Christians participate in Christ's death and resurrection already. This means baptismal theology is first done in the rites of initiation: The witness of baptism is a present way of life, the new creature is appearing. The church as the baptismal and baptizing community is itself to be a sign, a living witness to the hope. Hence liturgy and its consequence in how Christians are to live out the baptized life anticipates the world transformed. The radical equality found in the baptismal promises enacted and taught in the catechumenate is primary: In Christ there is "no longer Jew or Greek, there is no longer slave or free, there is no longer male and female" (Gal. 3:28).

Baptism is not limited to the act of the water bath with prayers and laying on of hands. At a surprisingly early period, a lengthy and sometimes elaborate process of formation led those seeking baptism through powerful immersion in biblical teaching, training in prayer and a way of life, and through a series of particular ritual moments. This catechumenate period we may regard as a kind of eschatological formation. For many of the Christian communities, such as that reported by Hippolytus, the baptismal preparation was a formation in practices of a way of life governed by dominant images. The point of the catechumenate in these early centuries was to form those on their way to baptism in a doxological life, not to teach theology as propositions about God to be believed. The theological understanding of God was, as it were, embedded in practices such as hospitality and articulated in images of a new life as citizens of God's reign.

We can appreciate something of the eschatological character of this formation by reviewing the range of images that first occur in the New Testament literature. Such images permeate the texts and teachings used in the catechetical process. These in turn link the culminating water bath and the first sharing in the Eucharist with the whole preceding process. Later baptismal theology often concentrates on one or two of these images to the exclusion or neglect of others. In this manner, the "secondary" baptismal theology of official church teaching is certainly less ample and perhaps even more misleading than are the rites celebrated. The symbolic enactment of the rites is the arena of primary theology of the new life in Christ, wherein the promises of God begin to be "lived."

One of the primary eschatological images lies at the basis of the Christian life itself: dying and rising with Christ. Paul, in writing to the church at Rome asks:

> Do you not know that all of us who have been baptized into Christ Jesus were baptized into his death? Therefore we have been buried with him by baptism into death, so that, just as Christ was raised from the dead by the glory of the Father, so we too might walk in newness of life. For if we have been united with him in a death like his, we will certainly be united with him in a resurrection like his. (Rom. 6:3-5)

This brief baptismal instruction shows that the baptismal ritual act of going into the water was, from the earliest stages, a physical mimesis of burial. The promise of being resurrected to new life was literally acted out in the course of the baptismal liturgy. This provided, after the initiation rites were concluded, a language of interpretation and explanation of what the baptized person had undergone. The proleptic dying (going down into death) was necessary to receive the promise of rising to new life (coming out to light and life and the feast of the Lord's table).

A second predominant image is that of being washed clean from sin. This is found in many passages in the New Testament and in the early writings of the church that may not mention baptism explicitly, but which refer to the character of the baptized life. This is often, as in Peter's sermon at Pentecost, linked with receiving the gift of the Holy Spirit. "Repent," Peter exhorts his hearers, "and be baptized every one of you in the name of Jesus Christ so that your sins may be forgiven; and you will receive the gift of the Holy Spirit" (Acts 2:38). It is not necessary here to unravel questions concerning the various strands in the New Testament witness to how the cleansing in the water and the reception of the Spirit are conjoined. My point is simply that the forgiveness of sins and the empowerment of life by the Spirit are eschatological realities. These are signs of the new age already taking effect, and are in turn grounded in the death and resurrection of Christ. Being baptized "into Christ" is to be made a participant in the life bestowed. The centrality of this image and its related concepts explains in part why the issue of post-baptismal sin became a critical question, especially when sin became, in the Western churches, the primary locus of theological teaching about what baptism does.

The receiving of the Holy Spirit is also imaged under the figures of illumination or enlightenment. Justin Martyr reports in his *Apology:* "This washing is called illumination, since those who learn these things are illumined within."[12] Clement of Alexandria, writing toward the end of the second century in Egypt, contributes this striking progression of images:

> Being baptized, we are enlightened: being enlightened, we are adopted as sons [*sic*]; being adopted, we are made perfect; being made complete, we are made immortal. . . . This work has many names; gift of grace, enlightenment, perfection, washing.[13]

Baptism as illumination is especially prominent in the Johannine Gospel and some of the Pastoral Letters in the New Testament. The great Johannine images of light that propel the prologue and articulate who Jesus Christ is have much to do with light and glory. From "the Light shines in the darkness" to "I am the light of the world" the motif of baptismal illumination moves through the evangelist's account. One is reminded of the remarkably witty account of the man born blind whom Jesus heals. As his accusers engaged in dialogue, pressing him ever harder, they see less and less, and he is more and more enlightened about who healed him. It is the Eastern church traditions that use the imagery of illumination in the baptismal rites more than the Western churches. This accounts in part for some of the differences in baptismal theology as well.

Adoption as sons and daughters is another key image connected with baptism, as we saw in Clement of Alexandria. The image of "adoption" refers to being made inheritors of the promises of God in Christ, especially when this is applied to the

Gentiles. The Pauline Letters speak of those baptized into Christ as being joint-heirs with him of the promises of the resurrected life. This is not the naturally inherited birthright of the Christian Jew, either. It marks a distinctive incorporation into a new society and into new citizenship in God's coming reign. Furthermore, the early baptismal liturgies make it clear that being adopted is not simply the matter of a future life after death. It is precisely this new status that empowers Christians to "walk in newness of life" (Rom. 6:4). Put succinctly, "If anyone is in Christ there is a new creation" (2 Cor. 5:17). Here the baptized person becomes a living icon of what God promises to bring about in the whole of the cosmos—a new creation.

Closely related to those already cited is the image of new birth, of being born again "into a living hope" (1 Pet. 1:3). This image gathers to itself a range of associations with restored innocence and even ontological transformation. So Jesus' dialogue with Nicodemus in John's Gospel is an exploration of the meaning of what it means to be baptized. In order to grasp the eschatological promise of conversion to the way of Jesus, one must, like Nicodemus, overcome our literalistic tendencies. To be born into life eternal is to participate in that which is not conceivable under the old categories, biological or otherwise.

We have seen how Christian baptism in its earliest expression contains a striking combination of images. These together provide a rich, many-splendored language with which to speak of the new creation already moving into the course of human life. A detailed study of the early catechetical process, the rites of initiation, and the sermons and teachings given to the newly baptized (the *mystagogia*) reveals that the liturgical rites were, in fact, radically oriented to the reality promised in Christ.[14] But the very action of the gathered assembly of the baptized making new Christians is also a sign of the church as the future promises of God for the work coming to social realization in an actual community of human beings. These features are found in the juxtaposition of texts, symbols, and ritual acts of Christian initiation across many cultures. It has been a singular aim of twentieth-century baptismal reform to retrieve this powerful range of images and practices.

These may be found in nearly all the newer baptismal liturgies, and especially in the *Rites of the Christian Initiation of Adults*.[15]

Eucharist

If baptism contains the enacted theology of the rule and reign of God present and yet to come, then Eucharist carries this out over time in the life of the community and in the faith experience of the individual. Gathering about the Lord's table for the meal, distinctions of class and social standing are reordered. Paul's struggle with the reality of actual eucharistic assemblies in Corinth sheds light on the permanent tension we face here. On the one hand, there is no class or rank in Christ, on the other hand, every social arrangement is itself based on some form of power that excludes or marginalizes someone (not by morality but by class and rank). So the very gathering brings social customs and practices which are characteristically brought to the celebrations of the Eucharist. Thus a permanent tension is created, not simply between the "already" and the "not yet" of the Kingdom in some large sense, but in the actualities of the concrete, specific assembly of Christians about the word and the table.

So it is that Baptism and Eucharist as the initiating and continuing sacramental actions carry a radical theological claim: Christ is present, the rule of God is very near, in fact the gifts given in the water bath and in the holy meal obliterate the conditions that keep us separated and alienated. We are reconciled to God and to neighbor. The communion is a foretaste of glory divine and a foreshadowing of the new Jerusalem.

We do not presume here to fully grasp this. But the words of the institution, "Do this in remembrance (for the remembrance) of me" indicate a double process of memory. We are to remember what Christ gave for us and the world, but we are appealing to God in the very act of the common meal to remember what God has promised in the Law and prophets, fulfilled in Jesus Christ. Thus, each time we celebrate Eucharist, we pray for the Lord's coming, we proclaim anew the beginning of salvation, and we experience anew the blessing of the final realization of what Christ initiated. The living memory (*anamnesis*) of all God has accomplished in Christ is dependent upon calling upon God's Holy Spirit bringing the assembly to life in the signs and the prayers. We will explore the relation between invoking, remembering, and supplicating in the Lord's Supper in Part 2.

The gap between this reality that is offered, and what our social body is capable of receiving is sometimes excruciating! We recall that this was part of the very first generation's own struggle. This excruciating gap is what led Paul to speak severely to the Corinthian congregation: "When you come together, it is not really to eat the Lord's supper" (1 Cor. 11:20). The human character of the assembly can thus contradict or deny what is offered in the promises of the meal. How vulnerable this seems to be if the sacrament of the table is to be a fundamental theological act. That is, if the practice of Jesus' memory and the calling upon God to make real the signs of bread and wine is to constitute our primary theology as Christians, is this not a most fragile foundation? With all the abuse and corruption, alongside the relatively innocent forgetfulness of the assembly (or simply our dullness), how can we even maintain the Eucharist, how can we even hope that Christian baptism can speak of justice and the final righteousness of God? This seems an absurdity!

There is no need to deny the fragility of sacramental actions of the Christian assembly seen from a human point of view. Nietzsche, Freud, Marx, and others rightly see the weakness and human vulnerability in these practices. For them such practices are, amidst a world such as ours, an illusion. But the Eucharist and Baptism are precisely the divine vulnerability. For at the heart of Eucharist are the broken symbols of suffering and death—God's humanity made visible and palpable. The risk is both divine and human. At the center of this is limit, the self-emptying (*kenosis*) of God in human form and death. We should expect this feature of Christian faith to surface especially in how we face death as a community. And it does.

Christian Funeral Rites

Let us examine briefly some features of Christian funeral liturgies as yet further evidence of the eschatological character of

Christian worship. Among the so-called "pastoral offices," or Christian rites of passage in the Christian tradition, funeral rites provide us with an explicit form of personal and communal eschatology. It is no coincidence that a close connection between baptism and Christian funeral liturgies developed early. Since one of the primary images of baptism is "dying and rising with Christ," the funeral is, in a sense, the literal test case for the truth of baptism. Thus funeral rites of a wide variety of Christian traditions exhibit baptismal reference and resonance. This is particularly striking in the reformed rites following the Second Vatican Council. We will presently examine a specific example found in the United Methodist rite, known as "A Service of Death and Resurrection."

Before a reading of the funeral liturgy, it is well to reflect on death itself as personal eschaton. Certainly the biblical tradition speaks of death as part of the created order. Psalm 90 expresses the mortality this way:

> The days of our life are seventy years, or perhaps eighty, if we are strong; even then their span is only toil and trouble; they are soon gone, and we fly away. (Psalm 90:10)

We are creaturely and mortal; the fact of death shows this. So it is with every living creature. In a striking passage Hans Schwarz states the matter strongly:

> Death gives each moment of our life its singularity and we cannot repeat one act of our life. Unceasingly and unresistingly we are on our way to the eschaton. Whether we want it or not, we exist truly eschatologically, since the potential presence of the eschaton at any moment of our life gives our life its peculiarity.[16]

The way of linking the particularity of a life understood from the standpoint of its ending is analogous to the idea of human history not being fully understood until its ending. The analogy with the whole cosmos constitutes a limit beyond which we cannot think except to posit the analogy: this is how we come to form an idea of the finite world as a created order, a limited whole.

Death of human beings confronts us with the God question. The fact of death reveals our creatureliness, but it also shows alienation from God, and is our object of fear—fear of face-to-face confrontation with God, imaged as judgment. The Christian claim is that Christ conquered death. As the Orthodox Easter troparion sings: "Christ is risen from the death, trampling down death by death, and to those in the tombs, bestowing life!"[17]

But the eschatological promise does not merely refer to the eternal life after death God's grace confers to believers. It has a social-historical reference, and finally a cosmic reference. Precisely these connections are made in Christian funeral rites: the resurrection of Christ is restored to the center of the liturgical gathering. Hence we are beginning to reconceive.

The classical function of the funeral is to care for and dispose of the bodily remains, to comfort the bereaved, and to praise God for life, proclaiming the hope of the resurrection. The meaning of resurrection can only be fully disclosed in light of the apocalyptic view of human history and the yearning of the created order for restoration in God. The hope expressed in the texts of the prayers, the force of the symbolic acts, especially with the renewed connection with Baptism and Eucharist, is a full-orbed biblical hope.

When Christians gather to bury or to memorialize the dead, two basic things are done. The reality of death and the pathos of bereavement are faced in the presence of God and the assembly, and the resurrection gospel is celebrated in the context of God's baptismal covenant with the church in Christ Jesus. While there are many variants, such as whether the remains of the dead are present and will be buried as part of the whole rite, the central ritual enactment juxtaposes the resurrection hope with the specific life now brought to its earthly closure. The specific human and cultural contexts vary greatly, as we shall examine in Part 3 of this book, but the eschatological force of this assembly remains the most fundamental theological point.

As with baptismal and eucharistic rites, nearly all major Western Christian churches have undertaken the reform of the funeral rites in the late twentieth century. Let us consider a few features of one example, the "Service of Death and Resurrection" of The United Methodist Church.[18] The very title of the service signals a theological retrieval and restoration of biblical imagery and more ample classical funeral rites. The fundamental reality to be celebrated is christological and triune. The direct references to the significance of baptism is unmistakably present in the opening words:

> Dying, Christ destroyed our death.
> Rising, Christ restored our life.
> Christ will come again in glory.
> As in baptism *Name* put on Christ,
>   so in Christ may *Name* be clothed with glory.[19]

This deliberately echoes the acclamations found in the liturgy of the Lord's Supper that is there uttered by the whole congregation. And it is put directly together with the clothing image of baptism into Christ. At the level of text, the definitive theological affirmation is made as the ritual procession into the church begins. So the entrance rite makes explicit what the action of bringing the coffin or urn into the midst of the assembly intends. When there is no procession and no pall is placed upon the coffin beforehand, the opening "Word of Grace" begins the service: "Jesus said, I am the resurrection and I am the life." This text has been used for centuries in funeral rites, conjoined with the refrain found in Revelation: "I am Alpha and Omega, the beginning and the end, the first and the last." Thus the eschatology expressed at the beginning of the funeral is at once transcendent of human time and relevant to all finite time. "Because I live, you shall live also."

After the opening greeting that speaks of the praise of God, the witness to the church's faith, the acknowledgment of human loss and a plea for God's grace, the congregation sings an appropriate hymn. The prayers that follow address God with the character of the psalmist's pattern: lament and praise:

> O God, who gave us birth,
> you are ever more ready to hear
>   than we are to pray.
> You know our needs before we ask,
>   and our ignorance in asking.
> Give to us now your grace,
>   that as we shrink before the mystery of death,
>   we may see the light of eternity.[20]

Reminiscent of Psalm 90, this prayer is followed by confession and pardon and by Psalm 130, "Out of the depths I cry unto thee," concluding the opening liturgy.

In the following section of the rite, scriptures from the Hebrew prophets, especially from Isaiah, are read next to Psalm 23 which has been used in Christian burial from earliest times. The readings from the New Testament are on the resurrection (1 Cor. 15; the vision of the new heaven and earth and Rev. 21:1-7; and the "neither death, nor life, nor angels . . . nor anything else in all creation, will be able to separate us from the love of God in Christ Jesus our Lord," Rom. 8). The preferred Gospel reading is John 14, Jesus' words of comfort, declaring that a place is prepared for those who follow him, and that the Holy Spirit will bring to remembrance all that Christ has accomplished, leaving God's shalom with all—the living and the dead. From the juxtaposition of these readings, a sermon proclaiming the gospel in the face of death is given, followed by naming the deceased and opportunity for witness to that life in the context of Christian faith. A congregational hymn and/or affirmation of faith follows, concluding the "liturgy of the Word" section.

In the Commendation that follows, the completion of the funeral rite with a celebration of Holy Communion is here restored, or when not, a prayer of thanksgiving is used that offers thanks for Jesus, "who knew our griefs, who died our death and rose for our sake, and who lives and prays for us. . . ." completed by the assembly's joining in the Lord's Prayer. In the words of commendation to God found in the new United Methodist funeral service, the eschatological promises are made clear again to the deceased, and to the church: "Receive us also, and raise us into a new life. Help us so to love and serve you in this world that we may enter into your joy in the world to come."

Certainly we can "read off" of the texts of the prayers a profound recovery of eschatological imagery and themes. My point, to be explored in more detail when we discuss the nonverbal dimensions of liturgy as theology, is that these texts are set into a living ritual context. It is the context of human grieving and its range of pathos, mostly "too deep for words," and especially the rhythm of ritual enactment that provides the primary theology here. Taken *together*—the gathering, entrance, readings, singing, proclamation and witness, prayers, the act of commendation and the celebration of the eucharistic meal and final blessing—it is the whole pattern of the liturgy that embodies the eschatological hope. Well celebrated, this funeral rite is now reshaping the faith experience of many United Methodists. The verbal dimensions of the texts, with all their interaction, must be understood as gesture, as integral to the sign-actions of the whole rite.

Thus, while specific theological work has been done to recover a deeper range of biblical and theological eschatology, the primary theology is done by the gathered community. It is the community at prayer and in ritual participation that gives voice to what the texts indicate: to "what is the breadth and length and height and depth . . . of the love of Christ which surpasses knowledge."[21] This suggests that the eschatological character of the funeral liturgy is not simply *in* the texts, and therefore is dependent for its power on the quality and authenticity of its actual celebration. This, it seems to me, is especially true in the contemporary social/cultural context where the living hermeneutic of the worshipers must be considered as integral to the "meaning" of the rites. By this I refer to our new awareness of how the social and cultural forms of perception and self-understanding are part of the interpretation of symbol. Understanding liturgical participation requires tracing the active role of social subjectivity.

The biblical images found in the texts we have cited, put together with the physical signs enacted in the community's keeping of time, the water bath, the common meal, and the burial of the dead, carry the living theology of Christian hope. Even a simple gathering to listen, to sing, and to pray, becomes an act of hope. Every prayer uttered under the sign of death and resurrection in the name of Jesus is a resistance against hopelessness and death.

The paradox discussed in chapter 1 concerning the intersection of human pathos and divine ethos of the Christian assembly may now be clarified in two ways. First, the hope in God and trust in the mystery of Christ's self-giving requires the active remembering over time of the whole life, teachings, and resurrection of Christ. At the heart of that is the *kenosis* of God in the passion of

Christ. The world's history of suffering and death, and the forces of injustice and oppression are figured in the cross. The divine passion for all creation and for us as human creatures is the basis for hope, even in a time of the "absence of God." This is the glory of the cross that many Protestant hymns sing, and that is at the heart of the Paschal mystery. Baptism initiates us into this, and the Eucharist, with its juxtaposition of Word and holy meal, continues to offer it.

The second aspect of the paradox is located in the invoking of the Holy Spirit to bring to remembrance these things. Having "given us a new birth into a living hope through the resurrection of Jesus Christ from the dead" (1 Pet. 1:3) is radically dependent upon the Spirit of God animating the liturgical assembly. Every prayer, as Karl Barth reminds us, is: "Come Holy Spirit."[22] The Eastern liturgies have preserved this more prominently than have most Western rites, except perhaps for the Pentecostals and the Quakers.

Yet there are also promises of goodness, of blessings, and of the walk by faith that characterizes the baptized life. The promised return home out of exile and the presence of justice and peace are nonetheless real. As Jewish prayers lean toward the hope of fulfillment of Torah and the kingdom of God, so Christian liturgy leans always toward the fulfillment of these in the One called Alpha and Omega.

But this makes actual human history a crucible itself. Our lives, socially, politically, and individually, become the testing place of the expectations. The eschatology of *primary theology* enacted in the liturgical assembly thus looks to and works within the arena of history as the arena of God's glory. This is poignantly expressed again and again in the songs and preaching of the African American traditions: "Keep your lamps trimmed and burnin,' keep your lamps trimmed and burnin'. . . the time is drawing nigh!" This is an Advent faith. But it is vibrant in the very act of being sung in the company of hope, trembling with power: "I want to be ready, to walk in Jerusalem just like John" means opening to a future beginning now, in this time and place. Yet still, beyond what can be made real in social and political history, there is the vision: "My Lord, what a morning, when the stars begin to fall." Such a final judgment of all life and all creation requires a reticence and a sobriety born of the joy that is the hope of all the world.

The realized eschatology embedded in the liturgical action of the community at prayer in Jesus' name is not simply a recall of the "fact" of a resurrection in the past. Rather it bespeaks and enacts the impossible possibility of the future becoming present. The present outpouring of the Spirit that brings all things to memory about the whole history of God's passion for the suffering, groaning creation, is a crisis in time, for the Spirit enables us to remember what has not yet come to be in history. Here we dare, even in our not comprehending, to join in the ending cry that is our beginning, "Maranatha!"

For all the explicit theology in these liturgical texts about the promises of God, there is a *not knowing* as well. The New Testament is, for the most part, reticent about the end time: "But about that day and hour no one knows, neither the angels of heaven, nor the Son, but only the Father" (Matt. 24:36). The eschaton is God-given, literally not conceivable in human schemes. Not a date, but a promised faithfulness. Not something guaranteed by proper liturgy, but a radical risk of faith. We shall see this again in considering liturgy as prayer.

We are up against the limits of language, and the limits of human knowing. Yet we do use language and we do employ human images to speak of these things, from the parables of Jesus, to reports of Emmaus, to the liturgy in the book of Revelation. The reticence and the power are held together in the liturgical imagination that traces the self-emptying of God.

What, then, is the hope expressed in the juxtaposition of these readings, prayers, symbols and ritual acts? It is the future of God that can only be invoked and cried out in the present circumstances, knowing the history of human pathos. It is the journey *through* Dante's words over the entrance to hell: "Abandon all hope, ye who enter here," to the eucharistic acclamation: "Dying you destroyed our death, rising you bestow new life; Lord Jesus, come in glory!"

C H A P T E R

4

LITURGY AND THEOLOGY: CONVERSATION WITH BARTH

Ultimately, the liturgical problem of our time is . . . a problem of restoring to liturgy its theological meaning, and to theology its liturgical dimension. Theology cannot recover its central place and function within the church without being rooted again in the very experience of the Church (in thanksgiving and supplication). . . . Theology must rediscover as its own "rule of faith" the Church's lex orandi, and the liturgy reveal itself again as the credendi.[1]

What we believe, acknowledge, and become by praying are deep features of what we profess about God. The human activity of listening for and addressing God shows something of what may be said and known about God. In this way the language with which we address God gives more than a hint of the shape that theological doctrine about God must take. That is, praying to God and speaking about God in relation to the affairs of the world are intimately related, as Alexander Schmemann suggests, but in complex ways.

In this chapter some reminders are assembled about the relations between liturgy as the ongoing prayer of the church and the task of theological reflection that takes liturgy as a source for learning how to refer all things to God. This is, admittedly, a form of liturgical theology, and it must be distinguished from a simple "theology of prayer" or "theology of worship." These latter enterprises usually take the form of applying already formulated theory or doctrine to the "practices" of prayer. By contrast, I propose that the explication of various modes of prayer already sketched in chapter 1 yields doctrinal insight. Furthermore I propose that Karl Barth, despite the cliché that he stresses objective revelation to the exclusion of human liturgical activity and expression of faith, may be understood precisely as doing this, though not as an announced program.

But why Karl Barth? In his *Introduction to the Theology of Karl Barth,* Geoffrey Bromiley remarks that one of the unappreciated aspects of Barth's *Church Dogmatics* is "the ultimate orienting of theology to worship."[2] This neglected reading of Barth as a special kind of liturgical theologian is, I am convinced, crucial to any attempt to demonstrate the political and ethical strands in Barth's theological interests. More to the point, however, is the fundamental role gratitude and acknowledgment of God play in rendering language about God intelligible. To show this I will not exposit his "theology of worship," or simply apply his antecedent theology of revelation to the practice of prayer. Rather, my reading of Barth focuses upon the manner in which liturgical concepts are implied by and, in some cases, illumined by his central concerns for knowledge of God and the Christian life.

My focus is therefore upon an obvious but neglected orientation of Barth's theology to liturgy as the ongoing prayer of the church.[3] There is, as I will attempt to show, an indelibly liturgical character to Barth's doctrine of God that sheds light on the way he thinks about human ethical and political experience. Everyone who comes into Barth's field of force is aware of the problematic character of relations between divine and human agency and, in particular, issues generated for "religious experience" by his resolute focus upon the integrity of God and the divine self-disclosure. So a liturgical reading of Barth's doctrine of God, with its attendant anthropological implications, is not, on the surface, obvious. Yet the doxological themes are there, and a way of thinking about doxa and doctrine that attracted the Catholic theologian von Balthasar.[4]

As a young pastor, Barth once admitted that he had an aversion "to all ceremonial in worship."[5] His friend Gunther Dehn once observed, following a worship service in the Popplesdorf Kirche in Bonn at which Barth had presided: "Sermon, first class; liturgy, fifth class."[6]

Certainly Barth had expressed skepticism concerning the liturgical renewal in the German Lutheran Church, and even of the World Council of Churches' Faith and Order debates and proposals over sacramental practice, liturgy, and ministry. The "art of liturgical worship" elicited by "historical models and aesthetic ideals" he thought to be a matter of theological fancy! Many of his actual pronouncements on liturgy seem discouraging to my line of inquiry here. He would doubtless agree with C. S. Lewis's famous critique of those who get the "liturgical fidgets." [7]

Theology is a critical investigation into the language that the church employs in order to speak faithfully in accordance with the pattern of God's own actual self-communication. The revelatory event of God's self-disclosure displays a trinitarian logic; or, if you will, a relational onto-logic that shows the very form and content of the divine life as triune. Theology is, on this construal of Barth, essentially a grammatical inquiry; that is, the explication of the rules governing intelligible discourse about God. This is impossible without attending to the activity of prayer as graced human acknowledgment—Barth will speak of the "miracle of acknowledgment"—and dialogue with God.

In *The Humanity of God*, Barth states this unequivocally:

> It is imperative to recognize the essence of theology as lying in the liturgical action of adoration, thanksgiving and petition. The old saying, *lex orandi lex credendi*, far from being a pious statement, is one of the most profound descriptions of theological method.[8]

This strand in Barth's theological reasoning renders theology itself a self-critical offering and a sacrifice of praise and openness to God. In this way his conception of the critical character of theology must itself be rendered in terms of specific liturgical themes and concepts. Critical theological thinking is secondary and therefore derivative of the first-order theology shown in praying to God.

In the opening volume of the *Church Dogmatics*, Barth announces that the subject matter of theological reflection is our language about God.[9] In this respect the force of his enterprise is intentionally modern. This does not mean that he is discontinuous with the apostles, the early councils, and the patristical sources, much less the Reformers. Nor does Barth wish to posit a philosophical scheme or metalanguage with which to interpret the Scripture and revelation. Rather, his idiom for clarifying Christian doctrine incorporates the linguistic turn of recent analytic and phenomenological styles of thinking. Proclaiming and acknowledging the truth about God, the world, and the church is a fallible matter. Therefore it must be subject to critique and not simply be "read off" from the pages of Scripture or the texts of the church's prayer, or applied from tradition in some "cookie-cutter" style.

The task of theology is, according to Barth, a critical formulation of rules governing intelligible discourse about God. At the same time we think about how we are to proclaim and to speak of God, we must remain open to speaking about the church and the whole cosmos, as it were, *with God*. While the divine self-disclosure is given to the church, Christian theology is the rule-formulating reflective activity that provides norms and criteria for any faithful speech about God. The relevant aspect of Barth's project is that we must use language (fallible as it is) about God to address God and the worshiping church and the nonchurch world. Theology unfolds the grammar of language about God in order to become truthful and intelligible about the church, humanity, and the whole created world—"heaven and earth."

The conventional reading of Barth regards prayer and liturgy as secondary to the positive revelation of God. This trades on the idea that he is against any appeal to human response or awareness. But a careful investigation shows that this contrast between "objective revelation" and "human faith," if taken as a neutral point, is inadequate to the logic of truthful theological work.[10] The church's language about God must be grammatically appropriate to its true object—the One acknowledged, received, and petitioned. In this way Barth shows us that theology itself is not knowledge of God, but is, rather, the grammar of what is known when God is appropriately acknowledged, praised, invoked, and supplicated. Indeed, critical theology itself is conceived as an offering, a response—hence it shares the pattern of all faithful prayer. The "divine service" (*Gottesdienst*) is precisely the event in which God's speaking and human answering correspond. Since the community that is the church comes into being in praising and worshiping God, theology as a function of this community attends to the patterning and to the tacit understanding of God revealed by prayer and proclamation.

In this manner Barth's theological reasoning, early and late, opens the way for a deep interdependence of prayer and the doctrine of God. Since he begins with the actuality of God's self-disclosure rather than with human consciousness or some general notion of religious experience, God's initiative is at the center of all references to prayer and liturgy. The categories of personal agency and God's freedom are basic to his account of the divine life and to any human knowledge of God, hence, to any human self-knowledge. Personal agency and freedom, are, I contend, liturgically constituted categories, and not metaphysical or ontological in some neutral sense. In order to show how theology "begins and ends in prayer" for Barth, we need to understand the liturgical themes and concepts entailed by his actual procedure in dogmatic exposition of God's self-communication to a community constituted by prayer and proclamation.

Relations Between Prayer and Theology

A brief examination of Barth's discussion of prayer and theology in his *Evangelical Theology: An Introduction* will illuminate my point about the general relations between dogmatic exposition and ongoing prayer as response and dialogue.

"The first and basic act of theological work is *prayer*."[11] This claim sounds a theme heard throughout the whole of the *Church Dogmatics*. Theology, while requiring historical knowledge and conceptual refinement, is dependent upon our having been addressed by God in such a manner as to respond freely in return. In the early volumes this theme is largely implicit, but it becomes explicit in Barth's 1962 lectures. Theological work "does not merely begin with prayer and is not merely accompanied by it; in its totality it is peculiar and characteristic of theology that it can be performed only in the act of prayer."[12]

The task of formulating a trinitarian doctrine of God, for example, is not simply motivated by prayer, its logic follows out the pattern given to prayer. There is an essential unity between prayer and the conceptual side of theology. Thinking about God and speaking the truth of the gospel are possible insofar as they address God faithfully. The whole motif of "God in Christ reconciling" must illuminate every topic in theology and hence display a unity, necessity, helpfulness, and beauty that is grounded in prayer to God. But it also specifies the status of the "object" of prayer by taking its stance before God. For Barth, the essence of prayer is the acknowledgment and recognition of God's gracious turning in mercy and judgment to the world. In this sense, prayer is a way of knowing God by virtue of responding to the Word-formed encounter with God. We are drawn more deeply into prayer by our very search to understand that "God is the one who rules."[13]

Second, the object of theological reflection is the "Thou" we encounter, not a thing to be grasped such as an idea of the Highest Good or of the ground of being. Here Barth asserts that doctrinal language about God must flow from a graced response to God. This implies that doctrines about God must take their logic and content from the address of God—precisely as a fruition of God's address to humanity. "Theological work must really and truly take place in the form of a liturgical act."[14]

Third, since theological thinking is itself dialogical, we cannot rest with building upon the certainties of earlier systems of thought. Rather, turning and returning to God in prayer means, for Barth, "beginning once again at the beginning." To conceive of God as living and redeeming the world is possible only by the graced receiving anew of the present activity of God. Theology itself becomes an offering to God, an invocation.

Finally, theology cannot guarantee the grace of God. It must follow Anselm's prayer, and his logic, in the *Proslogion*: "Reveal thyself to me." Certainty in our knowledge of God lies not in the formulated doctrines, but in the petitioning that God will truly dispose us to God's Word and active being. Doctrines then are communally authoritative rules that govern speech, intention, action, and faithful responsiveness to God and neighbor.[15]

In light of these later remarks linking prayer and theological doctrine, we may observe how Barth's whole trinitarian doctrine is instructive for our inquiry. Two crucial themes emerge from religious praxis to form the necessary background for constructive dogmatics: the themes of thanksgiving and doxology. Both are to be understood in light of Barth's focus upon God's self-communication. Nevertheless, the theme of thanksgiving is intrinsic to any knowledge of God. Likewise, Barth connects the theme of glory—both as *doxa* and *doxologia*—with the reality of God. These emerge for human thought so far as God is acknowledged. To acknowledgment as a graced human activity we must turn in detail.

Acknowledgment of God

The concept of acknowledgment is key to the relationship between prayer and the explication of God's self-giving. It expresses the manner in which the creaturely and the human can be referred to God so as to supply the human mind with analogies, and hence with experience which is truly of God. Acknowledgment defines what it is for humankind to be an active subject in the event of the divine self-disclosure and the divine self-giving. Put abstractly, acknowledgment of God in prayer is a responsive capacity, and it is graced. The invocation, and recalling of God in thanksgiving, praise, and petition expresses the grammar of Barth's fundamental but implicit "canon" of prayer.

Acknowledging God is, we might say, the central hermeneutical key to understanding the internal relationship between God as "revealed" and the modes of prayer appropriate to God. Barth makes this point extensively in *Church Dogmatics* III/3, where he asserts that the essence of prayer is "an asking, a seeking and a knocking directed towards God."[16] Prayer is, in essence, the church's constant petitioning. This is the one thing "which corresponds . . . to this . . . revelation."[17] True prayer and worship, which both remembers and invokes God, is the receiving of God's self-giving. The character of prayer as petition in the modes of thanksgiving, invoking, remembering, praising is grounded in the reality of Christ's eternal intercession for the world. Acknowledging God, then, is a fully responsive human activity; but it is given its content and its capacity by the very "canon" or ruled range of modes of prayer appropriate to the God who allows himself to be petitioned. Thus, God "is God in the fact that He lets man apply to Him in this way."[18]

Theology itself is a *critical* sacrifice of praise grounded in the epicletic (invoking) and anamnetic (remembering) nature of how God is acknowledged in and through praying with Jesus Christ. This is precisely why Barth can speak of acknowledging God as miracle (*das Wunder*). "In the possibility of acknowledgement of the Word of God there . . . consists the possibility of experience and therefore of knowledge of the Word of God."[19] This implies that the acknowledgment that comes with praying faithfully in and through Jesus Christ is pivotal. It refers to what it is for human beings to be active subjects in the very event of divine revelation.

The ongoing prayer of the community's worship of God is governed, according to Barth, by this logic of acknowledgment. The very invoking of God is thanksgiving—in this sense is eucharistic. To give thanks, Barth claims, is "to acknowledge (*anerkennen*) as such a gift, freely given."[20] Recognizing and receiving God's free gift of self-giving is what is due. As the eucharistic prayers begin: "It is our duty and delight to offer you thanks and praise!" God accepts our thanksgiving "as 'Eucharist,' as acknowledgment (*Anerkennung*) of his grace."[21] But to invoke God is also doxological as we will explore in the following chapters of Part 2. Thanksgiving acknowledges God's having graciously acted, and drives toward praise for God's own being-in-act. This in turn leads to "multiple petition"—the concrete expression of the request for God to continue to act and to reveal the divine will and purpose in accordance with God's covenant Word of promise.

Barth's development of these points is extensive in the *Dogmatics* and in the later writings such as *The Christian Life*. This is a neglected aspect of the "logic" of his trinitarian exposition of revelation. Acknowledgment of God as a recognitional capacity comes into its clearest focus, perhaps, in Barth's analysis of the act of faith in the Doctrine of Reconciliation section of *Church Dogmatics* IV/1. While Barth's polemic against natural human agency is not negated, it is nevertheless clear that he characterizes faith as the theological disposition realized and actualized in prayer.[22] He proceeds to analyze the act of faith in relation to the terms we have noted: acknowledgment, recognition, and confession. Such terms, according to Barth in IV/1, show that the act of faith "is a knowledge."[23] Thus human beings, in praying, take cognizance of God in the form of obedience and a confession of radical dependence.

To acknowledge God is to call upon and to remember in thanksgiving, praise, and petition. But this very graced activity is also an analogical capacity. In other words, acknowledging God in this patterned way with the community involves the rational and critically reflective capacity to form fitting analogies of God. The being and the work of Jesus Christ as the one who leads us in the prayer determines this. Barth here connects prayer and theological reflection explicitly. To ask what we must do in obedience to God's promise and command is already "the beginning of the human reaction proportionate to God's action."[24] So invoking and remembering God in thanksgiving, praise, and petition is that which constitutes human "cooperation" in the history of the covenant.[25]

We may say, then, that the acknowledgment of God in prayer and worship gives rise to thought about God's revelatory activity. It is given correspondence in human thought and specific determinacy. "Analogy" is therefore not some common metaphysical factor between God and humanity described in terms of a general concept of being. Rather, it is the reflective side of the *analogia fidei* ("analogy of faith"). The capacity to acknowledge God generates awareness of the *analogia* of God. Thus, even though Barth does not pursue this as a systematic principle, fitting analogies of God are indeed formed by reflection upon the language of prayer and the logic of acknowledgment, especially with respect to the eucharistic logic of God's self-giving. God is a gift received in thanksgiving. God is the Giver of all thanks recognized only by depth of praise, God is consistently the One who turns to us in mercy as acknowledged in our very act of seeking, asking, and, petitioning God to come to us.

Throughout this conversation we have noted that prayer is not defined as generic human longing, as for example, in Schleiermacher. Rather, it is defined by its goal or summit. So the final point to be made is that prayer in all its modalities is conceived by Barth as an eschatological activity. The most fundamental aspect of prayer is that it is gift, and that God answers prayer. The assurance is in God, not in the human experience of prayer. Yet, strangely, Barth can say: "Prayer exerts an influence upon God's action, even upon his existence. This is what the word 'answer' means."[26] Thus prayer illuminates the very character of God in relation to the world. This is fundamental to the method of liturgical theology underlying this book. By yielding to human address, to our supplication, God shows the kind of majesty and greatness that is God's alone. This is a key aspect of *kenosis*, or God's vulnerable action toward the creation. Thus Barth wishes to claim that, properly understood, prayer is a practice of the future of God already present. In the lectures of 1929 Barth boldly claimed:

> Prayer is the actualization of our eschatological reality that is possible here and now . . . we actualize our eschatological reality in prayer.[27]

In this way the whole sphere of ethical problems can be seen in light of the ongoing prayer of the people of God. Ethics is illuminated by regarding human intention and action eschatologically (the subject of chapter 14). In paragraph 15 of Barth's *Ethics* this is pointedly clear under the title "The Command of Promise." To speak theologically and hence ethically at all, we must take up the standpoint of God's future for us in Christ. Prayer is what allows us to conceive ourselves not merely as creatures and sinners saved by God's gracious reconciliation, but as children of the promises of God. Recognizing the possible problems in appealing to Barth's 1929 lectures, I nevertheless contend that his point about prayer is basic in his later work as well. All petition to God that is faithfully grounded in praying with Christ is eschatological in the sense of manifesting our openness to God's future for us, while revealing the reality of God's intention to act toward us in accordance with God's unfailing promise.

This is borne out in a striking passage in "Ministry of the Community" from IV/3/2:

> In prayer the community keeps God to His Word, which is the promise of His faithfulness as the Word which calls, gathers, upholds and commissions it. It keeps [God] to the fact that its cause is His. Appealing to His free grace, it expects quite simply that He will let Himself be kept to His Word and therefore that its cause which was [God's] yesterday will be His again tomorrow. In its thanksgiving and intercession it thus enters . . . not hypothetically but confidently, into the dealings which God has initiated between it and Him, becoming an active partner in the covenant [God] has established.[28]

By virtue of prayer itself being a graced capacity to participate in God's future for us and for the whole creation, it is possible to claim that God chooses to be disclosed in the very activity of human response.

The connection with ethics is made quite explicitly in Barth's later lectures on the Lord's Prayer as well. In commenting upon both Luther's and Calvin's treatment of the Lord's Prayer, Barth speaks of our being immediately invited to ponder the inner essence of Christian prayer as solidarity with all humanity. To pray the Lord's Prayer with the church is to address God in and through Jesus Christ on behalf of all humanity. This is basic to the vocation of all baptized Christians. As we have noted, this theme emerges boldly in Barth's reflections on the community's ministry, both in IV/3/2 and in the 1962 Chicago lectures, *Introduction to Evangelical Theology.*

With both Calvin and Luther, Barth sees the whole of the Lord's Prayer as an invitation from God for us to participate in God's reign and life, both here and now and in the life to come. The Lord's Prayer is but the epitome, to use Tertullian's phrase, of all Christian prayer—it is radically eschatological in point. The Word of promise of what God has done and is yet to accomplish "on earth as in heaven" permeates the whole prayer. Every petition sounds this note, but the last petition on the "eschatological temptation"—the absolute evil that threatens us with oblivion—drives this point home. The eschatological character of the whole prayer, hence all Christian prayer in Christ, is linked to Barth's fundamental claim that God is faithful to God's self-given Word: the Kingdom, the power and the glory are finally, in Christ Jesus,

God's alone. The prayer is an eschatological cry based precisely on the acknowledgment of God's name, will, and reign. All the particularities of our ethical struggles and actual human needs with which we petition God are themselves signs of yearning for the future which is already claimed in faith—though never grasped or possessed, no matter how profound the human faith or experience of prayer. In his *Ethics,* Barth specifies the sense in which we "actualize" what we have not or cannot do for ourselves. "Because we actualize our eschatological reality in prayer, . . . to be living in Christ, Christian prayer must say finally, 'Not my will but Thy will be done. . . .' "[29]

Could it be claimed then, that for Barth, our "eschatology" is to be prayed? If this brief exposition and line of reasoning is anywhere near the mark, the answer is in the affirmative. In one respect, our eschatological claims are unsayable—a point taken up in chapter 13. God's future is not said, but *shown* in and through the work and prayer of the community gathered in Jesus Christ. At the same time, because the graced activity of acknowledging God in the entire range of Christian prayer and worship also discloses who God is, we may trust the "fitting analogies" and images given in Scripture that characterize the kingdom of God for which, and because of which, we pray. In this way Barth's theology begins and ends in prayer. The double mystery revealed is at one and the same time God's gracious turning toward us and the creation, and the deep things of humanity before God. A passage in *The Christian Life* puts this unmistakably:

> As only God himself can be at issue in the prayer of Christians for the coming of the Kingdom, so only man can be at issue in their other thinking and speech and action. Man himself is he whom God loved, for whom Jesus died and rose again, and for whom he will come again as Judge and Redeemer. To him as such, Christians owe righteousness, their whole attention and concern and mercy.[30]

All of this could be true and still we could have missed the point. The "miracle" of acknowledgment constitutes human receptivity to the rule and reign of God as "future present," to use Marianne Micks' provocative title.[31] There are resistances in Barth to easy claims about social political norms, and most certainly there is a permanent "hermeneutics of suspicion" in him with respect to the presumptive and idolatrous tendencies, let alone their unholy wedlock, which emerge in both church and state. Such resistances and such permanent vigilance regarding the presumptions and idolatries of the human heart and of our social engines and programs, emerge not from conservative political theory in Barth, but from the eschatological character of life before God, which must always be a life of prayer and worship. In this way prayer and the ongoing liturgy of the church is not simply a devotional atmosphere or an emotional context for thinking hard about the sufferings and complexities of human social existence. Faithful liturgy is a logical context for discernment; or rather, is that graced activity of acknowledgment (praise, thanksgiving, invocation, and petition) which exercises the *analogia fidei* and *imaginationis*. All the time we note that the uses and abuses of prayer and liturgy to cajole, manipulate, self-congratulate, suppress, repress, and deny human reality are legion!

A reticence and a revelatory picture of theology's being and ending in prayer emerges. Could we say that authentic prayer is both reticent and revelatory? Reticent because of the situation of those praying creatures, sinners saved by grace; revelatory because prayer is itself the miraculous acknowledgment—the "graced" point of contact that generates fitting analogies for God. Praying with the community disposes all that is creaturely toward the finality and future of God's self-giving. In this way Barth's theology begins and ends in prayer, and there can be no ethics without faithful liturgy, nor faithful liturgy without a community obedient to God's will.

While there is much in Barth's theological reflection on the sacraments and on liturgy to disagree with, my reason for conversing at length in this chapter is to explore the restoration of theological significance of Christian liturgy, and to show the liturgical dimension of theological thinking. It is one thing to set forth the formal conditions surrounding the mutuality of the *lex orandi* and the *lex credendi*. It is another to explore specific ways in which the liturgy prays "primary theology." To that task we now turn.[32]

PART TWO

Liturgy as Prayer

CHAPTER

5

PRAISING, THANKING, BLESSING—GRATITUDE AS KNOWLEDGE OF GOD

Worship in the gathered community of faith takes the form of enactment. Remembrance of God is, as we noted in the previous chapters, "active"; requiring shared texts, symbols, and ritual actions. Praying, proclaiming, responding, and celebrating the baptismal bath and the common meal are the very means by which the "future-present" of God is possible. Selected and "canonized" memories of the people of God are contained in the biblical books and in the continuing deep structures of the prayer-actions that constitute Christian rites.[1] Thus, in reading, singing, preaching, and hearing the word, in the silences as in the sacramental actions, the present community—in whatever age or cultural circumstances—encounters what is remembered of God and the divine promises.

While not everything in liturgical rites is specifically prayer, it is illuminating nevertheless to think, as we did in chapter 1, of the variety of Christian rites as "schools of prayer." So far as the glory of God is acknowledged in praise and thanksgiving, and biblical prayer speaks of ascribing to God the honor and blessing appropriate to God's holiness and to the mystery of God's being, we may speak of liturgy as prayer. Liturgical worship therefore begins and ends in praising, thanking, and blessing the reality of God. This is, as we have seen, a theological act. This is what Kavanagh, Lathrop, and others call *theologica prima*, primary theology.[2] Here is the revolutionary notion at the heart of liturgical theology: to pray to God is to be a theologian. Thus the gathered church at prayer is doing theology, from which more abstract forms of critical reflection and "secondary theology" emerge.

At this point we need to explore how praise, thanksgiving, and "blessing God" are themselves forms of knowing God. I will speak of liturgical rites as "teaching us to pray." This does not mean that we simply imitate the texts of the prayers. Nor is the chief function of liturgy "didactic." Rather, if we are to speak of knowledge of God it must be a passional knowing—a process of being formed in specific affections and dispositions in the way we live that manifests what is known about God. I shall argue that the pattern and imagery of the classical eucharistic prayers are places where a particular gratitude toward God is formed. Such acknowledgment and grateful blessing of God is itself, as our discussion of Barth indicated, a way of knowing God. No praying ever guarantees the presence of God, but when authentic praise and thanksgiving are offered in response to the divine initiative, the conditions for receiving the divine self-communication are made alive. In this sense, authentic Christian liturgical prayer is born of both gratuitousness in God and human pathos—and these most intensely copresent in our celebration of the Eucharist, the common holy meal.

Christian liturgy, we have claimed, is the ongoing prayer, proclamation, and life of Jesus Christ—a sacrifice of thanksgiving and praise—offered to God in and through his body in the world. That is, Christian liturgy is our response to the self-giving of God in, with, and through the One who leads us in prayer. The community is called into being to continue that prayer on behalf of the whole world. So we must continue to gather in praise and thanksgiving about the book, the baptismal font, and the eucharistic table in order to know a home. This extended definition highlights the christological nature of Christian worship and its dynamic historical and temporal character. Yet it opens the way for a discussion of the relations between gratitude and God's grace. As Geoffrey Wainwright has trenchantly observed:

> In worship we receive the self-giving love of God, and the test of our thankfulness is whether we reproduce that pattern of self-giving in our daily relationships with other people. Of course, the test already begins with our attitudes and behaviour as brothers and sisters in the liturgical assembly.[3]

We shall return to this linkage between liturgy and ethics in chapter 13.

Before turning to an analysis of how specific liturgical prayers teach us to pray, two points must be made. First, Christian prayer and prayerfulness can be distinguished from the reciting of texts of prayers. As David Steindl-Rast reminds us, "Sooner or later we discover that prayers are not always prayer."[4] His point is that prayer is ongoing communion with God, whereas "prayers" are texts we pray, whether written or in oral tradition. What makes our prayers authentic *prayer* is wholehearted attentiveness or attunement to God in and through the utterances. The intention and the state of mind of prayer he terms "recollection," drawing upon classical Catholic tradition. We may analyze prayer texts and interpret liturgical actions and yet miss the heart of the matter. Prayer in the Christian tradition is opposed to an indifferent, passionless, or distracted frame of mind. The thanksgiving offered in response to God, as Romano Guardini observed, "consists in accepting life, with ever-growing awareness, as God's gift."[5]

Prayer as living communion with God as awareness of existence as divine gift is beyond the "language" of liturgical prayer texts; this is the very pattern of affection and intention in the lives of those who pray. My point is not to construct a dualism of "inner" experience and "outward" language and ritual act, but to show how the affections of gratitude and praise are learned in and through such language as ritual gesture. *How* to give thanks and praise to God is formed in us by coming to participate in the reality referred to in the descriptions and ascriptions of God as creator, judge, redeemer, sustainer, and consummate lover of all creation. This requires conceptual determinacy and hence is not mere "feeling" or inchoate experience. One has only to consider the frustration of parents trying to teach young children to be grateful. It is a marvelous experience when a child moves from merely repeating words under duress to the first fully spontaneous, "Thank you, Mommy." So it is with thanks to God, but with an entirely new subject unto whom gratitude is expressed.

Praying in the Christian context moves through understanding the memories of the church witnessed to in the Scripture, the narratives, images, and the depictions of the divine life in concrete human terms. This is why, among other things, love of God requires love of neighbor. It is also why there is a constant tension of anthropomorphism in language used to speak of God: "Father of mercies," "God, whose mothering care," "shepherd," "searcher of hearts," and "Holy One of blessing." Such learning about God from participation in liturgical action can never be a matter of didactic content. Coming to know God involves a personal encounter and not just a cognitive mastery of texts.

The second point concerns the manner that human beings acquire a capacity for sustained gratitude, in season and out of season. This gratitude to the divine for the gift of life and the benefits of the divine self-giving in history is not a mysterious "inner experience" so much as it is a pervasive attunement to the world in all its beauty, terror, and mystery. In this sense human maturity is involved.[6] A deepening capacity for gratitude and thankfulness of heart leads to a more comprehensive sense of truth about how things are. At the same time, thankfulness to God requires a reconfiguration of our natural desires. We may say that Christian prayer, so far as it is speaking God's name in praise and thanksgiving, is part of the discovery of our own humanity. This is suggested in the classical definition of worship as the glorification of God and the sanctification of all that is human. There are anthropological consequences. Let us speak of prayer, then, as a double journey—at once toward the mystery of God who invites relationship, and into the deep places of our own human self-understanding. This leads Guardini to say:

> It is therefore of the utmost importance that we should learn to give thanks. We must do away with the indifference which takes all things for granted, for nothing is to be taken for granted—everything is a gift. Not until man [sic] has understood this will he truly be free.[7]

We find in the texts of Christian prayers of thanksgiving the opposite of indifference as well as an invitation to human maturity. The freedom for spontaneity in relation to the world, for being "surprised by joy," is given only in and through the discipline of learning to attend to God and to intend all things to God. Understanding ourselves and the whole human family as receiving the gifts of God's good creation, sustaining mercy, and justice, is to reorient ourselves to the world and to other human beings with a continuous gratitude that renders both the praying and the living as a response to grace. The central mystery of gratitude in the Christian context is the reordering of relations between creature and the Creator.

This reordering of relations we find most intensely sounded in the texts of eucharistic prayers. While the pattern remembers the being and the deeds of God's specific acts in history, the focus is upon God's self-giving in Jesus Christ who is taken to be the recapitulation and the chief model of the divine self-giving. Thus in the Prayer of General Thanksgiving from the *Book of Common Prayer*, God is thanked for "our creation, preservation, and for all the blessings of this life," but chiefly for "the redemption of the world in Jesus Christ." The deep affections that are formed in continuing to pray this prayer are "interior"—relating to desire and a range of other affections such as compassion, repentance, and joy—and "relational"—relating to the social and historical contexts in which human beings live. Authentic prayer forms us in an affectional understanding of the truth about how things are.

In what follows we will see how the eucharistic prayers are the most intensive and extensive form of praise and thanksgiving in the Christian tradition. A full analysis is, of course, not possible here. Suffice it to say, the eucharistic prayers that emerged very early in the Christian tradition contain all the modes of prayer within the framework of thanksgiving: praise, adoration, confession, invocation, supplication, and eschatological doxology. Lamentation is only hinted at times, but we shall have more to say on this in chapter 7. We turn first to two of the most significant early forms of the eucharistic prayer as a way of illuminating the themes and proposals advanced thus far.

Inherited Patterns

The earliest Christians prayed to God and gave thanks with the language and gestures inherited from Judaism. The synagogue and domestic meal liturgies, and, to a lesser extent, the temple rites provided fundamental images and basic patterns that the earliest Christian communities addressed praise and thanks to God. The writings of the New Testament reflect this. These writings were themselves generated by the prayer and worship in the daily lives of the churches in the first two centuries.[8] In the Acts of the Apostles, the author tells us:

> They devoted themselves to the apostles' teaching and fellowship, to the breaking of bread and the prayers. . . . Day by day, as they spent much time together in the temple, they broke bread at home and ate their food with glad and generous hearts, praising God and having the goodwill of all the people.[9]

This is a picture of the earliest Jerusalem community. There is an obviously close connection between the structure and rhythm of prayer, and the fellowship and ritual action, especially in the continuation of praise and thanksgiving in daily meals as well as in the temple. Some scholars have seen in the phrase, "the breaking of bread and prayers," a reference to an embryonic eucharistic rite. While perhaps not a Eucharist in the full ritual sense of the term, this nevertheless gives evidence of inherited patterns of meal thanksgivings, now linked with the teachings of the apostles about Jesus' life, death, and resurrection. This is clear from the literary context in Acts where this description follows upon Peter's extended sermon concerning the meaning of Jesus' life in light of the crucifixion and resurrection, retold in the second chapter of Acts.

Blessing Prayers at Meals and the *Didache*

The points of continuity with Judaism are strikingly evident in prayer texts from the document called the *Didache*, or "Teachings of the Lord, given to the nations through his Apostles." Written

at the close of the first century or the beginning of the second, the
Didache records the following texts in chapter 9:

1. With regard to the prayer of thanksgiving (*eucharistia*), offer it in this fashion.
2. First, for the cup: "We thank you, our Father, for the holy
   vine of David your servant, which you have revealed to us
   through Jesus your servant. Glory be yours through all
   ages!"
3. Then for the bread broken: "We thank you, our Father, for
   the life and knowledge you have revealed to us through
   Jesus your servant. Glory be yours through all ages!
4. Just as the bread broken was first scattered on the hills, then
   was gathered and became one, so let your Church be gathered from the ends of the earth into your kingdom, for
   yours is glory and power through Jesus Christ for all
   ages!"[10]

Anyone even slightly familiar with Jewish traditions of prayer
recognizes the close connection with the blessing prayers prayed
at meals and the language used by the *Didache*. The language and
the gestures of blessing and thanking God in the *berakoth* (especially the Birkat ha-Mazon) echoes in these prayers. The use of the
Greek word *pais* ("servant" or "child") to refer to Jesus is evidence
of the antiquity of the prayer forms here cited.[11] At the same time,
the significance of the linkages between the actual prayer formu-
laries of various meal *berakoth* and the emerging pattern of prayers
at the Christian Eucharist is far too complex to investigate here.
For our purposes it must suffice to observe the intrinsic relation
of the inherited Jewish prayers of praise, blessing, and thanksgiving to the eucharistic prayer and ritual actions.

The most striking point about the *Didache* is that it takes the
pattern of a Jewish household meal in which the blessing of God
for wine and bread preceded the meal, and a series of prayers
concluded the meal. This final prayer was, in fact, a series of four
blessings. The first of these praised God as ruler of the universe
who gives good to all creatures. In the *Didache*, chapter 10.3, we
find the additional note of thanks for the "spiritual food and drink

leading to eternal life" through Jesus. The second element of the concluding meal *berakoth* focused upon the acts of God in leading Israel out from slavery. In the *Didache,* the Christian community also praised and thanked God for mighty acts in history, but the focus is upon the "knowledge, faith and immortality" revealed in Jesus who is described by St. Paul as "our Passover" in his Corinthian correspondence some thirty years earlier.

The third benediction prayed for mercy on Jerusalem and the lineage of David. The *Didache* prayer focuses upon the church, supplicating God to "gather it from the four winds . . . into your kingdom." This is directly parallel to the "gathering of the dispersed children of Israel" in the final table benedictions—an eschatological yearning for full restoration. The fourth benediction in the meal prayers consisted of a lengthy series of petitions constantly addressing God as "good and benevolent" or the "kindly lover" of humanity. In the *Didache* prayers of chapter 10.4, we encounter a short formula that may imply a series of spontaneous petitions, prayed gratefully: "Above all we thank you because you are almighty. Glory be yours through all ages!" The end of the chapter states simply: "Allow the prophets to give thanks as much as they wish."

From this brief excursion into one significant source of the earliest Christian eucharistic manner of prayer four points can be drawn that will permeate the remainder of our discussion. First, the patterns—shall we say, the "deep structures"—of Christian liturgical thanksgiving are indelibly Jewish in origin and cannot be understood without knowing their antecedents.[12] Second, God is praised and most especially thanked by remembering mighty acts as well as specific benevolences in creation, for example, the fruit of the vine and bread from the earth. The connections between creation and history are placed in the context of the glory of God's own being. Hence, praise for what God has done must not merely be an expression of the received "blessings" but also of the sheer acknowledgment of the glory of God in the mystery of God's own self. This is later to develop into a distinction between thanks for God for us and praise to God for God's own sake (*in se* or *a se*), to glorify God "in God's own being." In the third place, the Christian community from the beginning included the mediating role of Jesus in the very act of praise and thanksgiving. The distinctive fact of *eucharistia* was "in and through Jesus." The *Didache* speaks of "servant" or "child," while the characteristic ending "through Jesus Christ our Lord" developed in the doxologies and benedictions used in the Pauline letters and elsewhere.

A fourth point emerges: all petitions and intercessions are part of an eschatological dimension of all praise and thanksgiving. That is, not only is there a transfer of the eschatological petitions for Jerusalem and the scattered children of Israel to the community whose identity is marked by the person and work of Jesus of Nazareth, but the very act of prayer as petition or intercession for the whole world is an implicit prayer that the Kingdom (or final rule) of God may come to the whole world. Corroborating evidence of this is found in the initial petition of the Lord's Prayer, echoing its antecedent in the ancient *Kaddish* from the Jewish liturgy—"your kingdom come on earth." The final utterance of the book of Revelation is *Maranatha*, "Surely I am coming soon." Amen. Come, Lord Jesus! (Rev. 22:20). Thanksgiving is eschatological as well as remembrance of things past.

Eucharist Prayers in the Apostolic Tradition (Hippolytus)

With these four points about the earliest strata of Christian eucharistic praying in mind, let us examine the liturgical structure and themes of the earliest written text of a full eucharistic prayer pattern, that of Hippolytus as found in the *Apostolic Tradition* from the early third century. This text is not the only type used in the early liturgy at Rome, but it has become important in subsequent research (since its publication in the late nineteenth century) and, more importantly, in ecumenical restoration of eucharistic prayers in the twentieth century. It has become a paradigmatic model for nearly every major Christian body undertaking reform of its rites during the past twenty years.

After the presider and the assembled community share the ancient dialogue which concludes, "Let us give thanks to the Lord, it is fitting and just (so to do); Hippolytus' account of the prayer continues:

> We give you thanks, O God, through your beloved servant, Jesus Christ. It is he whom you have sent in these last times to save us and redeem us, and be the messenger of your will. He is your Word, inseparable from you, through whom you made all things and in whom you take delight. You sent him from heaven into the Virgin's womb, where he was conceived, and took flesh. Born of the Holy Spirit and the Virgin, he was revealed as your Son. In the fulfillment of your will he stretched out his hands in suffering to release from suffering those who place their hope in you, and so he won for you a holy people.[13]

After a brief section concerning the passion and death and its power to, "trample . . . the powers of hell," and of the manifestation of the resurrection, the so-called "institutional narrative" is included. Reflecting all of the Gospel accounts and the tradition that St. Paul had received orally (1 Cor. 11), this institutional narrative is also a command to, "Do my *anamnesis*."

> And so he took bread and gave you thanks, saying: Take, and eat: this is my body which will be broken for you. In the same way he took the cup, saying: This is my blood which will be shed for you. When you do this, you do it in memory of me.

This passage enjoins the ritual actions, and is followed immediately by what is known technically as the *anamnesis* segment of the prayer: "Remembering therefore his death and resurrection, we offer you this bread and cup, thankful that you have counted us worthy to stand in your presence and show you priestly service." Here is the thankful response to what God has already given. Even in the recital of the "words of institution" there is thanksgiving, and again in the very act of presenting the bread and the cup in oblation, thanks is rendered. The language *and* the gesture of grateful response coinhere, that is, form an indissoluble unity.

The prayer then moves to an invocation of God's Holy Spirit upon the gifts offered and upon the whole people gathered, known in Greek as the *epiclesis* segment of the eucharistic prayer.

We entreat you to send your Holy Spirit upon the offering of the holy Church. Gather into one all who share in these sacred mysteries, filling them with the Holy Spirit and confirming their faith in the truth, that together we may praise you and give you glory through your servant, Jesus Christ.[14]

Especially noteworthy is the reappearance of the eschatological plea, "gather into one" the whole church—with the implication of the whole human family and created order as well. The whole prayer then concludes with a great doxology: "All glory and honor is yours, Father and Son, with the Holy Spirit in the holy Church, now and for ever." To which the whole assembly shouts its "Amen." (Let it be so!)

Patterns of Thanksgiving and Praise

In reflecting over the whole structure of this prayer we immediately see the rhythm of praise, thanksgiving, and supplication, all mediated christologically. The creation of the world is effected through Christ. This recalls the opening prologue of John's Gospel. The Logos of God, now made flesh, is acknowledged as the same "word" (creative reason and power) by which all things were created. This same logos is also the utterance of God in and through the prophets now "in the last days" incarnate. Thus God is thanked and praised both for the holy acts in history and for the very glory of God's own life.

The structure of the ancient eucharistic prayer is again reminiscent of the heart of Jewish recitals found in such places as Psalm 136, in related canticles (Song of the Three Children in Daniel 3, for example), and in other liturgical prayers. God is praised and given thanks by recalling the mighty works. The distinctive note of reciting the word and acts of Jesus Christ provides a personal narrative element at the heart of Christian prayer. The "Do this" commands—his *anamnesis* by sharing bread and cup—a present experience of all that God has given in creation and redemption. This recital is not simply the recall of a fixed past event. Rather, it is a descendant of the remembrance at the Passover Seder. When the child asks the elders, "Why is this night different from all other nights?," the answer is given in the form of a narrative of the Exodus event. But it is clear also that on the *present* night—in this very prayer and ritual action of the meal—the liberating power of that past event is here and now, made actual among the community of memory and hope.

The pattern of thanksgiving in these early eucharistic prayers show a great range and depth. The act of gratitude makes the founding events present and the future as well. It is far more than "outward" ritual expression of "inwardly felt" gratitude. It is much more comprehensive than a simple recounting of one's "blessings." Such a pattern of praise and thanksgiving contains both an invocation for the present activity of divine grace and a plea for the saving power of God signified in the descriptions and ascriptions of glory and mercy in God embedded in the prayed narrative. Such a remembering includes a hope for the future, so that the thanks given and the praise rendered is directed toward God's future acts as well. In this way the thanksgiving is radically eschatological in force.

At the same time we must note the sacrificial element of self-offering to God implicit in the text. This is the double function of the *anamnesis*: the worshipers offer bread and wine in solidarity with the self-giving of the life of Jesus to God. These very gifts the community "offers" are possible only because they are first received as gifts from the hand of God to human beings. This exchange of gifts, then, is based upon the transformation of created material in and through the self-giving of God in creation and in human history. For the Christian community, all of this is concentrated in the way the life and deeds of Jesus Christ are like a parable of the whole creating and redemptive work of God. Thus, God's self-giving and the worshipers' symbolic self-giving at the table of the Eucharist embrace as the mystery at the heart of the eucharistic action. A radical paradox emerges. Christ is both the celebrant and the one given and received. What he embodies is God's eternal self-giving to the world. Thus what appears as "exclusivist" thanksgiving and praise is at the same time the most "inclusive" and universal praise. St. Augustine, more than two centuries after Hippolytus wrote down the primitive eucharistic liturgy, was to make the human consequences of this paradox explicit in his remark to the Christian community: "When you receive the eucharist, it is your own mystery you receive."[15]

The *epiclesis* element mentioned above emphasizes the fact that it is the Holy Spirit of God who animates both the gifts presented and those who are "worthy to stand before" and to serve God. In other words, the full range of meanings in Christian thanksgiving must include acknowledgment of *both* mutuality between God and the creation *and* the happy dependency of all things upon the grace of God. This is a "happy" or blessed dependency precisely because, in acknowledging with grateful hearts the creating and redeeming love of God and the life-giving Spirit, the human community fulfills its true nature: to praise and glorify God. The goal of human existence is reflected in liturgical terms by the very first question and answer of the *Westminster Shorter Catechism* (1647–48): "What is the chief end of man? Answer: "To glorify God and to enjoy him for ever."

In these two crucial instances of the origin and early development of the great eucharistic prayer at the heart of the central liturgy of the Christian faith we have the most intensive and complex form of prayer and praying. To be formed in the language and the gesture of this prayer is to acknowledge that all other forms of prayer and indeed, all forms of contemplation and action, are within the great embrace of praise and thanksgiving. So the concluding doxology reiterates the christological mediation of thanksgiving and supplication: "through him glory to you and honor . . . now and for ever!"

Knowing God

This all too brief exposition of early eucharistic prayers illustrates the four foundation points made earlier.[16] We can now explore further ramifications of our initial thesis. At the heart of Christian liturgical prayer and action is a pattern of thanksgiving and praise which, when addressed to its most fitting object (the God of all creation), opens a way of life and consequently a way of knowing God. Such a knowing is not simply doctrinal or cognitive, but is profoundly affectional. Prayers must become *prayer*, liturgical actions must become ways of relating to God, to creation, and to other human beings; otherwise the full implications of prayer and liturgy are never understood. Likewise, if other human emotions and intentions, no matter how virtuous or noble, are not brought to the praise, thanksgiving, and glorifcation of God, they do not find their true source and unity. Such a thanksgiving, when coupled with its christological mediation in the Eucharist, can be commanded but not coerced. It requires communal ritual expression that forms the believers in the appropriate deep affections. Eucharistic praise is thus an intention-action pattern for human existence.

One of the fundamental challenges to a life of gratitude is pain and suffering. This is heightened in Jewish and Christian traditions because pain and suffering are not regarded as illusory, but as historical and social realities. While other traditions' metaphysical views diminish the problem of evil and suffering, the very christological mediation of the presence of God in creation and history heightens the problem. Unmitigated suffering counts against being grateful. Death seems to be the final enemy of gratitude. So how is it possible for Paul to command the emotion of joy in "Rejoice always" or to command the believers to "give thanks in all circumstances"?

The first point is: This is no naive joy or thanksgiving. Paul does not command a simpleminded maxim for human happiness. The liturgy itself does not call for rose-colored glasses through which we see the world is not full of perplexities, pain, and sorrow after all. On the contrary, Paul knows suffering in his own life—in his own physical body. The doxologies that punctuate his correspondence with the early Christian communities, particularly in the book of Romans, are always seen against the background of the real vicissitudes of life. The praise and thanksgiving to God is like a reorientation to the essential relationships in life. Thus one does not thank God for evil and suffering. Rather, in the midst of suffering and perplexity one thanks and praises God for the gift of life and endurance. The thanking is itself an act of hope and resistance to what is evil—including the evil intentions and destructive desires that inhabit the human heart.

Here we must be cautioned about personal gratitudes that ignore the complexity of our social reality, including the social pathologies so destructively internalized in our time: anxiety, self-imposed guilt, fear of neighbor and stranger, and terrors from a loveless and capricious moral world. Metz remarks on our tendency to be overly positive in Christian liturgy: Because of an "absence of suffering in the official language of prayer" we "generally fail to notice what 'modern humanity' loses with the gradual impoverishment of the language of prayer."[17] What happens when *"eulogistic evasion of what really matters"* is our natural religious idiom?[18] We lose the only social language capable of expressing and sustaining our humanity in hope and love—therefore in true praise. Only to appease the individual conscience is to deny the trajectory, if not the essence, of biblically formed prayer. Here I have in mind the demanding emotional range of the Psalms that do not shrink from what really matters. To pray for, with, and out of suffering, forces the liturgy to yield its tremendous consolation and the depths of thanksgiving. For only here can we begin to discern and to acknowledge who this One is to whom we pray— the Lord who stretched out his arms on the cross to embrace all. Here liturgy can begin to form us in gratitude and praise which can encompass all our griefs and all our joys.

In the second place, the eucharistic prayer does not simply remember "good things" or some Edenic, idealized past; rather it remembers suffering and brokenness just at the most crucial point. Just as the memories of Israel recite that they were once in bondage to slavery in Egypt, so the Christian liturgy recalls bondage to sin and death and names brokenness of turning aside. More pointedly, however, is the fact that the christological narrative recalls suffering and death in the very act of rendering thanks. The fact of pain and death is not avoided, but recognized as part of the very means by which redemption is effected. In this sense, then, it is part of Christian gratitude to know the contrast between joy and suffering, between life and death, and between moral evil and virtue.

The vulnerability of the Christian tradition lies in the paradox of the extravagant claims made on behalf of a human life offered in radical obedience and full and thankful self-giving. Yet this is the crucial way in which pain and suffering and death are both remembered, in the act of rendering God thanksgiving for creation, redemption, and with praise for what is yet to be consummated for the whole cosmos. This is also why it can never be a merely "interior" state of mind or feeling, but thanksgiving must issue in a way of living that is eucharistic in character: giving thanks to God for who God is in all circumstances, whether immediately good or ill. This is echoed in other eucharistic prayers: "It is right . . . always and everywhere to give thanks to you, Holy God."

We have suggested that as faith and prayer mature in its experience of God and the world, the simple gratitude for specific acts intermingles more and more with the glorification of God for God's own being in itself. C. S. Lewis has a trenchant discussion of his own struggle to understand why praise and thanks to God was so central to the tradition. He admitted that he was at first put off by the thought that God should demand this. It distressed him that, in addition to gratitude, reverence, and obedience, he had to participate in a "perpetual eulogy." It seemed that God must be above such demands for gratification. He says later that he had overlooked the fact that all deep enjoyment overflows into praise unless it is deliberately prevented. This is simply a fact in human existence. Lovers praise the beloved, citizens their heroes and countries, and religious believers their saints. Moreover, he observed that the "most balanced and capacious minds, praised most, while the cranks, misfits, and malcontents praised least."[19] Thus he concludes that the psalmist's call for praise and thanksgiving was simply a call for what all healthy persons do when they address that which they truly care about and revere. We delight to praise what we enjoy, Lewis remarks, "because the praise not merely expresses but completes the enjoyment; it is its appointed consummation."[20] This is a corollary to the exchange of gifts at the heart of rituals of thanksgiving, which we saw at the heart of eucharistic offering. Just as the gifts of bread and wine, first gratefully received as God's to give are themselves offered in response, so the praise of God completes the enjoyment and delight in the acknowledgment of who God is and what human life becomes when "all things are referred to God."

Our understanding of gratitude and thanksgiving in the Christian tradition is incomplete without this intimate connection with praise. In all the great prayers of the church one finds this overflowing of thanksgiving into joy and praise. Might we say that there is a mutuality of affective understanding here? A proper understanding of the object of true praise attunes our hearts and our minds to the gifts and the giver. In theological terms, to know God and neighbor truly is to love and to serve both, precisely because, in worship, we come to understand the direction in which the mercy and compassion of God move—always toward the other. A full exploration of this point would lead to reflection on the inexhaustibility of glory and grace in the divine life. These qualities of God are never exhausted by our expressions of gratitude and praise. This is because, even in God's self-giving to the world, the divine being remains veiled, inexhaustible, and not comprehensible by the human mind. Yet the prayer and liturgical traditions within Christianity form us in knowledge of the divine life as one of glory and grace. Thus, in the act of thanksgiving, we acknowledge gift and giver, yet we cannot comprehend the fullness of God.

This leads us to an important connection between grace and gratitude that helps define the concept of human sin in the Christian tradition.[21] One of the most acute insights on this connection is found again, as in chapter 4, with Karl Barth. "Grace and gratitude belong together like heaven and earth. Grace evokes gratitude like the voice an echo."[22] This implies that the failure or absence of gratitude in the creature is a transgression, a sin (whether voluntary or involuntary) against the creator. This failing to ascribe honor and glory to the divine being diminishes the human enterprise. Hence, Barth claims, "Radically and basically all sin is simply ingratitude—man's [sic] refusal of the one but necessary thing which is proper to and is required of him with whom God has graciously entered into covenant."[23]

All this suggests that there are degrees of thankfulness and its relation to praise. The fullest praise in human life is reserved for the most worthy objects. Jonathan Edwards, among others, stressed the moral excellency and beauty of God as the supreme object of all holy affections.[24] The more excellent and worthy the object of human reverence and delight, the more intense the praise and gratitude will be. This theme is found in many different forms in the Christian traditions, especially in the early theologians such as the Cappadocians.

The modern writer C. S. Lewis links praise with beatitude in this remarkable sentence:

> If it were possible for a created soul fully . . . to 'appreciate,' that is to love and delight in, the worthiest object of all, and simultaneously at every moment to give this delight perfect expression, then that soul would be in supreme beatitude.[25]

This is a taproot of all elation and experienced joy in the religious life. Many traditions testify to this. There are moments in which sustained thanksgiving and praise allow us an experiential taste of bliss. In Christian tradition this is called an experience of the kingdom of God or the beatific vision. Such experiences in this life, however, are always partial, "through a glass darkly," never fully beholding the reality of God.

Yet even when the world is filled with death, we give thanks, for God's covenant endures forever, as Psalm 136 sings. Bitterness, despair, and hopelessness are not part of God's intention, but they are human contrasting possibilities. To continue in the prayer of acknowledgment of God in the midst of adversity as well as in good fortune is to understand more and more deeply who we are in light of who God is. Yet false and self-deceptive (self-congratulatory) forms of liturgy abound. Even these, however, cannot alter the central import of the most primary act of Christian life and prayer: to praise and thank God, and to grow in gratitude as the mystery of human existence before God unfolds.

Authentic prayer is born of extremity and in gratuitousness. Christian liturgical prayer, which from the beginning shaped prayer in solitude, is born in acknowledgment of life given by God in grace, that is, "without strings." Liturgy is also a rehearsal of the way we are to become related to one another and to the world. With respect to creation itself, one is brought to awe and wonder and gratitude when, suddenly, the familiar patterns of life are seen afresh. When the face or place encountered a hundred times before becomes luminous with what it is, there is gratitude. Gerard Manley Hopkins expressed this connection between liturgical praise and intense particularity well:

> Glory be to God for dappled things—
>   For skies of couple-colour as a brindled cow;
>   For rose-moles all in stipple upon trout that swim;
> Fresh-firecoal chestnut-falls; finches' wings;
>   Landscape plotted and pieced—fold, fallow, and plough;
>   And all trades, their gear and tackle and trim.
>
> All things counter, original, spare, strange;
>   Whatever is fickle, freckled (who knows how?)
>   With swift, slow; sweet, sour; adazzle, dim;
> He fathers-forth whose beauty is past change:
>   Praise him.[26]

Even greater than the sheer beauty of specific creatures—a rainbow, a sound, a bird in flight—is the sudden sense of the gratuitousness of all things. The wonder of being at all: this is the origin and the ever-refreshing source of gratitude in the human heart. Its power lies in the background of contrasts we have traced: light with dark, joy with sadness, the cup of water with thirst, the bread with hunger, and life with death. The eucharistic prayer contains contrast, a life of gratitude lived unto God learns how to refer all these to God.

We may regard Christian liturgy and its central prayer forms as an expression of the primordial gratuitousness of being. As communal prayer and ritual action it also forms human capacities to receive the world as gift and to live thankfully within it. To recite the wonders of nature and history to the source of all being, and to invoke the animating power of all life is to learn gratitude as well as to express thanksgiving and praise.

Prayer, in both its Christian liturgical and personal-devotional dimensions, is, as Brother David Steindl-Rast has pointed out, a coming alive to gratuitousness.[27] Only sustained prayerfulness over time opens up the relationships between God and the world because it participates in the mutuality of gift, giver, and recipient. Giving thanks daily, which marked the early community in the book of Acts, finds its culmination and fullest sounding in the eucharistic liturgy which is but a rehearsal of being eucharistic in the world in relation to neighbor. Praying with the church is thus a continual reminder and a training in the narratives and images that focus God's self-giving as the primal gift—the primary sacrament. But such gratitude cannot be gained in a single episode. It is deep only because it moves toward the whole of life. It takes time to unfold in the passing circumstances of temporal existence. But it is a double journey—both into self-knowledge and into the mystery of God's own being and self-giving. Only a lifetime lived in prayerfulness and gratitude can grasp who God is, much less, in the Christian context, the mystery of God's self-disclosure in and through the pattern of a human life who is both celebrant and grace in the Eucharist.

A final cadence must be sounded. The liturgy can only "teach us to pray" in gratitude because the triune life of God embraces us and calls the created world to its best being. The liturgy teaches us to become prayerful only because we continually cry out a request to the One who is present and celebrated, "Lord, teach us to pray." The liturgy can only teach us to pray because the life-giving Spirit who is invoked upon human persons, bread, wine, and water, continues to intercede for us with "sighs too deep for words."

Many go to church and many attend worship who do not find themselves praying. Dialogue, mutuality, and communion with the living God are never guaranteed. But the mystery of Christian liturgy well celebrated remains: God is faithful and waits. So the liturgy in its whole range—from daily prayer, to initiation rites, to Eucharist, to burying the dead—waits patiently for our humanity to be opened to it. The liturgy waits patiently, like the Scripture, like Jesus, like the whole life of God who, as Tolstoy once observed, "sees the truth but waits."

The greeting and singing, the reading, the telling, the praying, the offering, blessing, breaking, pouring out, and receiving always point to what God will yet do with us. Liturgy parabolically, symbolically, and metaphorically gathers us, carries us, and transfigures us to that which is not the merely visible, the evidently audible, the plain sense. Rather, liturgy carries us across and prepares us for "what eye hath not seen, nor ear heard" yet which, Scripture says, has been prepared for those who love God. Those whom God loves—and that is all creatures great and small—are meant for this. Liturgy invites us to a "home where none of us has ever been."[28]

All liturgical gatherings, ferial or festive, simple or elaborate, plain or splendid, are pregnant with the future. Or, we might say, every liturgy is an act of resistance against *no* future, against hopeless, loveless, unjust, and faithless worlds. So the oldest liturgical prayer testified to at the end of Scripture (Revelation 22:20) and in the *Didache* is but our beginning: "Come, Lord Jesus!" If Christian liturgy is to be the ongoing prayer of Jesus Christ in and through his body in the world, then all human vulnerabilities, complexities, and our primordial creaturely need to acknowledge the source and summit of human existence—all are brought to praise and thanksgiving "In, with, and through Jesus Christ in the unity of the Holy Spirit."

CHAPTER

6

INVOKING AND BESEECHING

Praising, thanking, and blessing God are essential features of Jewish and Christian liturgy. We have seen how these modes of prayer exhibit both theological and anthropological trajectories. While it is certainly possible and even desirable for some purposes to distinguish between praise, thanksgiving, and "blessing the name of God," taken together, they form a school for gratitude. To know God is to praise and give thanks. Chapter 2 established doxology as a way of perceiving God's glory, a central theme we found in conversation with Karl Barth in chapter 4.

The further we explore the interrelations of praise and thanksgiving, the further we journey simultaneously into the mystery of God and into the depths of our common humanity. But such a journey must be prepared for, learned, and guided. Learning to praise and thank God may be a primary mode of liturgical formation, but it may be the last thing we learn to do with a mature grasp of what to ask *for*. We come slowly to learn the *incomprehensibility*, and hence the glory of God. It takes time to learn the wisdom of Bishop Ignatii Brianchaninov:

> Do not theologize, do not be carried away by following up brilliant, original, and powerful ideas which suddenly occur to you. Sacred silence, which is induced in the mind at the time of prayer by a sense of God's greatness, speaks of God more profoundly and more eloquently than any human words. "If you pray truly," said the Fathers, "you *are* a theologian."[1]

This implies that our language of thanksgiving which may, as in the Eucharistic prayer, recite the "mighty acts" of God drawn from the witness of Israel and the early Christians depends upon something prior. I do not mean something necessarily prior in time, but rather theologically prior. I speak of invoking God.

We began this study by reflecting on the contemporary sense of the absence of God in our epoch. Certainly in an age of Holocaust and a media environment that renders evil banal by its television juxtaposition with seductively advertised consumer goods, the matter of experienced absence is close at hand. Practical atheism in everyday life, despite the language of prayer on Sundays and talk of Jesus in between, is made quite easy. One theologian has bluntly claimed, "People don't learn to be practical atheists by getting too involved in the world; they learn it in church—in the prayers they hear in church."[2]

But our age has no corner on experiencing the absence of God. There is a long and venerable history of this in the wisdom traditions, but even more pointedly in the Christian spiritual traditions that acknowledge the "dark night of the soul." The point relevant to our concerns in the next three chapters is the bearing of the presence and absence of God upon prayer, both liturgical and devotional. In turning to invoking and beseeching as modes of prayer, we must face the question: what part of God is veiled from us? Does the very act of "invoking" or calling upon God imply an absence?

Our earlier discussion of the eschatological character of Christian liturgy touched upon the cry for God. So the Lord's Prayer and the "Maranatha" were mentioned as two explicit instances of eschatological praying. Implicit in both, and in all honest forms of petition, is asking that God really be God. Of course, this includes our hoped for "projections" and potential idols as well as the received images of the transcendent Holy One. Human prayers are always toxic with our own religiousness. Prayer is, in this sense, a special form of "primary speech," as explored in the provocative book by Ann and Barry Ulanov.[3] Before considering the specific liturgical features of invoking as *epiclesis*, we first must address the issue of the implied absence of God in Christian prayer.

Prayer and the Absence of God

In devotional prayer as in public worship, most people think of "asking God for something" as basic. A case could be made that, left to our own devices, most of our praying would be placing our requests before God. That is, prayer arises naturally when we are in need. So our earliest prayers are petitions, "please, God. . . . " As we grow older, our invocation of God is often a desperate, "O God, are you there?" But even when we are habituated to public liturgy, our instinct is to call out for God to be God for us. Out of helplessness or turmoil, we need One who has the power to help or to relieve the distress. This suggests that praying begins not so much with a sense of presence, but with some intuitive or even painfully concrete sense of God's not being immediately present. The Psalms, as we noted earlier, contain the plea: "Where are you? How long, O LORD? Will you hide yourself forever?" (Psalm 89:46). Theodore Jennings claims that "If prayer has any basis at all in what we feel about God, it has that basis not in our sense of God's presence but in our sense of God's absence."[4] He continues in a manner reminiscent of Jacques Ellul, concluding that the only human basis for praying, at least of petition, is in our godlessness and godforsakenness. "If God is fully present with us, prayer is neither necessary nor possible."[5] This point of departure goes against the natural assumptions of piety. Most of the training we receive in church and Sunday school assures us that God is always "near." But from the perspective of the wider ranges of the biblical and spiritual traditions, this is only half true. The pathos of human existence raises the question of absence and presence. Perhaps more pointedly, the pathos of human existence *is* the question of God's absence and presence.

Suppose, then, that we regard prayer as a calling, an asking for God to become present in our lives. This, as Jennings suggests, is an expression of something we lack. We pray, together and alone, for God to be present, because we experience an absence. Thus: "We ask that God will sanctify his name, bring his kingdom, perfect his goal—because of the absence or hiddenness of these things and thus because God . . . is absent, hidden, or 'not yet who [God] will be.' "[6] Here once again we return to the basic point established in chapter 3, namely, that all prayer—whether liturgical or devotional—exhibits an eschatological yearning. But now we face the question of absence and presence in the very language and gesture of prayer. There is a deep restlessness in us, as Augustine of Hippo observed, that remains restless until it finds rest in the presence of God.[7]

Here we do well to distinguish those forms and situations of prayer that cry out of a sense of abandonment, from liturgical prayer that rejoices in the presence of God. The latter occurs most typically in the mode of praise and thanksgiving. Wholehearted praise and the joyful giving of the eucharistic prayers examined in the previous chapter, presuppose the community's acknowledgment of what God has done and rests in the promises that God will be present. But we also encounter biblical prayers that cry out of the void. The supreme case of this for Christians is the prayer from the cross. Here, at the end of Jesus' life we hear the anguish of Psalm 22:1: "My God, my God, why have you forsaken me?" (Matt. 27:46; Mark 15:34). More will be said in the following chapter on lamentation in relation to praise and thanksgiving. For now we need only observe that *both* a cry of desolation in time of "absence," *and* the communal act of giving thanks to the God who is present in grace and judgment are part of the biblical and Christian canon of the worship of God.[8]

But if prayer as invocation or the beseeching of God to be present is based upon the human experience of the divine absence, or at best, on the experience of "distance," how is prayer anything more? What is the basis for liturgical prayer that occurs in the matrix of hymns of praise, readings about the power and mercy of God, and the celebration of sacramental actions that the church deems as "means of grace"? The only reliable basis is found in what God has promised to be. It is a profound act of hope to pray, whether in the context of anguish outside the rooms of liturgy, or within the ordered patterns of ritual action. In this respect, Barth's reminder that prayer is itself a graced acknowledgment as well as a graced hunger in the human soul is unmistakably true. But our point is fundamental to the biblical notions of convenient promises: God will be faithful to the divine promise. This is who God is: the steadfastly faithful One who is the true "I Am." This is not an automatic guarantee of presence. The New Testament witness identifies this primordial "name" of God with Jesus Christ who is called the "Alpha and the Omega" in Revelation 3:8, echoing Isaiah's, "I am the first and I am the last; besides me there is no god" (Isa. 44:6). For the Christian community this is the presupposition of all prayer "in the name of Jesus."[9]

We still must ask: what connects the promises of God with the human activity of liturgical prayer? An adequate answer to this question would encompass the whole doctrine of the Holy Spirit. It is precisely the power of God's Holy Spirit that animates both the calling upon God and the efficacy of the church's prayer. This, in turn, may lead us to a reappropriation of the central role of the *epiclesis* prayer within the sacramental actions. From this point light may be shed upon the very possibility of authentic worship "in spirit and in truth." As we shall see, *epiclesis* cannot be confined to a single subunit of liturgical prayer, it is the necessary character of all authentic prayer in the name of Jesus.

Invoking the Divine Name and Spirit

At the heart of all Christian liturgical prayer is boldness and reticence. There is boldness in the act of approaching the God of all creation by calling upon the name of God. Such an act takes God's word of promise at face value. Much biblical prayer is spoken of this way, and the New Testament letter to the Hebrews claims that in Christ we have "confidence to enter the sanctuary by the blood of Jesus" (Heb. 10:19). Yet it is equally clear that, no matter how familiar with the language of Zion, we do not know how to pray. This is summed up in Paul's stark admission: "We do not know how to pray as we ought" (Rom. 8:26*a*). If he had left the matter there, we would remain in a kind of agnostic silence, no matter how many words we would needfully address to God. But, of course, the stunning truth emerges in the contrasting half of Paul's statement: "But that very Spirit intercedes with sighs too deep for words" (8:26*b*). The reticence of our calling out to God is born in our *not knowing* God or even our own deepest needs. The boldness comes from taking God seriously and from the promise made in Christ that the Spirit will come to the aid of our weakness. Thus we have no access to God apart from God's gracious self-giving and empowering life poured out. The Christian faith declares that in Christ the promises have become flesh and blood. In joining his prayer and work (the fullness of Christ's liturgy), we receive the Spirit's continuing intercession: for "the Spirit intercedes for the saints according to the will of God" (Rom. 8:27*b*).

It is easy for the habitual practices of religion to miss the paradox of prayer. Too much certainty about God leads to presumptive prayer. Presumptive prayer takes God for granted, and supposes that the presence of God is at our beck and call. Presumptive prayer, like presumptive behavior, ceases to respect its object, and soon all sense of awe, reverence, or "holy fear" is lost.

But presumptive prayer also results from proceeding to call upon God as if we truly know our human hearts and understand ourselves. Yet what do we really know of ourselves? What do we really know of God? These are the questions that are alive for communities of authentic prayer and worship. There is a gracious agnosticism in the "not knowing" which calls first on God the Holy Spirit to teach us how to pray. Like the first followers, our liturgical practice needs to begin always anew with their request of Jesus: "Lord, teach us to pray" (Luke 11:1*b*). Hence, authentic liturgy is a continual invocation.

Presumptive prayer and worship can be regarded as the seed-bed of idolatry. This, of course, is the constant danger of liturgy gone wrong when human beings settle for lesser gods. As Jennings has rightly observed:

> If we settle for less than God, we are likely to make that "less" *into* God, and thus "God" becomes the guarantor of the way things are. This is the idolatry of those who have settled down in the land—who transform Yahweh into Baal .... Under these circumstances prayer, too, ceases. Instead of asking God to be God, and thus to transform earth and heaven, we ask that heaven ratify earth.[10]

Here is precisely where the prophetic side of praising God emerges, as Walter Brueggemann has persuasively argued.[11] There is a transformative character to praise and thanksgiving because it in fact names and invokes the God beyond our religiousness. When these modes of liturgy become primarily a way of maintaining and legitimating certain social forms of human power in the name of God, then the prophetic force of invoking the Name of God once again must be exercised. This is precisely the ongoing story of worship in both the biblical account of God's people and of the history of Christian liturgies. When doxology comes to the edge of idolatry, the prophetic resources of invoking the God beyond our idols is essential!

In his discussion of worship as prayer, Peter Brunner begins by making what seems to be a contradictory claim to those just made. For him prayer presupposes the presence of God. Following Luther, he says that prayer "presupposes that presence of God in which God is present *for us* so that we may speak to Him as He [*sic*] speaks to us."[12] Such presence confronts us especially in the preached Word and in the celebration of Holy Communion. Yet he goes on to claim that the converse is also true. Thus, while liturgical prayer presupposes that the Word of God may actually be proclaimed and the Eucharist celebrated according to Christ's command and institution, such proclamation and sacramental celebration require invoking the name and Spirit of God. Hence both proclaiming the Word and celebrating the mystery of Christ's dying and rising are dependent upon the Spirit-gift of God. "That God approaches us through [the] Word and in [the] Meal with His incarnation-presence is not a mechanical, but a pneumatic event. Therefore we implore God for the gift of this particular presence."[13] In other words, the presence of God in word and sacrament is radically dependent upon God's own self-giving and not on the strength of our piety. This once again echoes the points made in chapter 4 concerning the relationship between prayer and theology.

There is something crucial, then, in beginning every Christian liturgical rite by invoking the name and Spirit of God. This is contained in the Reformed traditions' use of the opening sentence, "Our help is in the name of the Lord," to which the assembly responds in acknowledgment, "Who made the heavens and the earth." It is present in those traditions who use some variant of the trinitarian invocation: "In the name of the Father, the Son, and the Holy Spirit. Amen." In still other traditions it is an opening Christian *berakah* (see chapter 5): "Blessed be God and blessed be [God's] kingdom forever!" When such invoking of the name in which the church gathers is missing, something crucial is lost at the outset, even if prayers to the Holy Spirit are made later.

The distinctive character of Christian prayer was, from the earliest communities witnessed to in the New Testament, that it was made "in the name of Jesus." Just as one of the earliest baptismal formulas was simply the action of the water bath done in the name of Jesus. This in turn derives from the conviction underlying biblical prayer in Hebrew scripture that it is the Holy name of God that is to be honored. Blessing and praising the name of Yahweh was the characteristic mode of approach to the Holy One of Israel. The question of the unpronounced tetragrammaton is not the main point; rather to keep the name of God holy. So it is in the Lord's Prayer, as in its antecedent kin-prayer such as the Kaddish, that we acknowledge that God's name be hallowed— made holy *in us*. But this is itself to call upon the power of God to realize this in and through our praying and living. This, as we shall see later in considering liturgy and ethics (chapter 13), is the foundation of the Christian life.

Examples from Early Liturgical Sources

Let us return briefly to some of the earliest Eucharistic prayers of the Christian tradition where we find striking examples of invoking the name and the Holy Spirit. The *Didache*, chapter 10, gives thanks to God after eating the bread of the meal, and mentions the connection between the name and knowledge of God obtained through Jesus: "We give thanks to you, holy Father, for your holy Name which you have enshrined in our hearts, and for the knowledge and faith and immortality which you made known to us through your child Jesus."[14] The linkages between worship "in the name of Jesus" and true knowledge of God are evident in many other early sources as well. But the most significant pattern of invoking comes with the *epiclesis* prayers, literally the "calling down" of God's Spirit to sanctify persons and elements of earth—bread, wine, water, and oil—used in the ritual actions of the gathered assembly.

In the *Apostolic Tradition* of Hippolytus we read, following the words of institution from 1 Corinthians 11 and the remembrance (*anamnesis*) of Christ's dying and rising:

> And we ask that you would send your Holy Spirit upon the offering of your holy Church; that, gathering her into one, you would grant to all who receive the holy things (to receive) the fullness of the Holy Spirit for the strengthening of faith in truth, that we may praise and glorify you.[15]

Or, from the late third or early fourth century, the Egyptian Anaphora of St. Basil prays, "And we, sinners and unworthy and wretched, pray you, our God, in adoration that in the good pleasure of your goodness your Holy Spirit may descend upon us and upon these gifts that have been set before you, and may sanctify them and make them holy of holies." [16] The point here is not to give an analysis of these early examples, which may be multiplied, but simply to observe the crucial role of invoking the Holy Spirit in the context of the Eucharist itself. The appearance of the epiclesis section of the great prayer at the heart of the sacrament points beyond itself to the "epicletic" character of the whole prayer-action. "Come, Holy Spirit" underlies the whole prayer—the *canon* of the Mass in the West, the *anaphora* of the divine liturgy in the Eastern churches. That is, the whole prayer of thanksgiving, in all of its developing complexity in the early centuries, is dependent upon the work of the Holy Spirit when it is actually prayed in a gathered community at the table.

We find early evidence of the epiclesis "moment" of the Eucharistic prayer pointing to the consecratory force of the whole prayer in Hippolytus. Describing a celebration of the holy meal following the ordination of a bishop he cites the text as follows:

> Remembering therefore his death and resurrection, we offer to you the bread and the cup, giving you thanks because you have held us worthy to stand before you and minister to you. And we ask that you would send your Holy Spirit upon the offering of your holy Church; that, gathering (it) into one, you would grant to all who partake of the holy things (to partake) for the fullness of the Holy Spirit for the strengthening of faith in truth, that we may praise and glorify you through your child Jesus Christ.[17]

Here we see the interconnection of invoking the Holy Spirit as intrinsically related to remembering Christ's dying and rising, and to the life of the assembled community in the "fullness of Spirit." A century and a half later, Cyril of Jerusalem lectures to new Christians, explaining the significance of their participation in the Eucharist:

> Then having sanctified ourselves by these spiritual Hymns, we call upon the merciful God to send forth His Holy Spirit upon the gifts . . . ; that He may make the Bread the Body of Christ, and the Wine the Blood of Christ; for whatsoever the Holy Ghost has touched is sanctified and changed.[18]

There can be little doubt that these communities of faith carried in their practice a strong sense that, without the Holy Spirit, presence is not presumed.

The epicletic (consecratory) force of the prayer-action is also seen in early baptismal texts and accounts of the mode of celebration. In Justin Martyr's *Apology*, we find the invocation of the triune name of God to have this same function. In explaining the practice and meaning of baptism he writes:

> Those who are persuaded and believe that the things we teach and say are true, and promise that they can live accordingly, are instructed to pray and beseech God with fasting for the remission of their past sins, while we pray and fast along with them. Then they are brought by us to where there is water, and are reborn by the same manner of rebirth by which we ourselves were reborn; for they are then washed in the water in the name of God the Father and Master of all, and of our Saviour Jesus Christ, and of the Holy Spirit.[19]

In this vivid account we note that the catechumens (those who are to be baptized) "beseech God with fasting" in preparation. The invocation of the triune name of God is consecratory and renders the washing a true "illumination" by the Holy Spirit of God. This was, of course, one of the primary eschatological images of baptism we cited in chapter 3.[20]

The epicletic confidence of both Eucharistic and baptismal prayers gradually is diminished in the practice and theological understanding of the Western churches, while the Eastern churches tend to have preserved the epiclesis as more significant than the "words of institution" of Christ: "Do this in remembrance of me."[21] The history of the diminishing significance of the pneu-matological force of the Eucharistic prayer in the West is also a history of the gradual fragmentation of the whole prayer into segmented miniprayers. That history is not traceable here. But one of the most remarkable aspects of recent twentieth-century re-forms of Eucharistic rites among both Protestant and Roman Catholic traditions is the retrieval of the epiclesis. More impor-tantly, liturgical theology now stresses once again the consecra-tory force of the whole prayer-action. This, I contend, is integral to a renewed sense of the eschatological character of Eucharist and baptism. We will return to the theological and pastoral implica-tions of this in discussing the whole canon of Christian worship, and in the concluding chapter of the book.

If we are to fully appreciate how praising and thanking are a school for gratitude, we must also understand that invoking the name and calling upon the Holy Spirit is logically prior to these and all other modes of liturgical prayer. This gives testimony to the very act of worship as itself a gift from God. This does not deny human agency, but rather shows in some detail how the very activity of liturgical prayer-action provides a "grammar" of how to speak of God. The epicletic character of liturgy as prayer is required to enact the liturgy as rite faithfully. By invocation of the name of God (the unnameable "I Am" paradoxically imaged as triune life) and beseeching the Holy Spirit of God, the assembly foregoes all presumption. Yet how bold is the act: by the promises of God we call upon God to be God.

As in the case of the fruits of the Spirit, liturgical prayer-action as rite is done by real men and women in the midst of life. To invoke the Holy Spirit is to commit to being open to the gifts (charisms) God wishes to confer. While the gifts and graces are indeed social-relational powers, they are not simply our natural energies given a religious name. So liturgical prayer in the context of ritual action is something done by human beings. But all the while this "doing" is in relation to the continuing openness to the transforming power of the Spirit. For it is the Spirit, as John's Gospel tells, which is essential for the remembrance of what Jesus said and did. "But the Advocate, the Holy Spirit, whom the Father will send in *my name*, will teach you everything, and remind you

116

of all that I have said to you" (John 14:26). It is the Spirit that is continually animating the gathered assembly's worship and that is even greater than the religiousness of the human heart.

Boldness and reticence in approaching God are the earth of invocation, knowledge of God its fruit. The name we so easily call upon veils and reveals a reality beyond our religious projections, yes, even those drawn from previous liturgical experience. Without the life-giving, memory-conferring, and priestly-prophetic power of the Holy Spirit, no true thanks and praise will arise. Prayers will meet a "brazen heaven" unless we enter ever afresh into the epiclesis: "Come, Holy Spirit." The gesture of this vulnerable utterance renders Word and sacrament open to the presence of Christ, yet never controls that presence. We cry out to God in our sense of absence—whether in private desperation outside the church, or in communal faithful gatherings about the book, the font, and the table. The eschatological dimension of invoking the Name and Spirit of God is thus made clear: we take God's promises seriously. This, in turn, may reveal the mystery hid from our eyes and the plain view of the world—we are the "absent" ones: absent from God. The Spirit of God who searches all human hearts is the only power able to make us present to God in the midst of our forgetfulness of being.

Having established the interrelatedness of invoking and the modes of praise and thanksgiving, we have not yet fully faced our initial reflections on terror and the suffering. Lamentation must have its place if liturgy as prayer is to be truthful about our experience of the world.

C H A P T E R

7

LAMENTING AND CONFESSING: TRUTHFUL PRAYER

Those who say that they believe in God and yet neither love nor fear Him, do not in fact believe in Him but in those who have taught them that God exists. . . . Those who believe that they believe in God, but without any passion in their heart, without anguish of mind, without uncertainty, without doubt, without an element of despair even in their consolation, believe only in the God-Idea, not in God Himself.[1]

Christian liturgy is, first and last, praising, blessing, and thanking God. It is a continual speaking of God's name in gratitude and thankfulness for the self-giving of God to the world. On occasion it sings ecstatic praise for the very *being* of the source of all creation: *Te deum laudamus.* Yet every liturgical assembly, as every prayer in the name of Jesus, is radically dependent upon the gift of God's presence. Therefore all true worship begins and ends with a calling upon the name of the triune God, whose Holy Spirit gives life to our worship. This praying to God gives evidence to both absence and presence, and no human act in and of itself can overcome the gap between the experienced absence or distance from God and the divine presence. So we begin again and again by invoking the name and Spirit of God. Undergirding all authentic worship is a non-presumptive invocation. Here, too, we see the eschatological gesture in every true prayer. God is never contained in our liturgies. So we gather in the pathos and ethos of Advent, crying, "Come, Lord Jesus," and in the pathos and ethos of Pentecost, praying "Lord, send forth your Spirit, and renew the face of the earth" (Pentecost antiphon, Psalm 104).

All the modes of liturgy as prayer—praise, thanksgiving, and supplication—work in relation to one another. All are required for an adequate and faithful remembrance of who God is and a recognition of who we are in God's sight. In the next chapter we will focus on a crucial form of supplication that turns us toward others, namely, intercession for the world. For no praise and thanksgiving is complete without turning toward the creation. The blessing of God takes in neighbors to whom God incarnate comes with mercy. But all such modes of prayer must also be brought to the test of truthfulness and honesty in the experience of our ongoing life together. The crucible of testing is found in lamentation and confession of sin. Lamentation brings all gratitude, all hope, and all remembrance of God to the court of human pathos. Lamenting and confessing our sins before God brings us to face the truth about ourselves. Metz's warning about our easy "eulogistic evasion of the real" has already hinted at that to which we must now turn full attention.

Lamentation in the Psalms

Our inquiry began by naming the mixed texture of the world we encounter: its terror and its beauty. We raised the question of whether the liturgy could take into itself such a world. For many, the experience of absence and abandonment leads away from worship rather than toward it, though the cry of the heart for something (perhaps in place of the God no longer available) still is heard under a thousand disguises. We turn again to the book of Psalms, Israel's and the Christian tradition's common prayer book—a language where the terror and the beauty are found together. Now we need to examine liturgy as prayer in light of the criteria of truthfulness and honesty.

Many Christians have found the realism if not the harshness of the lament psalms too much. The history of Protestant worship contains a strong strand of suppressing the difficult psalms, especially the so-called "imprecatory" psalms of vengeance. These are often directly related to the prayers of anger over injustice and wickedness, but are also directed at "the enemy." John Wesley, for instance, found such a psalm as 137, with its furious image of dashing the enemy's children's heads against a rock, not fit for Christian tongues. And there is certainly a point to be made about psalms that seem to curse the enemy, especially in light of Jesus' teachings and example about loving one's enemies and praying for those who persecute the faithful (Matt. 5). Neither can we ignore the political and social differences between the original setting of the Psalms and our use of them today.

The desolation and abandonment expressed in Psalm 88 seems as difficult as the cursing psalms to those who believe that doubting God and experiencing the absence of God a sin. Here God is in the dock, as C. S. Lewis would say. If to call God into question is a sin, then much of the psalter is sinful indeed. But the point we must explore is the way in which lamentation is necessary for honest liturgical prayer. Along the way we can mark differences between individual and corporate lamentation and note differences between Israel's lament over being oppressed by powerful enemies, as in Psalms 74 and 79, and Israel's lament over natural disasters as in Psalm 83. In commenting on the two kinds of crises prompting communal laments—political crises and natural catastrophes—Claus Westermann observes that "communal laments in the psalms are invariably occasioned by enemies, while in the prophetic books . . . they are almost always a reaction to natural catastrophes."[2]

Throughout the rites of lamentation in ancient Israel, the nation was seeking God to turn again to them in kindness and mercy after such suffering, in war, or at the hand of natural forces. The psalms of lament are thus "one of the most important pieces of evidence for ancient Israel's understanding of history, an understanding which sees past, present, and future as bound together under God's control."[3] While communal laments are relatively few in number in the psalter, the individual lament psalm is the most common of all psalm types. These link the communal rites of fasting and penitence in the face of suffering, with the daily experience of individuals.

The child's question, "Why did God let Mommy die?" or our question, "Why is there so much innocent suffering in Bosnia-Herzogovnia?" help us connect with the psalmist's shifting contexts and types of anguish. Yet these questions are often suppressed in our public liturgies, or perhaps explained away. "God needed your mother more than we did" or "God is bringing a greater good out of the loss of these women and children's lives." Try as we may, there is no way utterances about God's will can deflect the force of the questions. For, if truly uttered in anguish, such questions already contain an acknowledgment of God. The silence of God cannot be silenced by easy rationalization, or by easy appeal to some self-evident will of God.

The difficulty of avoiding the psalms of lament and their contemporary sound in our liturgical assemblies may be put this way. Christian public prayer finds praise and thanksgiving far less demanding when lamenting is suppressed. Put differently, praise and thanksgiving grow empty when the truth about human rage over suffering and injustice is never uttered. Prayer may be sincere and God may certainly be praised and glorified in the absence of acknowledging such a truth about human suffering, but the revelatory character of prayer, liturgical or devotional, is diminished when no laments are ever raised. The Psalms wait to teach us this. Christian liturgy without the full range of the Psalms becomes anorexic—starving for honest emotional range. This is why some form of daily prayer with systematic coverage of the Psalms is so important in addition to more adequate musical settings of the Psalms for Sunday worship.

Claus Westermann's *Praise and Lament in the Psalms* puts this point clearly:

> Something must be amiss if praise of God has a place in Christian worship but lamentation does not. Praise can retain its authenticity. . . only in polarity with lamentation.[4]

If we see how the Psalms wrestle with human pathos in light of the covenant promises of God, can Christian liturgy convey something necessary about the very gospel it seeks to proclaim and the mystery that it seeks to participate? Consider some key features of lamentation.

According to Westermann, psalms of lament exhibit several variable features: (1) a complaint or accusation against God about something seemingly incompatible with the Covenant promises; (2) a complaint against enemies; (3) a sense of being threatened as God's people, not simply as individuals; (4) a calling to mind of God's past favor; and (5) an appeal to those favorable acts as the basis for hope in the present situation.

Some laments also anguish over sin and confess the faults of both previous generations and the present. We will return to the act of lamenting and confessing sin before the end of this chapter.

While not all the laments, individual and communal, sound all of these features, there is a web of interconnection being woven in these prayers. Their origin is in concrete political and social circumstances and Christian liturgy should not ignore them. But even within the Jewish tradition, these psalms provided a language of truth-telling about real suffering in generation after generation. Thus praying the psalms and singing them in various cultural contexts was a living hermeneutic, if you will, of ever-new instances of perceived incompatibilities with God's promises in the Covenant. The language is open-textured; hence the bitterness and anger of any time and place could be voiced in these songs. Perhaps the most anguished case in the biblical witness is found in the complaint over the destruction of Jerusalem in 527 B.C.E. "Are the deeds of Babylon better than those of Zion?" cries Esdra over the utter desolation of hope.[5]

Lamentation and Christian Liturgy

David Power has argued that, in our time, the Holocaust has retrieved the necessity of full lamentation. This is part of the weave of the suffering of Jewish people throughout history. But the reality of the Covenant was horribly called into question in a genocidal context at the hand of the Nazis. What language could both name this incomprehensible event and yet still recall God?

If the Covenant were to be kept as the foundation of the people's existence and identity, they felt the need to be able to recall it in a way commensurate with their awful sense of abandonment. How would it be possible to celebrate Passover service as long as it were not possible to find a way of containing the horrors of the Nazi hatred and violence within the remembrance of the Pascha. . . . Does a people silence this remembrance in order to continue to worship, or can it take issue with God over a brutality to which there is no divine response as far as any meaning is concerned and yet render praise in hope? [6]

I cannot presume to address the dilemma posed for the Jewish community, but I am convinced that the search for a truthful language about human atrocities and the ongoing inhumanity all about us is imperative. The point is not simply one of expressive honesty about rage and anger. The point is about God, and how lamentation is necessary to keep praise and thanksgiving from evading the real. It may well be that we cannot truly grasp the truth of Christ's cry of abandonment until we enter into the unimaginable pain of our fellow human beings. It is also linked to a question we cannot resolve here but which must be raised: what is the place of the people of God's Covenant in the eschatological promises of a "new heaven and a new earth"? Christian assemblies that ignore this not only avoid Paul's struggle in Romans 9–11, but do not fully grasp what it means that Jesus Christ is the "fulfillment" of the Law and Prophets.

The issue for Christian liturgy is whether the features of lament we noted in the Psalms, which appear in the prophetic and Wisdom literature as well, can be part of our prayer in the name of Jesus. As both David Power and Walter Brueggemann have pointed out, the language of praise tends to affirm security in God. Or, as I have attempted to explore, praise and thanksgiving tend to focus on the presence of God. But do we ever, in David Power's phrase, "allow the questions that a postcritical age puts to the inmost nature of God and of God's relation to the world [to] enter into remembrance and prayer"? [7] I contend that we must, no matter how difficult and theologically disarming this may be.

Lament must enter into Christian liturgy because, in a sense, it is already there. It is there in Good Friday, in the remembrance of Jesus' cry of dereliction from the cross. It is there when we pray honestly for those imprisoned, those who suffer innocently, and when we struggle to preach about the prosperity of the wicked and the pain of the faithful. Lament is implied by the broken bread and poured out wine of the Eucharist. And it certainly has begun to make its way into our awareness of how we human beings are slowly destroying the very natural order's viability.

Four principal causes of lament in the contemporary world are pointed out in Power's essay, "When to Worship Is to Lament."[8] First is the fate of the Jewish people in a post-Holocaust world; second is the enormous suffering of much of starving and war-torn humanity; third is the history of the Church's own complicity; and fourth, the "overidentification" of God with the actual unjust structures and preachments of the Church. These may not be everyone's definitive list—in fact, there can be no definitive list. But I find these connecting more and more with the very heart of the gospel to be proclaimed and the mystery to be celebrated. This is the nonpresumptive invocation of God's name and Spirit, where we can honestly acknowledge the terror and our own complicities in the very act of remembering that God is not our projected comfort, nor the guarantor of power in our image. Quite the contrary, the God whose very life takes on the suffering of all cries out with us against ourselves.

At the very least we must learn again to begin with lamentation of our sins. Here the rhythms of the liturgical year come to our assistance. Like the Psalms, the seasons of penitence are linked inextricably to seasons of thanksgiving. One without the other is empty. This is because the justice, mercy, and love of God figured in Christ addresses our tragedies and our sinful complicities, if we but have eyes to see and ears to hear. To discern the holiness of God may require, in this fragmented and peculiar age, a crying out on behalf of all creatures, of all creation.

Confession of sin has often been muted to a rehearsal of our personal vices. That we do have sins of omission and commission that require forgiveness and healing is true. But the deeper roots of sin are often linked with the terrors of society, and with those very injustices and sufferings over which we secretly lament, if we have a moral conscience at all. But confessing sins is not merely to lament them. In the Christian economy of salvation, the liturgy invites us to speak the truth about ourselves in order to find the truth in Christ. True confession of sin before God is not an indulging in our guilt or a massaging of our feelings of sorrow. Rather, it is directed toward amendment of life. This is why confessing is always in mutual relation to reconciliation and forgiveness.

So, for example, to pray with Jesus the Lord's Prayer, is to ask for forgiveness "as we forgive others." This is not a spiritual or liturgical bargaining chip. It is a condition for understanding how God characteristically forgives and liberates human beings from the captivity of self-preoccupation. Forgiveness is a restored social relationship, and hence a social healing.

There is a marvelous prayer used in many churches called the Collect for Purity that reads:

> Almighty God, to you all hearts are open, all desires known, and from you no secrets are hidden. Cleanse the thoughts of our hearts by the inspiration of your Holy Spirit, that we may perfectly love you, and worthily magnify your holy name, through Christ our Lord. Amen.[9]

Contained in this brief text is a profound theology of truth-telling. It is, in miniature, the indelible linkage between invoking the name and Spirit of God and the consequences of having worshipped God in spirit and in truth.

To worship God authentically is to face the truth about our world and ourselves. It is idolatry to name "God" and think we have nothing to face about evil, suffering, and our complicities. But the range of Christian liturgical life, conceived as a continually praying with, in and through Jesus Christ, will not let us go. Even the barest memory of Israel and the most simple remembrance of the life and death of Jesus acts as a check against our constant temptation to forgetfulness of God.

There is one more principal mode of prayer that is part of the facing of the truth about the world: intercession. If we truly pray for others, we cannot avoid, except when in the vice of self-preoccupied forgetfulness, being faced with the truth God knows. We must lament, but we cannot do justice to the biblical notion of lamentation unless we reconnect it with the promises of God out of which we make prayer for the world and for others.

C H A P T E R

8

INTERCEDING: REMEMBERING THE WORLD TO GOD

Remember, Lord, those in old age and infirmity, those who are sick, ill, or troubled by unclean spirits, for their speedy healing and salvation by you, their God.[1]

Without lamentation, our thanksgivings and petitions may founder. Thanksgiving may easily become, in Metz's words, a "eulogistic evasion of what really matters." But lamentation born out of suffering and the lacerations of the world must also be accompanied by facing and speaking the truth about ourselves and about our complicities in the very evils we deplore and find excruciating. Hence, praying truthfully in our liturgical assemblies requires naming the realities of our social-political world as well as the realities of our "inmost being."

If lamentation is not simply cathartic or self-indulgent, it flows outward into compassion for the sufferers, toward the oppressed and the oppressors. Intercession is a fundamental vocation of the church. It shows kinship with lamentation. We are to pray for the world in all its suffering. But this requires looking clearly and honestly at the world and at ourselves as we really are. To join Christ in his ongoing prayer for the world is to be plunged more deeply into the densities of social reality, not to be taken out of them.

So interceding for the pain of the world is itself an act in solidarity with Christ. In so being, this act of prayer commits those who pray to the intention to act in solidarity in the world of social-political forces. The liturgical act of interceding is thus a school for compassion. Literally this implies a suffering with others, not as an act of pious romanticism or of "pity on those less fortunate." Rather, entering into the dying and rising with Christ illuminates the world in all its actuality. Thus, to explore interceding for the world as integral to Christian liturgy is to explore the "primary theology" of Christ's compassion and the Holy Spirit's continual intercession.

Later we will raise the question of how liturgy is formative and expressive of Christian character and hence of the pattern of Christian ethical praxis. But here we will unfold that specific mode of prayer-action that links the truth of lamentation and confession with our turning toward the world. The actual world where ignorant armies clash by night is what Christ's passion and resurrection illuminates, and for the sake of which the Holy Spirit is called upon to empower us. It is in the recovery of the "prayers of the faithful" in twentieth-century worship that we gain an extraordinary clue to how we pray shapes what we believe about God and the world.

Patterns of Liturgical Intercession

Biblical examples of supplication to God for the people of God are too numerous to cite. Certainly one paradigm of this is found in Moses' continual dialogue with God on behalf of the Israelites as recited in Exodus. Abraham pleads for the cities of Sodom and Gommorah, and Judith and Esther intercede for God's people. Throughout the Hebrew Scriptures we find a continual reference to remembering the orphan and the widow, and the stranger within the gates. In both the Law and the Prophets the community is commanded to care for the poor and to give hospitality to the sojourner. Living in faithful obedience to God depends upon the reciprocity of cultic remembering and doing the works of justice and mercy. In the case of praying for the poor, it is God who continually reminds Israel to remember those outside the place of prosperity and power. But to remember the orphan, the widow, and the stranger is, in fact, to remember God.

As Moses was mediator between God and the people, so in the New Testament, Jesus becomes the chief mediator and interceding high priest. The writer of the Letter to the Ephesians prays in this light:

> For this reason I bow my knees before the Father, from whom every family in heaven and on earth takes its name. I pray that, according to the riches of his glory, he may grant that you may be strengthened in your inner being with power through his Spirit, and that Christ may dwell in your hearts through faith, as you are being rooted and grounded in love. I pray that you may have power to comprehend with all the saints, what is the breadth and length and height and depth, and to know the love of Christ that surpasses knowledge, so that you may be filled with all the fullness of God. (Eph. 3:14-19)

Few prayers in the Scripture rival in comprehensiveness this intercessory prayer for the ministry and the life of the church. In this passage we have both an example of interceding and a theological declaration of the coinherence of love and knowledge of God. In tracing the particular form and place of liturgical intercession we discover that the awareness of praying together in Christ for the world opens the possibility of maturing into our common humanity given to "all the saints."

In the First Letter of Timothy we find one of the earliest patterns for liturgical intercession in the New Testament. The writer is providing guidance for the leadership of a local Christian community. Among the regulations governing right worship is sketched a pattern of praying for others:

> First of all, then, I urge that supplications, prayers, intercessions, and thanksgiving be made for everyone, for kings and all who are in high positions, so that we may lead a quiet and peaceable life in all godliness and dignity. This is right and is acceptable in the sight of God our Savior, who desires everyone to be saved and to come to the knowledge of the truth . . . . I desire, then, that in every place the men should pray, lifting up holy hands without anger or argument. (1 Tim. 2:1-4, 8)

Depicted here is the linkage between thanksgiving, supplications, and specific kinds of intercession. But it also indicates the spirit of prayer and the physical gesture common to the early church. The community is to pray for both insiders and those outside the faith, especially for those who hold the fate of society in their power.

Less than a century later, Justin Martyr also speaks of the intercessions of the community. Following the water bath, the newly baptized Christian is brought into the assembly gathered to make common prayers:

> They then earnestly offer common prayers for themselves and the one who has been illuminated and all others everywhere, that we may be made worthy, having learned the truth, to be found in deed good citizens and keepers of what is commanded. . . . On finishing the prayers we greet each other with a kiss.[2]

This striking passage shows the importance of joining the prayers of the faithful. During the long baptismal preparation, according to Hippolytus, the catechumens were dismissed before such prayers occurred. Only the baptized into Christ could, in effect, join Christ's prayers in and through the intercessions of the assembly.

Liturgical intercessions, or "prayers of the faithful," have traditionally occupied one of two positions in the subsequent history of the eucharistic rites. Some are found at the conclusion of the liturgy of the Word, just before the offering of gifts at the table. Many twentieth-century reforms have placed them in this position. The other place is internal to the structure of the eucharistic prayer itself. In some cases very long intercessions were prayed in the presence of the eucharistic bread and wine. This is especially true of the Jerusalem liturgy (St. James), the Byzantine Liturgy of St. Basil, and still today in the orthodox liturgy of St. John Chrysostom.[3]

It has been argued that there is special efficacy of intercessory prayer when made while the eucharistic elements remain on the table before distribution. But the more important point is that the eucharistic assembly enters into a comprehensive prayer for the world and all that dwell therein. While each rite is marked with the specific accents of its particular cultural style, and with the particularity of those with whom the day or season is concerned, they all remember to God the entire range of humanity. Thus in a funeral rite, not only is the deceased remembered, but the whole world. In a marriage rite, not only are the bride and groom remembered before God, but the whole world. During Lent, not only are the catechumens remembered—as at the baptismal celebration of Eucharist the newly baptized are prayed for—but the whole world as well.

Leonel Mitchell has observed that when the intercessions occur within the actual prayer of the Great Thanksgiving, they are "an expansion of the *epiclesis* upon the congregation to include within the eucharistic action others for whom they pray."[4] Here we note the explicit connection between the invoking of Holy Spirit upon gifts and people, and the empowered prayer for the world.

But even when intercessions occur at the end of the liturgy of the Word, the point is that they flow from the heart of the community. The very reason for gathering is to receive the gifts of God and to join Christ's ongoing liturgy in the midst of the world. This means that, whatever the inherited pattern or structure—elaborate or simple—every social order must find its own reality to pray into the general pattern. The pathos of each community comes to expression here. In the case of so-called "nonliturgical" churches, intercessory prayer may be quite spontaneous and informal. In the case of Korean churches, for example, an extraordinary form has emerged called Tongsung Kido (literally "pray aloud"). Here everyone cries out their supplications and intercessions simultaneously while the leader also may offer a summary prayer.[5]

The virtue of following the themes and catagories of intercession from the classical early liturgies is in their comprehensiveness. All sorts and conditions of humanity are included, and the seriousness of the church's primary vocation to pray for and to serve the world is made clear. In gathering to praise God, to hear God's Word, and to celebrate the grace of God in the holy meal (or the water bath), the assembly must also pray with Christ.

Intercessions also occur in the structures of morning and evening prayer. While less elaborate, as in the case of the well-formed "suffrages" of the Anglican and Episcopal Prayerbook traditions, these nonetheless signal the ongoing prayer of Christ in and through the gathered assembly. In this case they are in close proximity to brief readings and especially to the Psalms. Here the juxtaposition of different psalms on different days through the whole psalter provides a rich liturgical hermeneutic for such prayer. In some cases a hymn or anthem, as in a Lutheran or Anglican choral office, extends the intercessions. This is not musical ornamentation, but a continuation of choral prayer by the choir or the whole assembly.

In the Prayerbook traditions the ancient prayer of St. John Chrysostom concludes these intercessions and the whole prayer office by asking God again that all the supplications may be fulfilled "as may be best for us; granting us in this world knowledge of [God's] truth, and in the age to come life everlasting."[6] The theological truth implied here is striking: God does not guarantee that our prayers will be answered with what we ask for, but rather, that (whatever the "answer") the very act of praying opens us to knowledge and especially to the *eschatological gift* of eternal life. This reminds us of the early church's teaching on prayer that emphasized "ask for the great things (the kingdom of God), and the lesser may be yours as well."[7] But this, in turn, is but a gloss on the primary teaching of Jesus: "Seek first the kingdom of heaven" in the Sermon on the Mount (cf. Matt. 5–6).

The Primary Theology of Interceding

The restoration and renewal of the prayers of the people (intercessions) in recent liturgical reforms focuses on a central theological claim: Christ is in the midst of his people praying with and for them for the sake of the whole world. Intercession is written into every Christology worth its salt, beginning with the Letter to the Hebrews: we have an intercessor who knows our pathos, and the sufferings of the world. If we truly make the request with the disciples of old, "Lord, teach us to pray," we will be attentive to his ongoing solidarity with the enormous pain of the world's body. The very act of praying for others is a declaration that God in Christ takes on the death-dealing, moral evil of the world.

A basic theological truth resides in the bodily, ritual practice of interceding: without prayers for others, our worship cannot possibly discern the fullness of how God is to be remembered. Whatever we say about the "presence" of God in the liturgy of word and sacrament cannot be disassociated from the neighbor in need and the social disfigurements of our age. Paul makes this clear, for example, in his critique of the church at Corinth whose Eucharists were a profanization of the body and blood precisely because they did not attend to the hunger of the poor. To forget, neglect, or willfully turn aside in the presence of Christ those we consider, or which society places, on the margins is to participate unworthily. More to the point, such a neglect or forgetfulness of the poor is a violation of the very meaning of the Eucharist. Hence when Paul castigates their behavior he renders null and void the very ritual actions they undertake. "This is not the Eucharist you celebrate." Here is a prophetic critique of the cultus because of a massive ethical failure. Here is a clear example of the theology as enacted. To recognize Christ's presence in word and Eucharist is to confess his presence in the hurt and in the very personhood of the neighbor as well. The former, rightly acknowledged and celebrated, discloses the latter. But not attending to the neighbor in Christ renders void any attempt to offer God thanks and praise in the common meal.

Prayers for others in the context of Christian liturgy show a fundamental christological orientation: as Christ had compassion, so must we; as he encountered the brokenness of the world, so must we; as he loved even in the face of death, so must we. Because his way of being radically open to God was to heal, restoring sight and hearing, and to proclaim in word and deed the liberating grace of God, prayer in his name is marked by his continuing intercession for the world. In this sense, to intercede is part of learning to regard the concrete world of human physical and social reality in, with, and through Christ. It is no accident that classical eucharistic prayers conclude with a sequence of prepositions—*through, by, with*—adding yet one more epicletic reminder, "in the unity of the Holy Spirit." The meaning and direction of our affections is schooled in this mode of prayer in two ways: toward those in need whom God in Christ loves; and toward the Intercessor who prays in and through us. Intercessions are the practice of being continually turned to act in the direction in which God's steadfast compassion moves.

Four Aspects of Intercessory Prayer

To pray with the community gathered in the Spirit around Jesus is to remember the world before God. To pray for others is a way of life that features our solidarity, not just our sentiments of pity or "sympathy" with the pathos of humanity. And not simply "humanity" in general, but the specifically hungry, oppressed, and self-destroying around us. This too, like lamentation, is part of the truthfulness of praying. Remembering others before God is part of remembering God. Four aspects of this mode of liturgical prayer are critical in the contemporary situation.

First, we encounter dimensions of ourselves as praying with and for others not otherwise encountered. Prayer, for the early church, was never isolated. Praying alone and praying together were conceived as two dimensions of the same ongoing life of the Spirit in Christ's body. A dichotomy between individualistic devotional prayer and the church's common prayer is foreign to the spirit of the early church. This may teach us about how we learn compassion. To "suffer with" our sisters and brothers is to receive a crucial part of our own existence. When prayers of intercession are conjoined with specific courses of action, we avoid "spiritualizing" the compassion of God. This requires a truthfulness about our own pain and our own sin toward others. Here the church must always be on guard against a counterfeit vulnerability of self-indulgence: where benign pity replaces the hard work of praying and working for and with others. Spiritual pulse-taking can never substitute for being disposed intentionally toward others as neighbors from God. Encounters with these dimensions of human beings are activated when the church becomes a ferment of intercession in liturgy and life.

Second, only in and through solidarity with those in need can we mean what we pray. In the human capacities released by praying for others, we can mature in our knowledge of how God's self-emptying love (*kenosis*) works in our tangled world. The "meaning" of prayers for others, therefore, is not so much the diction of our prayer texts as it is the manner of being disposed in compassion. To pray for others without allowing the ministries of the community to be visibly represented in the body renders them inadequate to their intent.

Third, we gain a moral intentionality in addressing the world to God. We plead with God to remember those for whom we pray. We cannot simply "enjoy" the forms of prayer and the affections of empathy. So we learn, outside the rooms of prayer, the risk of commending others to the grace and mercy of God. The most difficult thing here is that the church is called to trust God beyond our own highest capacity for love. Thus, to intercede for the world is to be attentive to God's hidden ways of mercy. The community of the people of God, Barth insists, "speaks by the very fact of its existance in the world; by its characteristic attitude to world problems; and, moreover and especially, by its silent service to all the handicapped, weak, and needy in the world. It speaks finally, by the simple fact that it prays for the world.[8] This manifests the christological force of such praying—Christ has promised to go before us and to be encountered in the hurt and the naked and the oppressed. The apocalyptic images of Matthew 25 make this clear: "Then will the righteous say, 'when did we see you . . . ?' "

Finally, intercessory forms of prayer forces us to recognize that religious faith must be lived in the world of power, conflicting passions, and in moral ambiguity. In our social circumstances prayer as praise must be linked with prayer as love of neighbor. This is the perennial tension between "prayer" and "action" in the Christian life. But my argument implies two further points relevant to this tension. The stress on compassion for neighbor does not entail the diminishment of love and adoration of God. Love of God and love of neighbor are not two sides of a balancing scale of affections. The double commandment of Jesus cannot be sliced in two. The summation of law and prophets does not put love of God and neighbor into inverse ratio, one to the other.

In the second place, we cannot assume that the tension between prayer and action is the same as the contrast between contemplation and action. This would identify prayer completely with "contemplative prayer." Joining the interceding work of Christ in the Spirit forms us in both "beholding" the suffering of the world truthfully and "intending" courses of action congruent with the vision of human well-being in the reign of God.

Once again we note that tensions are built into the Christian moral life shaped by common prayer. To pray with Christ is to face human forces we would avoid by staying only with the mode of praise and thanksgiving. To pray with Christ is to face temptations those who do not pray can hardly imagine. But these are not taken on as a matter of religious heroics. They are simply part of the uncommon journey toward the truth of things. Intercession is part of the call to holiness at the heart of Christian conversion.

Christ's own life is one of active prayer and prayerful action. It is therefore fitting to speak of his whole life as a prayer—a continual self-offering in love and obedience to the One who calls "Abba." In exploring what Christ's life-liturgy signifies, we ponder afresh the necessity of prayer and action in mutuality. These are what humanity needs to be whole, and the tension required by living particular moments of the liturgy—now beholding God, now making one's prayer a concrete act of mercy—is necessary to growing up into the "measure of the full stature of the Christ" (Eph. 4:13b).

Our lives and our liturgies are incomplete until we learn solidarity with others who suffer, and allow others to touch our suffering. Only in this way can we cease being alienated from our own experience of the pathos of the world. Christian liturgy leads to a deeper perception of the "tragic sense of life," to use Unamuno's phrase; but always in light of what has been promised.

There is no authentic liturgy without such a radical identification, and no true service of others without praying with Christ for them. Lamentation leads to heightened thanksgiving when the interceding mercy of God in Christ is interposed. This is because Christ is the vulnerability of God made present in our cry for the world. Intercessions thus manifest the deepest aspect of the Paschal mystery: God has taken on our suffering and our death, and, in offering ourselves to such mercy, we receive one another back. We receive, by grace, the vision of a transformed world. Once we "taste and see" this goodness, we are compelled to implore the Holy Spirit to empower us to act. Only then does the church's liturgical prayer enter fully into the ongoing liturgy of Jesus Christ.

While we see that all the modes of liturgy as prayer we have discussed in Part 2 are necessary, we then begin to understand that none of these stands alone. Furthermore, they are not confined to one sequence or order, though the history of the basic structures or orders of historic rites order them in specific ways. The prayed theology—the "primary theology" of the church—is at its most adequate and vibrant when the community of faith brings its full awareness to the intersection of all the modes. No praise or thanksgiving is adequate unless it also touches the heartbreak and the suffering of the world. But lamentation itself recalls the promises of God, and often leads to confessing our complicities in the very evils and injustices we cry out against. Truthfulness in praying and confronting the actualities of social, economic, and political life leads to interceding for the whole world. All of this is not our natural moral disposition. Rather, all of this is learned, slowly over time, when we stay with the liturgy of Jesus Christ. Out of our not knowing, nonpresumptive prayer calls upon the name and the Holy Spirit of God to transform us and the world in the direction of God's promises. In the end, all liturgical prayer is radically eschatological: "Come, Holy Spirit!"

PART THREE

Liturgy in Context

CHAPTER

9

BEYOND THE TEXT: THE SYMBOLIC LANGUAGES OF LITURGY

Only if we come to the liturgy without hopes or fears, without longings or hunger, will the rites symbolise nothing and remain indifferent or curious 'objects.' Moreover, people who are not accustomed to poetic, artistic or musical language or symbolic acts among their means of expression and communication find the liturgy like a foreign country whose customs and language are strange to them.[1]

Thus Joseph Gelineau, writing a decade ago in his insightful little volume, *The Liturgy Today and Tomorrow,* introduces one of our principal themes: the liturgy is itself a country we must learn to dwell in. It contains many languages and customs that form a crucible of experience, a multiple-layered culture if you will. In the present stage of twentieth-century liturgical reform and renewal, we sense with greater urgency than anyone could have realized in 1970 the double question of symbol in the liturgy and liturgy as symbol. We have learned to speak of the assembly gathered about the book, the font, and the table. Liturgical research has developed increasing depth and sensitivity in attending to the concrete problems of ritual participation by specific communities. We know, in theory at least, that enacted liturgy, while trafficking in texts, is much more than texts well translated and ordered along with their accompanying rubrics, even flexible rubrics no longer in red. To go "beyond the text" is to investigate symbol *in* liturgy and liturgy *as* symbol.

In the preceding chapters on particular types and strands of Christian liturgical prayer, attention was given to the texts. At the same time, the words used in praising, invoking, lamenting, or petitioning God are "more" than words. This is why *activity* and the intention to *do* things with the words were central to the elucidation of liturgy as praying. Now we ask, given the presence of words addressed to God, and language used to "listen" for God, in what sense can we go "beyond" the language?

The argument in this and the following two chapters, and which undergirds the whole project, is that the concrete circumstances of the worshipers, not simply the texts, are ingredients in the "prayed theology" of liturgy. This sheds light on how the ritual contexts, like the activities of various human arts, give the participants access to a way of perceiving, receiving, and reconfiguring the world. Before we can speak directly of Christian liturgy as an eschatological art in the final section of our inquiry, the symbolic languages of the liturgy, and the ways in which liturgy is enacted symbol, need to be opened to reflection.

Lawrence Hoffman's groundbreaking study, *Beyond the Text: A Holistic Approach to Liturgy*, begins with an account of why we must not confuse the texts of prayers with the act of praying. Analogously, I suggested at the conclusion of Part 2 that we must distinguish between liturgical texts, ancient or modern, and the field of force in which such verbal language comes alive. "We ought not," Hoffman urges, "to argue from the people to the texts, . . . but from the texts to the people."[2]

To focus solely on the verbal or surface language of liturgical prayer is to neglect the very way that the language gains meaning and depth. Liturgical language is radically dependent upon what is not verbal for meaning and significance. This is not surprising in light of our explorations of the modes of prayer and experience in chapters 6 through 8. This means, of course, that issues of power, class, and gender assumptions that are encoded in liturgical language are revealed. If there is truth to be found, it will be *in* and *through* the performed matrix of words and sign-acts.

The central issue is not "what are the theological truths contained and stated in the texts?" but "what is being said and done in the liturgical action with the use of these words?" This latter question cannot be answered by recounting the earliest version of the liturgical texts under study, or by analyzing the language of the prayers as such. Rather, the actual performance of the language is done by a community. Thus the "hermeneutics" of the assembly's social, economic, and political/ethical energies and patterns are central. And, as we shall note in detail later in this chapter in section 4, the "aesthetics" of liturgical celebration becomes profoundly relevant to liturgy as primary theology. So Hoffman's point is crucial:

> The holistic study of liturgy may begin with the text but must eventually go beyond it—to the people, to their meanings, to their assumed constructs, and to their ritualized patterns that make their world uniquely their own.[3]

"Full, conscious, and active participation" is only a receding slogan from paragraph 14 of the *Constitution on the Sacred Liturgy*[4] if we do not attend to specific questions concerning resistance and vulnerability to the nonverbal and symbolic dimensions of liturgical celebration in specific social/cultural contexts. In our haste to render the liturgy intelligible and accessible to the worshipers, we easily neglect the complex matter of participation in symbol and symbolic power and range of the rites. Preoccupation with reformed texts and rubrics neglects the most difficult challenge: to uncover the intersection of human pathos with the symbolic power and range of liturgical rites authentically celebrated. Put another way, the current situation, so tellingly reflected in the data of recent surveys of actual assemblies at worship, forces us to reassess how we have conceived and fostered liturgical participation.[5] We must think again about the second half of that famous sentence from paragraph 14 of the *Constitution on the Sacred Liturgy*:

The Church "earnestly desires that all the faithful should be led to that full, conscious, and active participation in liturgical celebrations which is demanded by the very nature of the liturgy."[6]

Ritual Symbol and Levels of Participation

Mary Collins, in *Worship: Renewal to Practice*, also addresses the effort in contemporary liturgical studies to attend to "actual local practice, the customary usage of particular churches." In a chapter on ritual symbols and process, she claims that the conciliar reforms generated a situation, especially in American Roman Catholic parishes, that throws worshipers back on their own resources in an unexpected way. She observes:

> They have worked with greater or lesser knowledge of the wider liturgical tradition and the official liturgy, past and pending. They have drawn on the depth or superficiality of their experience and understanding of the paschal mystery, the mystery of dying and rising which is celebrated in every liturgy. They have been more or less successful in distinguishing the truly archaic ritual symbols of the Christian liturgical tradition still capable of embodying faith, from the merely antiquated ritual forms of other eras. They have combined these archaic forms in new ways, or they have juxtaposed them with the cultural forms of this era. Sometimes local worshipers have created ritual forms of sufficient vitality that they warrant inclusion in the public repertoire of the Roman Catholic Church. At other times, the banality of the forms or their esoteric qualities invite conscious repudiation and even banishment from the ritual repertoire.[7]

The failure to distinguish the primary or truly archaic symbols from ritual forms only expressing the inclinations of the worshipers' present cultural modes of communication is a major problem across ecumenical lines. One set of problems faces the Roman Catholic tradition so recently struggling to come out from under restricted and fossilized symbolization; another set faces Protestant traditions with little sense of symbol, or even a deep suspicion of the symbolic realm. Victor Turner's account of the three fundamental characteristics of ritual symbols may assist us with respect to the "double question" now amplified: how can our actual participation in primary symbol be true to the nature of Christian liturgy, and how can our experience of the liturgy be truly symbolic of the mystery that Christian liturgy presents?

In his *Forest of Symbols* and "Forms of Symbolic Action: Introduction," Victor Turner proposes that ritual symbols possess: (1) multivocality, or a fusion of many levels of meaning; (2) the power to unify several disparate referents and experiences; and (3) the ability to accumulate meanings around both affective and morally normative values.[8]

All three of these characteristic features of symbol work together in a live ritual context. In such a context central signs such as bread, wine, water, or oil—embedded in communal actions such as eating and drinking, washing, or laying on of hands—articulate and express a particular range of meanings in the concrete situation of their being enacted by a community. Each liturgical celebration forms and expresses a selected range of the many levels of meaning inherent in the symbol, and brings together in a unified experience both the sensate human dimensions of what is symbolized and the mystery signified by the biblical word of the divine/human interaction.

It is *over* a period of *time* that the fullness of symbol may be comprehended, if comprehended at all, by the worshiping assembly. The biblical word and the range of sacramental sign-actions (become symbolic) provide a shared matrix of social meaning. With respect to Christian liturgy, these three interactive dimensions of symbol described by Turner depend in part on the discipline and the formed aesthetic imagination shared by the assembly. But this very discipline and imaginative capability must be congruent with the deepest range of meanings presented nondiscursively by the symbols activated in the ritual context. This is crucial to preserving the "otherness" of primary Christian symbols.

On the one hand, symbols can be spoken of as objects, gestures, utterances, or complex actions. On the other hand, ritual symbols are never merely things. This is because "things" like light, water, oil, or bread are already, for the Christian tradition, embedded in a history of shared social life.[9] Such objects are not themselves "symbolic" by virtue of using them to express our experience. Rather, only by being vulnerable to and learning to participate in the shared life toward which these symbols point is "experience of the symbol" possible. The paradox of ritual symbol is that, in order for us to participate, the whole human being must be engaged through the senses (visible, acoustic, kinetic, and the like) while at the same time acknowledging that liturgical action signifies realities beyond immediate experience. Understanding ourselves to be in relation to divine reality is itself a parabolic, metaphorical, and symbolic process, as Turner's three points suggest. Gelineau has put this point well:

> Ritual activity is not concerned with producing purely 'worldly' effects . . . but the coming of the Kingdom. Thus in the liturgy we do not eat only to feed our bodies; we do not sing only to make music; we do not speak only to teach and to learn; we do not pray only to restore our psychic equilibrium. The liturgy is a parabolic type of activity (which throws us aside), metaphorical (which takes us somewhere else), allegorical (which speaks of something else) and symbolic (which brings together and makes connections).[10]

This excursus into ritual symbol implies that the otherness of symbol to which we submit cannot be a simple naive operation. It requires a deeper entry into the biblical word that provides language, albeit inadequate and culturally embedded and particular (therefore requiring critical distance), descriptive and ascriptive of those mysteries into which we are invited and taken by the power of common ritual action. Even the word—read, spoken, sung, contemplated—therefore becomes symbol; unless, of course, we confine the word to its discursive or merely propositional level—reducing our preaching or hearing to listening for moral maxims and/or dogmatic truths, literally dispensed. This is the great flaw of all fundamentalisms—biblical or ecclesial.

Perhaps one of the reasons for my impression of a certain one-dimensionality of "symbol" in interviews conducted in both Roman Catholic and United Methodist studies is that relatively little connection is made with biblical catechesis (in comparison, say, with favorable or unfavorable responses to the content of preaching or the "experience" of the readings). When the referents and the narratives of Scripture are not available to the worshiping assembly, there is a diminishment of symbol. As Turner, Langer, Geertz, and other symbol theorists remind us, it is the multivocality and the unification of different referents and levels of experience—affective, cognitive and moral/volitional—which constitutes the power of ritual symbols for human lives. In the world of biblical minimalism the typological and "connecting" power of the liturgy is reduced to connections in the human range of experience we bring. Biblical minimalism increases subjective projection onto the symbol and, ironically, into the biblical texts themselves. The loss of symbolic imagination and the rise of "explanations" of what symbols "mean" impoverishes ritual participation.

The deeper power of ritual symbolism in the Easter Vigil or in the rites of reconciliation, for example, presupposes the "archaeology" (Ricoeur) or the otherness of the story and the reality beyond our experience.[11] The liturgy is not a static system or structure to which we bring our life experience; rather it is a crucible of meanings which, if entered with our whole humanity, makes experience possible: deeper gratitude, deeper awe, a greater capacity for suffering, hope, and compassion. Such emotional dispositions are not simply our cultural values found "in" the liturgy, but are in large measure patterned because of a special memory and a history *not* immediately ours.

Having said this we must then stress the fact that liturgical participation itself is symbolic and parabolic. That is, participation in the "sensible signs"—gathering, greeting, singing, listening, speaking, embracing, eating, drinking, and blessing and being blessed—is only the first level of participation. At the second level we discern that enacting the liturgy together is participation in the mystery of being the church. This is precisely why "doing the liturgy well" is not enough. We can, as Protestant evangelicalism should have taught us long since, worship in a lively, dramatic, and humanly engaging manner, and yet not conceive our assembly as participating in the mystery of God's self-giving to the church. Without this second level of participation, the liturgy itself will not symbolize.

This point was brought home to me in a pastor's remark:

It's like you dream . . . a vision . . . that people gather for prayer, worshipping, offering praise, thanksgiving, the music, the responding, singing. At some point they say "we could stay here forever." That's the kingdom.

Such awareness of the liturgy as symbol of the mystery of the church and the rule and reign of God is more than "doing the liturgy smoothly" or "making it work." Yet, such a sense of participation in liturgy as symbol nonetheless requires careful attention to the forms, to the choreography, the space, the concrete actions of reading, singing, praying, movement, and the like.

Perhaps this point could be summarized by observing in classical fashion that there are three interrelated levels of participation in ritual symbol in the context of Christian liturgy. First is the necessary attentive participation at the level of rites. Second, participation in the rites, fully, consciously, actively, must itself be discerned as an act of the church—of the people of God called by word and sacrament to become in the world who we are in God's sight. Third, participation in liturgical rites and symbolic range is itself a participation in the rule and reign of God (the Kingdom) already come and yet to come in fullness.

Symbolic Languages and Human Emotions

Now we are in a better position to turn to the question of how liturgy both shapes and expresses a community in affective life— in a patterning of emotions if you will. The awakening and sustaining of social capacity to respond to symbols is central. Perhaps the greatest task ahead is to restore a sense of history and transcendence to the symbols embedded in the ritual actions of the liturgy. This process is deeply catechetical. It must always be evocative, imaginative, and experiential—but constantly grounded in the biblical witness to a living tradition. We never have access to the unmediated "pure" meaning of symbols. The water, the bread and wine, the cross, and the word always reveal and conceal. This requires bringing our cultural experience and pattern of life into contact with the otherness of the symbol-embedded word and the word-permeated sign-action.

We should be cautious about assigning too much valence to the experienced "immediacies of feeling." Even when asked "what was most meaningful?" or "what were you feeling during the communion rite?" we can only speak from a first level of awareness. Revealed in the responses in reporting immediacy of feeling are powerful currents of human consciousness, triggered by particular features of the liturgical action and the symbols. This is seen in one example from Holy Redeemer parish in the person who came to the liturgy aware of her father's illness. At several points this person drifted into the sense of "a lot of pain" in the world. She became very involved in the singing of the "Gloria," and at various points in the liturgy. Then she observed, "But . . . again I think I was thinking about my dad." Later, during the eucharistic prayer in the post-sanctus she remarked, "I remember thinking about my husband's grandmother who passed away. And an aunt of mine." These are vivid reports of consciousness triggered by participation. What we do not see is how, over a period of time, liturgical participation may have given and/or deepened her capacity to make the connections.

Thus immediacy of feeling must be distinguished from depth of emotion. It is the "depth of emotion" that only shows up over time. Only when connections are made in human existence and in our struggles to live the Christian life, alone and together, can we begin to discern the way that the symbols form and express the Christian pattern of affections. We may be profoundly moved by a gesture, or by the homily, or by the music. These are certainly signs of attentiveness and conscious participation. And we do recognize in the reportings various levels of maturity in the apprehension of these elements of word, ritual action, and symbol. But the deeper questions appear only when we allow worshipers to speak about how the liturgy has formed them in deep dispositions over time: in profound gratitude (receiving the world and other human beings as gifts), hope (even in the face of limits, suffering, and death), or awe and delight (of the sense of grace in ordinary meals), because one has been present to many Eucharists—some dull, some alive. This is not a call for liturgy that cannot speak to human emotional needs, nor is it a dismissal of the need for "affective immediacy." Rather, it is a call for grounding the formation and expression of human emotion in the deeper reaches of the symbol and the ritual process of symbolization—in increasing awareness of the "hiddenness" of participation.

The Christian life has depth and resiliency and liturgical shape precisely because there is an intrinsic connection between the word and sign-actions and the formation and expression of central emotion capacities in the assembly. Being capable of love, hope, remorse, and gratitude requires much more than the ability to "be moved," though we should never deny the fact that liturgical prayer and the rites may bring intense periods of "feeling" such emotions. Liturgy can be regarded as the community gathered about the word, the font, and the table where ritual action shapes and expresses persons in deep emotions. Such affective dispositions orient us to the mystery of God in creation and in redemption, and in a sense for the consummation of all things in God. In this sense liturgy well-celebrated should permit us, over time, to refer all things to God, and to learn how to intend our lives and the world to God.

There are limits to construing the liturgy exclusively as communal prayer. The whole economy of the rites enacted, as Aidan Kavanagh has pointed out, is more than prayer.[12] Yet, the liturgy is the ongoing prayer of Jesus Christ in and through the gathered assembly. It is therefore our ongoing place of communion and dialogue with the divine self-giving. In light of this, let us sketch briefly how the rites of the Sunday assembly as liturgical prayer can be said to shape and express us in fundamental emotions. "Feeling" such emotions as joy, welcome, remorse, encouragement and so on is only part of such emotions. Gratitude to God, sorrow for one's sins, compassion and intentional identification with the suffering are emotions native to our judgments and assessments of our lives and our world. Thus, to tell and to hear stories of God and to address God in the vocative of prayer means to undertake a certain way of existing and to behave in certain ways toward others. This is the linkage between the formation of certain emotions in liturgical experience and the becoming certain kinds of persons—the formation of character, if you will. How this sheds light on relations between liturgy and ethics will be the topic of chapter 11.

Thus to thank God, to lament evil and injustice, to confess sins, to receive forgiveness, and to intercede for others—these are ways of giving and receiving the self in relation to the world. What is done with the words of praise and thanksgiving is part of the meaning of what is said. Insofar as liturgical prayer begins and ends in praising, thanking, and blessing God for creation, preservation, and redemption, it is being formed in a passional regard for the divine self-communication. So gratefulness for life and for the created order as God's gift is part of coming to live gratefully in the world. This is at the heart of the Eucharist. It is therefore a cautionary note in the data when relatively few find the participation in the eucharistic prayer memorable. A person who appreciates the musical quality of worship in a large urban United Methodist parish mentioned that she often stays away on the first Sundays because of Holy Communion. Commenting briefly on how long the eucharistic prayers seem she remarked: "I'm not sure why I don't know how to go about finding out why it bothers me." To pursue this reveals not only personal problems with the death-memorial in the meal, but also the disturbing issue of cultural attitudes ingested but unavailable for reflection.

Yet the eucharistic prayer-action, regarded as a whole, still may work at levels of impact below the conscious awareness of thankfulness. At the same time, lack of intention to offer thanks with the presider indicates a low perception of being part of the whole church's prayer. The more we can enter into the prayer-action of giving thanks, the more likely the formation of deeper, sustained connections between eucharistic action in the assembly, and eucharistic dispositions in daily living. But the psychological and social causes of resistance to this may be very complicated.

The liturgy of word and Eucharist is more than thanksgiving and praise, as we have noted. It also involves recalling and encountering a memory of a people. Such a rite enacts a complex story and requires a passing over into something other than personal or social experience. Entering into the memory of Israel and of the New Testament witnesses is also a deepening of awe and wonder. These memories flooding through the readings, the homily, the songs, and the very heart of the eucharistic action itself draw together a wide range of emotions and referents. Formation in the word thus forms the assembly in the art of making connections between the symbols and the patterns of experience in life—suffering, aging, struggling with decisions, mixed loyalties, and the like.

Authentic liturgy also brings us to acknowledge who we are in the sight of God. To address God and mean what we say in word and in gesture is to recognize our limits and our complicity. In this sense the liturgy explores and continually reveals the difference between who God is and who we are. If praising and thanking are essential to full humanity, so is acknowledgment of sin, of limit, of human ambiguity. This is why there are deeper emotional levels available in nearly every dimension of the liturgy, not simply in the penitential rite. The experience of being released, of being freed to live truthfully and without fear or compulsive guilt, is a crucial element in liturgical participation.

We did not see as much of this in the Georgetown Study of Roman Catholic parishes because there were relatively few questions of responses in which the recall of liturgical experience was made in the context of daily life. I suspect, however, that many persons in these parishes could give us valuable insights into how the liturgy does, in fact, shape and express this range of emotional capacity—the capacity for self-examination and for being released to speak the truth in love. A dramatic instance of this occurred, however, in an interview I conducted with a layperson in a prominent United Methodist church in the Southeast. After describing a fairly conventional upbringing in Protestant church life, including receiving Holy Communion four times a year as a "solemn remembrance of Jesus' death for me," she told of a friend's severe cancer that had made eating more and more difficult. When she was asked to take the communion elements to the friend's bedside, she did so reluctantly. But during her friend's joy at receiving, despite her difficulty in swallowing, she realized "that this was the only meal that mattered" to her friend. "I saw the Holy Communion as a true feast of grace for the first time." Now, months after her friend's death, she seeks the Eucharist each week. "I know what All Saints' Day is all about. For me it's every time we do the Communion service."

The loss of our experience of the primary symbols in our daily lives—water, bread, light, fire, earth, oil, touch, sounds, silence, and gestures—is a loss of our humanity. The diminished sense of biblical memory and connection is a loss of the soil for liturgical participation and growth. So our problem, illustrated amply in both Roman Catholic and United Methodist surveys, is not that we lack "experiences" in the liturgy. It is that we do not have a strong sense of the discipline and the vulnerability to the mystery of God's self-giving that such depth of experience is possible.

The way that contemporary American culture forms us contributes greatly to our inability to pass over into a social memory not of our own. This was brought home to me in another interview with a layman who said, "Why do we have to listen to so much Bible and history? I don't care what King David did, or who begat whom. I don't think you people who make up these new liturgies should pay so much attention to old history. A more modern psychological approach based on our life-experiences would be closer to what we really need in church." This obviously intelligent layperson was reflecting an increasingly influential number of persons in that church.

We cannot untangle all the issues raised by some of these interviews and observations. Liturgical theology and liturgical praxis are just beginning to join in the problems of culture analysis and critique.[13] The current concern to adapt liturgy to different cultures simply illustrates the point of this chapter: living liturgy, unlike the texts in liturgical books (or the repeated oral "texts" of much "Free-Church" worship), is always culturally embedded and embodied. But of course even the texts and rubrics "in the books" are nevertheless cultural products. In other words, we must always go "beyond the text" in attempting to understand the theology that is actually being articulated and expressed in particular celebrations.

Texts and Symbolic Languages

We began this chapter by observing that the words we use in liturgy, whether in reading, praying, singing, or preaching, are dependent upon a wide range of nonverbal factors for their meaning and point. Christian liturgy, elaborate or simple, is a *performative* context in which language is activated by what is not verbal.

Even if we were to focus entirely on texts, for example in the lections, the Psalms, prayers, and hymns, we would be driven to consider how they are juxtaposed. The setting together of different passages of scripture for different days already alters how we "read" and hear those texts when they are considered singularly. This juxtaposition of readings from the Hebrew Scriptures, the Letters of the New Testament, and the Gospels sets up patterns of interaction. Here Christian traditions, the integrity of the Old Testament pericopes in their own context, tends to be the rule of active listening and interpretation in preaching.

This aspect of the readings has been explored brilliantly in Gordon Lathrop's recent book, *Holy Things*.[14] In his view the dynamic character of Christian liturgy already shares in the continual process of juxtaposition and reinterpretation that we find in Scripture itself. So prophecy is set next to letters, and letters to the churches are set next to a narrative of Jesus' actions and interposed by a psalm. This creates, at the level of the verbal structures, a set of generative associations, tensions, even conflicts. When these are "performed" in the ritual context, they themselves become verbal icons. In this way the verbal liturgy is more than verbal. But, of course, this is the habitual way of poetry and all imaginative human utterance.

The interaction of the readings *with* the prayers (we shall see this in the collects for Advent in chapter 14), and the sung texts in hymns, antiphons, and anthems is ever more densely layered. Here great chains of imagery in the texts are activated by visual symbols, by gestures, and by the principal ritual actions of the body of the assembly itself.

Verbal language is also subject to variability of time, space, sound, sight, and to movement. The same words do not have the same significance when uttered in different ritual contexts by different persons at different times. Saying, meaning, and understanding are thus bound to *uses* of language about God, not to the dictionary or even to the "doctrinal" meanings assigned to them by secondary theological reflection. The meaning and point of language used to praise God, to exhort, or to comfort and reconcile is a function of what the particular community of Christian discourse is "doing" with words. So "Jesus loves you" can make authoritarian attitudes toward a congregation as well as be guileless and transparent to the healing power of Christ.

Understanding what is meant by such images as "shepherd of Israel," Jesus as the vine and believers as branches, or "messianic banquet," depends upon a complex range of tacit understandings. While this requires familiarity with the chief narratives and the details of Scripture, many of the tacit understandings are formed by and encoded in *bodily* participation in the ritual acts. These are not primarily cognitive, but kinetic and affective. Such capacities to understand are not "theoretical" or discursive, but are part of the "knowing how" to participate. This requires a different sort of training than does learning to read the texts. To this point we return in chapter 10.

No study of liturgical texts can do without the study of the cultural patterns of communication and the character of social interaction that constitute these more "tacit" dimensions of the celebrating assembly's life over a period of time. In fact, the more adequate study of texts forces us to go "beyond the text." Yet the texts cannot be left behind, or be more absorbed into questions of power, or social status, or cultural determinacy, either. They function as language in the ritual context of living symbols. Language about God and language addressed to God has the character of depth and mystery because such discourse is part of a web of life, a disciplined yet open-textured "form of life."[15]

Such a form of life involves symbolic interaction with a social world. Here we confront the desires, attitudes, and guiding stories about what is real and what constitutes human good, as well as the social, political, and economic forces shaping the life of the church and religious communities. It is this world that Christian liturgy depends upon for its modes of communication. But it is also this very world that Christian liturgy also wishes to prophetically reorient to the promises and grace of God. We attend to this critical function of the basic structures of liturgy in the next chapter, and again in the closing reflections of this book.

CHAPTER

10

THE LITURGICAL "CANON" IN CONTEXT

Liturgical celebrations, both festive and ordinary, employ cultural modes of communication to address God and to address human beings. In a sense this is simply a tautology: Christians have no other language and gesture, no other music and bodily actions than the human ones we have received and within which we dwell. We must wear the clothes we have and breathe the air where we live. But this is precisely the point emerging from the last chapter. The words we use in liturgy, whether in prayer, reading, singing, or preaching, are dependent upon the cultural "languages" for their sense and point. Yet, we do change styles of clothing and we monitor the air for pollution, aware of our dependency and complicity. So liturgy lives in cultural modes of communication, but uses these to critique the inherited religious assumptions that become worn out or toxic.

Paul Hoon's *The Integrity of Worship* presents an anatomy of liturgical communication indicating five "directions," sometimes simultaneously, in the church's worship: (1) from God to the assembly; (2) from the assembly to God; (3) within the assembly from one to another; (4) by the worshiping congregation to those "outside"; and (5) by those "outside" to the gathered assembly.[1] We have noted how the verbal language used in prayer to God and as listening for God is *more* than words. The same is true for the discourse within the assembly in preaching, reading, singing, and hearing. And, in the ritual action, the language of exchange as in greeting, "The Lord be with you / And also with you," is not information but ritual gesture. But so, too, the communication from outside to inside is more than language. The architecture of the building speaks to the outside as well as the inside; and the arts—whether of "high culture" or "popular culture"—exercise a powerful influence on the discourse and behavior within the assembly for worship.

Christian liturgy, whether in an Anglo-Catholic parish on Easter or an informal lakeside camp celebration of the Lord's Supper, is always a *performative* context in which many languages are activated. So it is that the same texts and the same words uttered live do not have the same significance when they occur in different ritual situations, spoken by different persons. Saying, meaning, and understanding are bound to *uses* of language about God, not to the dictionary of definitions of the words. The meaning and point of language used to praise God or to exhort, or to comfort and heal, is a function of what the particular community of discourse is "doing" with the words. "Jesus loves you" can mask authoritarian and oppressive attitudes as well as be disarmingly without guile. Understanding what is meant depends therefore upon a complex range of tacit understandings, many of them bodily knowledge, which come from living with a particular community's stories, ways of behavior, and patterns of social interaction.

The particular patterns of listening for God and to one another —as well as to the surrounding culture—in a local community are part of the larger social matrix of symbol and bodily activity. Hence the study of liturgical texts is necessarily a study of cultural patterns of communication within which human understanding is made possible. Language about God and language addressed to God has the character of depth because such discourse is part of the complex "form of life."[2]

Such a "form of life" involves symbolic interaction, as contemporary ritual theory discloses. Our attention has also focused on the desires, attitudes, emotions, and intentions, that are shaped and expressed in the guiding narratives and the gestures of prayer that constitute the larger tradition. Chapter 11 will concentrate on how liturgy offers a set of stories, teachings, and ritual acts that comprise a vision of the good, and that have the power to form "character." This chapter explores some of the ways that the inherited patterns and structures of Christian liturgy intersect with the social/cultural fields of force in which the assembly lives.

Before considering the larger patterns and basic structures of Christian worship that constitute a "canon" of a distinctive kind, we turn first to a brief sketch of the symbolic languages hinted at toward the end of the last chapter. We shall see how the continuing interaction of texts, symbols, and ritual acts constituting the "rites" as living worship necessarily involve time, space, audibility, visibility, kinetic dimensions, and sensory tangibility. In other words, we first explore some general anthropological features of worship, and then turn to what constitutes a distinctive set of essential elements and structures—the "canon" of Christian worship. These, I shall argue, provide continuity amidst culturally diverse settings while paradoxically *requiring* diversity of style.

Symbolic Languages and Human Experience

From the standpoint of ritual analysis, Christian liturgy shares certain basic elements with non-Christian forms of religious ritual and ceremony. Growing awareness of signs and symbolic languages in twentieth-century thought has contributed greatly to our understanding of the complexity of any act of communal worship.[3] This complexity is a result of the interplay of many different kinds of elements and factors in specific social/cultural settings. In this way, understanding how Christian liturgy is theological requires attending to the anthropological phenomena that allow the art of celebration to take place. In calling time, space, sound, sight, and the kinetic dimensions "languages" we are reminded that verbal communication rests upon that which is nonverbal.

The phenomena of time, space, sound, gesture/movement, and the community itself may also be called "signs."[4]

Time

First, the symbolic language of time. We have already mentioned the eschatological significance of Sunday and the temporal patterns of the liturgical year in chapter 3. Time and temporality are necessary to theological meaning. For example, the significance of eating and drinking together takes time. In ordinary life, we come to understand what we have shared with one another only after having had meals on anniversaries, on birthdays, after funerals, and through the subtly changing seasons of life on ordinary days. Eating together, holding conversation, telling stories of the family—all this gathers meaning over seasons of intensity and seasons of leisure. This point applies directly to the eucharistic meal of the Christian liturgy, but also to the accumulative experience of all structures of worship over time. The narratives of Jesus and Israel, hymns, and the symbolic actions that surround the stories deepen as we mature with them. This is the secret of what we may call liturgy's nonverbal inexhaustibility. We keep bringing our ever-changing temporal life to the temporal unfolding of the church's year of grace.

The language of time requires a patterned discipline of days, weeks, and years. Time is essential to the remembrance of God, and to who we are. The particularity of what God promises to do in the sign-acts of the church and in the created world is marked in time. Jewish liturgical cycles of time were carried over as a kind of depth grammar into the Christian community's patterns, now done in the name of Jesus. Hereafter, the primary action of eating and drinking together and the water bath are forever marked with the narrative of Jesus. Hence the liturgical year is an unfolding of what God in Christ said and did. It marks his advent and birth, his ministry and teaching, his suffering and death, resurrection, ascension, and Spirit-giving.

But our finite temporality is also engaged by this narrative. At the heart of Christian celebration of the cycles of time is the mystery of how, by the power of the Spirit, our temporal human lives become interpreted by the life of Jesus who is the incarnate story of God. It is no accident that the ancient baptismal creed, known as the Roman Symbol, is *both* a declaration of essential belief and a miniature of the cycles of time. The declarative language of the Apostles' Creed depends upon the nondiscursive "language" of moving through weeks and years, participating again and again in remembering Jesus. In the early church the Creed itself was given to the catechumens in the temporal process of preparing for baptism. Reciting the narrative of the trinitarian work of God thus was a sign of initiation into the "new time" of Christ.

Space

While it is true that Christianity spiritualizes the Temple and speaks of God being worshiped everywhere, it is the case that the assembly of Christians always is in *a* place. "On the day which is called Sunday," writes Justin Martyr, "all who live in the cities or in the countryside gather together in one place."[5] First in houses, in catacombs, then in civic buildings gradually adapted for liturgical celebrations, and through an ever-changing history of architectural settings. Each place has, in turn, shaped how the assembly speaks, hears, and acts. Celebrating Eucharist around a table in a second-century house church accents the domestic character of the holy meal; celebrating in an orthodox cathedral with its elaborate iconostasis brings forward the intrinsic "dramatic" mystery.

Christian worship assembles in time and space. The places where people assemble have always had a profound influence upon the elaboration and simplification of the rites. In fact, new spatial arrangements and architectural environments are responsible for the elaboration of beginnings and endings of particular actions. The axis of a cruciform Gothic cathedral permits, even invites, solemnity in movement and a slow rhythm of speech and song. A storefront church with acoustic tile in the low ceiling requires electronic amplification and lively, rhythmic musical forms. Other spaces are static and sedentary, focusing more on listening to someone sing or speak, as in many Protestant auditoriums. My point is simply that we must always understand the orders and structures of Christian worship as being activated in quite different ways in different spaces.

Where the room of assembly is heavily ornamented, the visual theology of the stained glass, the iconography, the wall frescoes, or the statuary, is part of the prayed theology of the assembly. The images heard in texts and in music and preaching, are "read" against the history of seeing the depiction of biblical scenes in the art of the room. In this sense the architecture "contains" the visual and aural possibilities of the texts and ritual actions.

It may be useful to distinguish two basic dimensions of how the language of space and a sense of place affects participation in liturgy. These also bear directly upon how we perceive and understand primary religious symbolism.

On the one hand, there is the embodied history of meeting in a particular building and inhabiting the interior spaces. This is an accumulative experience over time of having gathered for generations where Sunday liturgies, baptisms, weddings, funerals, and all other rites of passage have taken place. The bodily memory of having knelt at an altar rail, or of sitting in a specific place becomes part of the theological significance of the rites. The sound of song and prayer is internalized in the particular space, and thus the power of association and the emotional depth of memory work to fuse together habits of the body with the present experience. The sense of place and of local history of worship is part of the theological language of that community, though it may rarely be articulated. This may lead, of course, to the domestication of religious experience in worship. This occurs when the generative character of bringing ever-new life experience (pathos) to the liturgy is lost, or when the texts and ritual actions are done lifelessly or without attention to their multiple levels of meaning.

On the other hand, the arrangement of space as an environment for symbolization and ritual enactment is an intentional aspect of liturgical celebration. In our age of liturgical reform, increasing attention has been paid to the necessity of a gracious, hospitable, and a strong environment.[6] The aesthetics of space bears directly on the range of perception and experience the assembly may have. The "aesthetics of the holy" will be our concern in chapter 13.

The arrangement of furnishings in space is a physically embodied theology: the placement and material form of the altar, reading stand, pulpit, font, seats, and musical instruments all determine the quality of what is seen, heard, and physically touched. Here we encounter physically embodied expressions of particular understandings of God and of how God communicates to humans. These are brought to and "built into" the architecture and the interior spaces. In other words, the art of space initiates a certain theological vision so that it may form and express how God and people encounter one another.

These aspects of space and its role in liturgical celebration help account for why the same order of service or prescribed rite may be celebrated and experienced quite differently in two different churches. The very same music and words may be used, but what is heard and perceived and therefore "prayed" will differ. Quite apart from more profound cultural differences, the very spaces in which we worship determine a pattern of selectivity in the rites enacted.

Whole theological histories may be noticed in the arrangement of the space in diverse traditions. A central stone altar speaks of the centrality of sacramental mediation of God, whereas an elaborate central pulpit witnesses to the centrality of preaching so characteristic of many Protestant traditions. A large baptismal font with flowing water located at the entrance or nearby the entrance to a sanctuary speaks of the importance of baptismal theology and the primary symbol of water, whereas a hidden or perhaps non-existent font speaks of the lesser significance of baptismal themes in the community's theological self-understanding. There is, therefore, a tension between the "normative" theology of worship expressed in the architecture and its furnishings, and the accumulated "cultural" attitudes that a congregation brings. In periods of extensive liturgical reforms, church architecture becomes central, and conflicts result between accumulated experience in space and recovered theological and/or aesthetic norms.

Sound and Silence

A third symbolic language is that of the acoustic shape of liturgical action. We not only hear the sense of words, but we always understand liturgical utterance as ordered sound. In short, the liturgy is intrinsically musical.[7] Music is the extension of human speech, so that even spoken or read parts of the liturgy are taken in by the worshiping assembly as having rhythm, pitch, intensity, tone, and other characteristics normally associated with music. This is the case even with preaching that seems at first to be the most discursive form of speech in the liturgical context. This was brought home to me many years ago following a sermon I had preached in a little country church. A member greeted me at the door saying, "That was a fine talk, son, but it weren't preachin'." She explained later that I just didn't "sound" like any preacher the church had heard, but she understood the words.

The acoustical properties and musical characteristics of prayers, readings, and other verbal forms are part of what the community is formed by. The sounds of worship often carry the emotional power and the memory of association when the actual words or texts cannot be remembered. This is obviously the case with hymn tunes and the musical settings of various texts—psalms and antiphons, for example. The remembrance of the words is carried and prompted by the melody and sometimes the harmonic and rhythmic elements. This creates disonance for worshiping assemblies when familiar texts are set to new tunes.

The silences between words are as important as the sounds themselves, for both are taken together in the process of primary participation. Likewise, silences for reflection and spaces between readings or specific liturgical units create a particular style of participation and celebration. The same rite will have remarkable differences in tempo and intensity because of the relations between silences and sounds. In all music, sound and silence work together. The act of reading and hearing the church's corporate memories in Scripture may be done in a variety of styles. Particular congregations are, for good and for ill, "evangelized" or habituated into these styles. Some Christian traditions deliberately accent silences, thus providing a more contemplative environment for texts and ritual action. Quaker worship is the most austere form of this. Others tend to fill the space with sound, even using instrumental music to "accompany" silent or verbal prayer. This, too, becomes a habitual way of praying. The music is part of the *gestalt* of the prayer.

This suggests that the aural character of liturgy is powerfully formative of our embodied theology. The art forms of music—congregational, choral, and instrumental—grow naturally out of this fact. Thus differences in musical culture make theological, and not merely psychological differences. A plainsong musical setting of the psalms of the eucharistic liturgy brings forward certain features of the texts, while a contemporary "folk" setting accents others. At the same time, questions must be asked about the gains and losses to the liturgy in the move from one musical culture to another. We cannot make purely musical judgments here, since the music is also serving the rites and providing (or suppressing) connections between the people's culture and the style of celebration. We will return to this point in considering how the cultural context is both "within" the assembly and addressed by the basic structures and forms of Christian liturgy.

Visible Language

The fourth symbolic arena of liturgy is its visible language. One of the most neglected aspects of Protestant worship is how people pray with their eyes. As a Puritan is reported to have quipped, "better to pray with one's eyes shut and book closed than to go to hell." Protestant visual iconoclasm aside, the visible signs of grace are nevertheless present, if only in an open Bible, in the person of the preacher, and the bread, and the cup. But, of course, the theological significance of what is seen is more thoroughgoing than that. This is why, when the visual dimensions of liturgy overwhelm the aural, and the sensual delight *distracts* from participation in the assembly, one can understand the attempt to "purify" or simplify by removing excesses.

Suffice it for our purposes here to observe that, with the exception of the sight-impaired, vast ranges of participation in liturgical rites involve "seeing." One only has to think of seeing other persons, the vestments, the art of the paraments and hangings, or of noticing the light-fall in the room, or the lighted candles. Especially we see the unfolding of the liturgical action itself. Some traditions such as the orthodox churches, fill the room with icons, splendid vesture, candles, and the ever-present Pantocrator

Christ on the dome of the room. Here, as in the stained-glass windows of Western Gothic cathedrals, much of the experienced theology is visual. The visible reveals the invisible world—that which the natural eye cannot see. In those instances we might think of the primary eschatological sense being sight. Hence the prominence of the root metaphor of "seeing God," or "beholding the mystery."

The visual dimension of liturgy is a means of communication and a sign itself of the incarnation. As Adrien Nocent claims:

> The liturgy must indeed be incarnated because of the incarnation of Christ, yet the adaptation involved must also take account of the fact that Christ became incarnate in a given historical culture, and one must therefore respect the visual dimension of this incarnation.[8]

His remark suggests that different cultural contexts and different historical epochs place differing values on the visual languages used in Christian liturgy. This is true, of course, also for the auditory and musical aspects of liturgy.

We will return to the way in which the visible can reveal the invisible in the final chapters. For it is crucial to Christian liturgy that the God who is praised and who is available through visible and tangible signs also remains hidden. When the Johannine prologue speaks of beholding the "glory" of Christ, it means to say that the reality of Jesus' person and work was more than what was seen to the physical eye. How what is seen reveals what is not yet seen bears directly upon the eschatological import of all worship.

The Kinetic and the Tactile

A final group of symbolic languages have to do with gesture, movement, and touch. All of these are present in Christian liturgy, but "high" and "low," and ordinary and festive. Specific signs such as kneeling to pray or to receive the eucharistic bread, passing the peace with handshakes or embraces, or even the simple act of standing to sing—all of these are ingredients in liturgical rites. In some respects our bodily movements, gestures, and dispositions may be the most deeply theological aspects of communal worship. For the human body is itself a primary symbol of God's glory. Again it is the fundamental conception of God incarnate in a human being that gives such theological significance to bodily action.

It is interesting to describe communal worship as a "dance" to worshipers unacquainted with this in their traditions, or who harbor suspicions about bodily movement in general. To redescribe coming into the sanctuary, greeting friends, sitting down, standing for singing and certain prayers, moving toward the altar for prayer or for Holy Communion, and movement out of the building as a slow, complex dance can be revelatory. For in fact, this is a deep feature of the experience of worship for many.

But once again we note that the power and the role of gestures, movements, and of touching other humans (or food, or water) varies greatly from one cultural context to another. So not only are there theological differences in the role of explicit gestures such as bowing, kneeling, making the sign of the cross, or shaking hands, but each of these in turn carries different cultural valences outside worship. Here we should also include the sense of smell, as in the use of incense, or in the case of freshly baked bread for the Eucharist. The more directly the body is involved, the more theological conflict there is likely to be between traditions. This is why, for example, conservative Protestants may have more trouble with the use of the sign of the cross or genuflection than with more explicitly doctrinal differences with Roman Catholics. The bodily signs carry theological convictions at a deeper cultural level than do rationally expressed "beliefs."

Our explorations of these symbolic languages may begin to illuminate three major points about the relations between Christian liturgy and cultural differences. First, the very nature of liturgy engages and affects all the senses. This is true for most Christian traditions. Even in the case of severe iconoclasm or puritan tendencies to deny the physical or sensual aspects of worship, the fact is that human beings must gather at a time (and over time), in a particular space, using language and silence, and what is seen as well as how the people move, in order to participate in the celebration of the gospel. All these show wide cultural variation.

The second point is that all these symbolic modes of perceiving and communicating are culturally specific. That is, the patterns and styles of worship must necessarily show variation because these "signs" or symbolic languages are necessary to communal worship. If cultural anthropology and ritual studies have taught us anything, it is that such symbolic modes are distinctive from one culture to another. This does not mean, however, that there are no commonalities remaining or available to communities of Christian faith, life, and worship. It means that the enduring structures such as the holy meal or the water bath in Christ's name show different theological understandings as they enter different social/cultural settings. There are complex issues concerning cultural adaptation of Christian rites we cannot address here. But the crucial point is that considerations of music, dress, bodily posture, and movement are the heart of the matter if the worshipers are to have something to bring to the liturgy. In other words, Christian liturgy, by its central story, requires the bringing together of human pathos to the ethos of the praise and celebration of God.

The third point concerns the inexhaustible richness of what Christian liturgy attempts to say and do. Could it be that it takes a wide variety of cultural styles and modes of celebration of the basic structures of Christian liturgy to bring forward ever-new aspects of the Word of God and the paschal mystery of Christ? Perhaps the rapid expansion of early Christianity into the polyglot world of many cultures is the model we have. For despite the wide variation in cultures, Christianity took hold. And, in the first great sharing across traditions beginning in the fourth century, we can see remarkable commonalities as well. The present circumstances of a diverse, global Christian expansion provides a testing ground for a generative series of tensions. Such tensions are between inherited theological assumptions in the West and the new polyglot of cultural and socioeconomic settings into which Christians are evangelized to gather for worship in the name of Jesus.

Having explored some initial features of cultural modes of communication that constitute the anthropological basis of Christian celebration, we turn briefly to another question: Are there distinctive Christian structures or basic orders that provide a continuity over time and through variable cultural contexts?

What allows us to recognize Christian liturgy amidst the bewildering historical and social diversity of its expression?

The "Canon" of Basic Structures: Cultural Receptivity

In some respects the question of what constitutes a continuity of identity in Christian worship is analogous to the question of what constitutes the core literature taken as revelatory. This is the question of a "canon" of Christian liturgy. Some of the same ambiguity obtains in both cases. The church makes a decision to rule certain books in and others out of the canonical set. But that process was itself influenced by nontheological factors. So, too, determining the essential elements or defining structures of Christian liturgy is influenced, to a certain extent, by cultural and political factors. Nevertheless it is possible to identify a certain set that have endured the test of time.

Several liturgical scholars have concluded that there have been four major structures persisting since the origins of Christian worship.[9] These are: the rites of Christian initiation (baptism-confirmation-first Eucharist); the eucharistic liturgy (with its two-fold synaxis and Eucharist pattern); the daily prayer offices; and the cycles of time (calendar of seasons and feasts). A fifth element of the canon is a less formalized set of liturgical orders sometimes called rites of passage or "pastoral offices." These include marriage, ordination, anointing of the sick, reconciliation (penance), and burial.

To name these as persisting orders or forms of Christian worship is not to exclude a wide range of others in the history of Christianity. For example, the standard Protestant preaching service might be considered, or prayer meetings, blessings and consecrations of buildings and persons, foot washing, Moravian style love feasts, and the like. The reason for not usually including these is, in part, their derivative character. The Protestant "Sunday service" is a truncated version of the full liturgy of Word and Table, although the specific form of evangelistic services has some things in common with the earliest public preaching of the gospel.

We need not rehearse the origins and historical development of these basic structures. Our point is to show in brief how each of these lends itself to a wide range of cultural styles. Furthermore, each of these structures may be seen to be eschatological precisely because they lend themselves to cultural variety.

In a deeply illuminating recent study, Gordon Lathrop discusses the basic patterns of the *ordo*, or shape of the liturgy, which has provided continuity throughout the history of the Christian faith.[10] His concern is to uncover the presuppositions behind the ritual ordering of Christian patterns. This has to do with how "[m]eaning occurs through structure, by one thing set next to another."[11] Having established a biblical pattern of how ancient words and actions are juxtaposed to ever-new historical situations, and in the breaking open of the old images and stories, the old language is revelatory of something new. He argues that the patterning of the basic Christian structures show the same process. It is the juxtaposition of the received ritual patterns (including their rhetorical resources) with new and image-breaking circumstances that releases the revelatory power of the tensions within the liturgical act.

Thus, the basic pattern of the Eucharist is a setting together of the liturgy of the word and the liturgy of the table. This reciprocity brings forth a creative power for the assembly. Because the Eucharist celebrates that which cannot be understood in any direct manner—namely the resurrected life of Christ now present to the world and the assembly—it must always work by juxtaposition. "For Christians, all texts and all rituals are the wrong words. All have to be broken to speak the Christian faith, the resurrection, the encounter with God in the crucified Jesus, the new vision of the world."[12]

This implies that ancient biblical texts set next to the meal remembering Jesus' work parabolically and metaphorically to disclose new referents. All of the rich meaning of images drawn from the readings also expand the symbolic range of meanings enacted in the eating and drinking together. At the same time the prayer of thanksgiving (the eucharistic prayer) recites what empowers the meal and how this is an encounter with the presence of God in Christ by the power of the Spirit. "The thanksgiving prayer gives words to what happens in communion. The eating and drinking, juxtaposed, are together the thing over which the prayer gives thanks, yet the eating and drinking are always more than the prayer can say."[13]

This approach to the basic ritual pattern of the Sunday assembly for Eucharist illuminates all the structures that constitute the "canon" of Christian worship. Just as the Eucharist conjoins the juxtaposition of texts and preaching with food and thanksgiving and thereby speaks of God, so with the structures of Christian initiation. Here the interaction is between the complex web of teaching (formation in *practices* during the catechumenate), and the water bath:

> ... which may be metaphorically called "new birth" or "dying and rising with Christ" or "crossing the Red Sea," can never be earned nor given as a kind of graduation. It stands in tension with learning, is greater than the teaching; the bath itself teaches.[14]

In this reading we can see that the pattern—the catechumenate, the washing in the triune name by invoking the Holy Spirit, and the holy meal—is not culturally determined or limited. Rather, it may take unto itself the actual human life of any culture. Provided, we must add, that the teaching uses the biblical accounts in all their tensions to help form those on their way to baptism in who Jesus Christ is and what he does. Or, in the case of those traditions now who baptize infants, the faith-formation process must exhibit the same revelatory juxtapositions of old and new.

In the daily prayer patterns emerging early in Christian liturgical life, we find the juxtaposition of psalms, readings, and prayers. In the case of evening prayer, these are put next to a ritual with the lighting of the evening lamps. But these, in turn, are construed as the "Light of Christ." The modes of praise and thanksgiving are placed in ever-fresh tensive relation to psalms of lament, instruction, trust, and praise. But since to join in this ongoing prayer of the assembly is to join in with Christ who leads the continual prayer of the church, the old texts are made to speak an ever-new prayer. So the intercessions found in the daily prayer patterns echo and give utterances in our words to Christ's intercession.

The cycles of time help order the memory of Christ's whole life, teachings, death, and resurrection. But they do this by ordering the whole of Scripture, now made to speak of what God has done in Christ. So the great sequences of Advent-Christmas-Epiphany and Lent-Easter-Pentecost are christological treasures. This is not simply because the New Testament Gospels narrate his life, but that his death and resurrection in turn illuminate the whole of Scripture, bringing out the continuing rhythm of presence and absence.

Viewed from this standpoint, the "canon" of Christian worship, while tied to the particularities of the biblical witness, is not tied of necessity to any one cultural ethos. This is already clear in Scripture, especially in the New Testament witness to both Jewish and Gentile participation in Christian liturgy. But most remarkable is that these basic structures are clearly discernable in the diverse family of liturgies that emerged from the fourth century on. From the beginning of the spread of Christianity, the liturgy carried the theology. The liturgical assembly collected and read the Scriptures in light of the ritual actions intimately linking them with the life and teachings of Jesus. Persons of many different cultures were evangelized into these patterns. Yet each culture brought its own distinctive modes of communication to the liturgy.

Thus we can discern these five basic components of the liturgical canon in East and West Syria, Jerusalem, Asia Minor, Alexandria, Rome, North Africa, Gaul, and on into northern Europe. It is as though the fullness of how Christ reveals God could not be contained in any one culture's ethos and style of celebrating baptism, Eucharist, daily prayer, or the cycles of time. Neither could sometimes vast differences in local customs and practices obscure the patterns found in Christian burial, care for the sick, and marriage.

All cultural contexts have something to contribute to the meaning of what Christian rites signify. This is not because all cultures equally understand the claims of Scripture, or share the same universal gestures or symbolic capacities. Rather, the features of human social existence—time, space, the visible and tangible world—all are engaged and given orientation in the mystery of God proclaimed and celebrated. And a universal eschatological vision is offered *in* and *through* the incarnate, creaturely signs.

Though the image of a restored world is spoken of as "Zion" or "Jerusalem," the actions and juxtapositions of the liturgy invite every culture to discover their own translation of this city promised by God. The broken symbol at the heart of Christian liturgy takes the history of human suffering and the yearning into itself, leaving room for all human diversity.

At the same time, the liturgy does not simply absorb local culture, it also criticizes that which is incompatible with God's gracious turning toward the world. As Lathrop remarks:

> Not everything that is cultural is capable of carrying the intention of the meeting; and everything cultural that does come into the meeting must undergo a reordering, a new centering on the mercy and truth of God, the creation of a hole in the cultural system this material represents.[15]

How the liturgy carries the seeds for its own prophetic self-critique is thus disclosed. It is the same as makes authentic Christian liturgy prophetic of all human social order.[16] This takes us to the edge of relations between liturgy and ethics, the subject of chapter 11.

CHAPTER

11

FOR THE SAKE OF THE WORLD: LITURGY AND ETHICS

T. S. Eliot puts it well in his "Choruses from *The Rock.*" What life have you if you have not life together? / There is no life that is not in community, / And no community not lived in praise of God. That question, "what life have you if you have not life together?" is about liturgy and ethics, about the church's prayer and work. Pressed upon us by the fragmentation and anxiety in contemporary life, the question is asked of the churches by people in the streets, and increasingly by those who, seated comfortably for years in the pews, are quite familiar with the language of Zion. In a time of profound moral ambiguity and the privatization of ethical concerns, the question must be addressed to all who lead and serve God's people. For we, in our gathered assemblies, have been considerably less than communities "lived in praise of God."

In his famous study, *The Shape of the Liturgy,* Dom Gregory Dix reminds us that "the study of liturgy is above all a study of *life.* . . . Christian worship has always been something done by real men and women, whose contemporary circumstances have all the time a profound effect upon the ideas and aspirations with which they come to worship.[1] The Scriptures grew out of the experience of a worshipping people whose social and political daily life and

---

liturgical assemblies were a testimony to life before God. Scripture is a record of God's mighty acts; but it also records the struggle of a people to live according to a vision of the good believed to be given by God. Any account of this communal life must show the relationships, for good and for bad, between worship and ethics.

By "ethics" here I mean the concrete way of life rather than the theoretical interpretations of ethical theory. The concrete living of the covenant community in Hebrew Scripture, and the followers of Jesus in the New Testament, shows not only a set of norms and practices, but a continuing remembrance of the vision. In this sense, as we shall try to show, ethical norms and practices are not simply or "purely" ethical. They are guided by and are often in tension with the continual recalling and re-entering what God wills as the good for humankind. Liturgical celebration of word and sacrament and the domain of social justice are equally grounded in the self-communication of God in Jesus Christ.

This means that questions concerning Christian ethics and the shape of the moral life cannot be adequately understood apart from how Christians actually worship God. Thus communal praise, thanksgiving, remembrance, lamentation, and confession of sin, and interceding for the world are part of the matrix that forms intention and action. How we pray and how we enact the holy meal and water bath in Jesus' name is linked to how we live—to the habits, attitudes, guiding affections, and desires which govern our relationships to persons and institutions. But as we have noted in earlier chapters, there is a disturbing gap between how we live and what we do and say in our liturgical assemblies. Even though the social forces outside liturgy may exercise greater influence over how we live than does Christian liturgy, it is nevertheless true that the liturgical commemoration of God's being and acts intends a vision of the good to be lived out. Awareness of the "gap" itself becomes a matter of learning how to confess and to speak truthfully about ourselves before the God of creation and covenant. Unless the liturgy has become hopelessly idolatrous—a possibility in every age—it will be ethically normative in some sense.[2]

Christian moral intention and action is embedded in a form of life portrayed in and commanded by the whole sweep of Scripture focused in the teachings, life, suffering, death, and resurrection of Christ. There is at the heart of the liturgical use of Scripture a narrative understanding of the world that places human life in relationship to human life and the whole created order before the face of God. The stories supply a narrative grasp of the good, evoking and teaching what it is to remember God. In specific commands, narrated lives of the people of God, and in accounts of how the community is to worship (e.g. "in spirit and in truth," "praying constantly," "ascribing glory to God," and the like), the Scriptures shape the life of faith in specific ways. While there are rules and teachings concerning behavior, the narrative sweep of the Bible portrays qualities of being-before-God as the most significant patterns of common life.

Of course a description of ethics and of the moral life can be given in complete independence of liturgical considerations. But if this is done, something essential to Judaism and to Christianity drops away.[3] Christian ethics, I contend, are best illuminated by tracing how particular affections and virtues (gratitude to God, hope in God's promises, sorrow over sin, for example) are formed and expressed in the modes of communal prayer and ritual action. In what follows we will explore how convictions and intentions to enact the good God wills are dramatized and appropriated by worshipers over time by participation in the ongoing prayer of the church.

Christian Liturgy and the Ethics of Character

Christian worship, through a complex symbolic pattern of words, gestures, and symbols in ritual action, forms and expresses dispositions belonging to a way of life before God in relation to our neighbor. These dispositions are given specificity by the distinctive modes of prayer discussed in Part 2. Gratitude, truthful lamentation and confession, compassion in solidarity with others—all these take God as their ground and object. In this sense they are ingredient in the moral regard of the neighbor and the created order itself. So, for example, love of God and neighbor are bound together in both the language and the form of the ritual action, especially evident in baptism and Eucharist. Such dispositions are part of the acknowledgment of God. They are requisite features of understanding who God is and what God requires of those who worship and seek to serve in the name of Jesus Christ.

Particular structures and patterns in communal worship come to express the community's life before God. The moral struggles and the awareness of ethical dispute and conflict are, if we have ears to hear and eyes to discern, found in the readings, the Psalms, and in the broken symbol at the heart of the Eucharist. Furthermore, if preaching is honest and deeply honed in the Scripture and contemporary human experience, the tensions in attempting to live out our religious ethics are made clear and taken up into the sacramental character of prayer. Ultimately this is a liberating feature of authentic liturgy: our moral anguish and our inabilities to live in accordance with the demands of the gospel are named and placed in an eschatological hope.

On the one hand, there are normative patterns of affection and virtue commended by and formed in the liturgical prayer-action of the community at worship. As God is holy, so the worshipers are called to be holy. On the other hand, our intentions and actions fall short, and our affections are rarely pure motives for well-doing in actual everyday life. But just at this crucial point, Christian liturgy in its texts, symbols, and ritual acts recognizes this gap, offering truthful repentance and reconciliation. Recognition of the gap itself is part of what authentic liturgy forms and expresses in our lives.

The Christian life in the world can be characterized as a set of affections and virtues. There are, of course, limits and possible misunderstandings in such a characterization. Yet this approach to the relation between liturgy and ethics is more adequate to the larger biblical-Christian tradition and to the contemporary situation than we first may think. Rather than speaking of the "ethics of obligation," this allows us to utilize the "ethics of character" in interpreting the shaping and expressive power of authentic liturgy. The Christian moral life is the concrete embodiment of a pattern of affections and virtues revealed in the pattern of God's self-giving in Jesus Christ. While many in our present social climate long for the certainty of conformity to a closed set of rules for behavior, Christian liturgy authentically celebrated compels us beyond the first-level certainty of "God said it, I believe it, that settles it!" There are certainly clear moral and ethical teachings in Scripture. And surely the commands of Jesus are often remarkably difficult: "Love your enemy," for example. But it is not sufficient to imitate the pattern of Jesus' behavior in the Gospel portraits. Neither the achievement of moral ideals as such nor the adoption of Jesus' "morals" is adequate to the full range of ethical and moral issues in the contemporary world. What is required is an actual reorientation of life, a process of conversion of the heart and social imagination to the rule and reign of God that Jesus proclaims and embodies. This has everything to do with "life together."[4]

Affections and virtues grounded in the saving mystery of Christ constitute a way of being moral, but do not offer a solution to every ethical dilemma. Rather, gratitude to God, joy in the mercy of Christ, hope, penitence, and a passion for justice and love of God and neighbor are grounded in the narrative of who Jesus was and is. This is celebrated in the "canon of Christian liturgy" we referred to in chapter 10. The exercise of such affections in life requires a continual re-entry into the paradox of Christ's death and resurrection. This is the reality initiated in the life, teachings, passion, and glorification of Christ, but which is yet coming toward us from God's future we do not yet fully comprehend. It is precisely this future-orientation that makes Christian ethics distinctive because the affections, intentions, and actions are focused in the promises of God, and not primarily in social structures and goods already achieved.

In his work over a period of time, Stanley Hauerwas has argued persuasively that the continuity and identity of self embodied in our character has deep moral significance. "The individual Christian character," he contends, "is formed by [the person's] association with the community that embodies the language, rituals, and moral practices from which this particular form of life grows."[5] This is possible only by coming to understand who God is and what the divine intention for human existence is as revealed in Jesus Christ. This coming to understand is precisely what good liturgy and faithful communal prayer can provide. There is a "deliberate rehearsal" at the heart of this process of bringing every aspect of character into harmony with God's intention for the world. This is an apt description of the imaginative force of good liturgy for the formation of Christian character. The various modes of prayer explored in Part 2 are part of the rehearsal of the great narratives of creation, fall, redemption, and future hope in Christian liturgy. Patterns of prayer, reading, proclamation, and sacramental action are precisely the practices of communal rehearsal of the affections and virtues befitting "life in Christ": the baptized life of faith in the world. This is no mere "imitation of Jesus." Rather, communal worship is a participation in the mystery of God's life poured out into the human condition. The symbolic forms and actions of liturgy are the school for conceiving and receiving such a pattern of life.

Responding to remarks on the primary symbols of faith made by H. Richard Niebuhr, Hauerwas speaks of the "enlivening of the imagination by images that do justice to the central symbol of our faith."[6] The liturgical assembly is the place where enlivened Christian imagination is formed and expressed. Normatively considered, faithful liturgy is the fundamental imaginal framework of encounter with God in Christ which, in the power of the Holy Spirit, forms intentions in and through the affections oriented to God revealed in Christ as their goal and ground.

Yet it is also true that Christian liturgical prayer must respond to a world in which moral ambiguity abounds. Archbishop Anthony Bloom reminds us that, "Prayer is not simply an effort which we can make the moment we intend to pray; prayer must be rooted in our life and if our life contradicts our prayers, or if our prayers have nothing to do with our life, they will never be alive nor real."[7] Not only does prayer shape intentions in accordance with the primary symbols of faith, it must be accountable to the way we make actual decisions, and undertake courses of action.

The connection between liturgy and ethics of character we are exploring opens up the inner relation between praying and being. How honestly such a form of life confronts the suffering and gladness of the world is something liturgy itself cannot guarantee. Spiritual self-deception is always possible because praying is always done in the human sphere of forces. Prayer and praise in heaven, we may assume, no longer fall prey to deceit. In hell, self-deception has become a compulsive way of life. Prayer that seeks withdrawal from the realm of human forces—social, economic, or otherwise—and seeks only to enjoy the "experience" of consolation in the symbols, fails to exercise fully the religious affections as motives in well-doing. To be moved by the love of God in Christ requires engagement with the principalities and powers of this world.

A powerful instance of this point is found in the high priestly prayer of Jesus in John's Gospel. In addressing the Father, Jesus is overheard to say, "I am not asking you to take them out of the world, but I ask you to protect them from the evil one" (John 17:15). The prayer of Christian liturgy faces the world's ambiguity and evil. It is precisely in the world that God is to be glorified by doing the works of God. Yes, common worship ascribes glory to God alone; but unless the glorification is shown in works of justice, mercy, and love faithful to the divine will, Christ's liturgy is not fruitfully enacted. In every age the tension between cultic and ethical activity must be rediscovered for the sake of the world. At the same time, their coinherence and mutual reciprocity provides the matrix of this critical tension. The glory and holiness of God is shown *both* in the otherness of God as the object of prayer and worship, *and* in the intimate self-giving of God in the servant-hood of God's people.

In our age, especially in the American social climate, there is a tendency to define prayer primarily by its effects and by our own consequent actions in the world. The prayerful life is shown by its fruits, assuredly; but it can never be reduced to its "results." When praying becomes a special technique or instrument for getting things done, prayer slides toward magic. A one-sided concern for the "effectiveness" of prayer leads, in Urban Holmes's phrase, to a spirituality of "prayer as production."[8]

Despite such misunderstandings, liturgical prayer does respond to a broken and often inexplicable world. Christian prayer is beholding the world in light of the narrative of God, told, heard, pondered, and enacted in proclamation and sacrament. Such worship is linked both to the raw needs of human conflict and to the world imaged as the arena of God's glory. The question "to *what* does prayer respond?" is ultimately reoriented by the question "to *whom* does prayer respond?"

The real issue is whether we can pray what we mean and mean what we pray without being drawn into the way in which God's vulnerability views the world. The meaning of praying, as we established in Part 2, is not a matter of uttering the "right words," or reciting the most literate prayer texts. To pray out of baptism into Christ is to become a living text before God. In this sense, meaning what we pray requires more than the onset of lively feelings. Meaning what we pray involves sharing a form of life in which the affections, desires, and dispositions to act are oriented toward God's promises. Discovering the meaning of what we pray in community includes the discovery, alternately joyous and painful, of our fears, angers, loves, hopes, and the contexts of life over which we can weep and rejoice together. Thus Paul's admonition to "Rejoice with those who rejoice, weep with those who weep" (Rom. 12:12) is about liturgy and ethics.

Consider a simple analogy: when do we say and *mean* "I love you"? Sometimes we say the words without much feeling. A good companion may then remind us, "Once more with feeling, please." We may be able to say it with a little more felt affection. But the test of the language of love cannot be measured by a one-time episode in its use. While various "feelings" connected with, for example, romantic love may wax and wane, they are not necessarily put to the test; but authentic love is put to the test of time. Only over a period of loving and giving, misunderstanding and being understood, being preoccupied and yet welcomed and loved again, do we say "how much our love has come to mean!" Here the utterance is far more than words said with urgent feeling. This is the difference between infatuation and maturing love.

In this case we see how the language of love may become access to truth and falsehood. A lifetime's learning to grow in love may be required to catch the deeper echo of what it means to experience the range of human loves. How much more is that *agape* of which the New Testament speaks to be measured, not by episodic intensities, but by steadfastness? Of God, the psalmist continually sings: "for God's love endures forever" (Psalms 118 and 136). From steadfast love, intense affectivity may arise; and, upon occasion, such a love may be the motive for laying down one's life for another. From an overwhelming experience of being mercifully loved and known, a human being may find entirely new capacities for steadfast love growing. Yet the holy affection of love, as Jonathan Edwards would point out, consists in the ongoing exercise of that love over time.[9]

In a letter to the Thessalonians, Paul exhorts the church to a Christian way of life. He lists first the things that prevent life in Christ. They are familiar: we are to avoid evil in all its forms, to put away revenge, malice, and the destructive passions and vices. We are to put on mutual respect and love. In the midst of the exhortation, he calls upon them to "rejoice always, pray constantly, give thanks in all circumstances" (1 Thess. 5:16). Here occurs a most improbable commanding of the human emotions of joy, gratitude, and love. These are not the kinds of affections that can be worked up on the spot as a matter of feeling. What is called for is a deeper joy that can abide in all circumstances, good or bad. The constancy in prayer is not some incessant pouring forth of words about God; it is, rather, a life lived prayerfully and with attention to the grace of God for which one can be continuously grateful, and in which one can continually rejoice, despite the rise and fall of all worldly fortunes and enthusiasms.

Prayer begins in gratitude, and its constancy in season and out of season is given definition by the steadfastness of its "object"— God in Christ. To pray with the community of biblical faith is to give ourselves to the Christian story in such a manner that the emotions and virtues exercised in life are nourished by the texts, symbols, and ritual actions of the liturgy. But prayer will be on occasion, and perhaps for long periods of time, dry and "meaningless," in the popular sense of the term. Where affectivity is lacking, we may lose sight of the larger narrative of God, and the fruitfulness of a prayerful life may be in eclipse. These are times of seeming abandonment Jacques Ellul and others reminded us of at the beginning of this study. Such a lack of meaning cannot itself be overcome by cultivating "feelings," no matter how exaggerated, apart from recovering the depth and range of the story. Here our moral lives are to be brought back to the story of creation, redemption, and the future promises of God to be qualified and shaped by it. The "meaninglessness" here must always be met with a waiting and an attending to the Word of God. Such attending is often prompted by the very moral tensions we encounter in daily life.

Having explored basic modes of prayer in preceding chapters, we now see that praying with Christ requires living in light of the gospel such that we may rejoice whatever the circumstances and persist in hope. To pray constantly is to be disposed to intend the world from the power of God's vulnerability to it. Liturgical prayer is thus not a technique, psychological, or otherwise, for living a spiritually healthy or ethically sensitive life. Rather prayer is historical solidarity, and integral to a life formed in joy, gratitude, awe, and compassion before God. These "graced capacities," as noted in chapter 4, we learn to call "gifts" when rightly understood. They are directed toward God and all the created order. We respond to the world and to others because we behold them "in Christ." Yet God is never "contained" in such praying. After all this has been said, the connection between liturgy and ethics is qualified by the fact that Christian liturgy is an eschatological gesture and utterance. Always uttered in the present, but always proleptic (looking for the Advent of God), and thus never "possessing" much less "dispensing" God.

But what about the community's own ministries within the liturgical assembly? Are there features of how worship is celebrated and ordered that bear upon the relationship between liturgy and ethics? What agencies within liturgy as cultus (*leitourgia*) prompt and give evidence of the people's liturgy in the world (*diakonia*)?

Liturgical and Diaconal Service

In gathering around the Word of God in reading, teaching, and preaching; around the table of the Lord for the common meal, and for the rites of initiation, a patterning of service is already activated. A glimpse of such patterning of human agency in the early church is captured in Acts 2:42: "They met constantly to hear the apostles teach and to share the common life, to break bread, and to pray" (Revised English Bible). We are told that they agreed to hold everything in common, and to distribute to everyone according to need, praying daily at home and in the temple, breaking bread "with glad and generous hearts," as they praised God and won the favor of many outside their community. As the book of Acts unfolds, we read of how the community had to order its common life and worship, and how early patterns of orders of ministry emerged. The growing local churches required the ordering of both their liturgical and diaconal life. The servanthood *within and for* the gathered community at prayer flowed into the servanthood *to and from* their daily life, including to those outside the community.

Among the images in the New Testament for the character of the Christian community, one of the most striking is that of the "royal priesthood." The First Letter of Peter speaks of Christians as being "living stones" built up into a spiritual temple and a holy priesthood who offer right worship to God through Christ. They were to offer themselves to God in both worship and daily service. Such a double work of liturgy is the true vocation of the church: "But you are a chosen race, a royal priesthood, a holy nation, God's own people, in order that you may proclaim the mighty acts of him who called you out of darkness into his marvelous light. Once you were not a people, but now you are God's people" (1 Pet. 2:9-10). In other words, this persecuted community comprised mainly of converted Gentiles was to live out faithfully their pattern of life as "good stewards" in all their varied and specific ministries.

Passages such as these, along with the basic picture of the church in the Pauline Letters, makes it clear that *together* Christians are called to belong to Christ's ongoing ministry in the world. We partake of his priesthood and his servanthood which are one life. Individuals will have different gifts, as listed in 1 Corinthians 12 and Romans 12, but the "whole people of God" are called to worship and service. All this flows from the grace shown in the priestly self-giving of Jesus. As the Letter to the Hebrews claims, "Since, then, we have a great high priest who has passed through the heavens, Jesus, the Son of God, let us hold fast to our confession. For we do not have a high priest who is unable to sympathize with our weaknesses, but we have one who in every respect has been tested as we are, yet without sin" (Heb. 4:14-15). This priesthood, like none other, has taken on human pathos fully, and continuous intercession for the world. This, as we saw in chapter 8, is the basis of the church's continuing to offer intercessory prayer—to remember the world to God in every time and place.

Christ's priestly work was at one with his prophetic and servant work. So must the church's be. Any claim to baptism into his life and death is therefore the source of all common ministries, and is the theological heart of Christian ethics. All Christians, not just "specialists," are to offer prayer, praise, acts of mercy and justice, and to continue in compassionate solidarity with all who suffer. This is the "living sacrifice," acceptable to God as our "living worship" (*leitourgia*) spoken of in Romans 12:1. To be a community called to worship and service in Jesus as Lord leads us back to our earlier definition of liturgy: the ongoing prayer and work of Jesus Christ in and through his body in the world. Now we must add: worship that shows creation and human history as the arena of God's glory. Theological discussions of ethics have to do with this complex arena.

All this implies that our liturgy as a gathered assembly is Christ's before it is ours. Jesus proclaims the reign of God by word and deed. Thus, what he said and did, witnessed by the New Testament and earliest worship traditions, he *now*, in our gathered assemblies, continues to say and do. But he has promised to be present in the midst of our worship in the world, until the rule and reign of God comes in fullness. Common worship is thus his liturgy both "where two or three are gathered" in his name, and in the service of our neighbor. Gathered to allow God to speak and to act in, with, and through Christ, in the power of the Holy Spirit, we also speak and act for the sake of the world in his name, enlivened by the same Spirit.

The gathered assembly requires many gifts and the differentiation of roles. Not all can be pastors, or teachers, or administrators, or serve the assembly. Practically speaking, not all are equipped to do so. Authentic liturgy as service of God and neighbor must hold together two things: leadership roles partaking of the collective priesthood of Christ, and the whole community representing the fullness of his prayer and work in the world. Ministries such as reading, serving, leading the congregation's song, leading prayer, presiding at the holy meal and the water bath of baptism have their reason for being in the promise of Christ to be present *in* the whole congregation. Likewise, every act of mercy, and each ministry outside the rooms of worship, has a priestly character whether done by laity or clergy. Prophetic and servant work flows from the liturgy of Jesus, and also serves to critique the abuses of power in the name of priesthood.

Implications for *Diakonia*

In the chapters on liturgy as prayer (Part 2), we established that authentic liturgy continually holds the world in all its actuality to God. Now we see that liturgical action and ethics as a way of living are interdependent, even though our lives may not often show this, and our liturgies may even contradict this truth when various cultural captivities take over. This is why careful attention is to be given to how we order the congregation's life of worship and ministry to the world. How should the ministries of the community be ordered to be faithful to the mutuality of liturgy and ethics, or prayer and work?

In the early church we can identify, in addition to bishops, presbyters, and deacons a wide range of recognized roles for persons serving the community of faith. The *Apostolic Tradition* of Hippolytus of the early third centuries mentions widows, readers, subdeacons, confessors, virgins, and healers.[10] The Syrian churches of the third and fourth century mentions cantors, doorkeepers, and others. My point is simply to remind us that the church has always recognized and named specific ministries that affect and effect worship. Vibrant and authentic Christian churches envision a variety of ministries as enabling the whole people of God to worship and to live faithfully. Originally the Greek term *kleros*, from which we derived "clergy," referred to *all* the persons within the church. The tendency to clericalize the authority and the leadership roles, early and late, has obscured this powerful fact from Protestants and Roman Catholics alike.[11]

The basis of the moral agency in the Christian life is *diakonia*, the service of God and humankind manifest in Jesus, the Christ. Different historical traditions have set aside a diaconate of those whose ministry is focused on the needs of the poor, the oppressed, the sick, and the neglected. All these ministries are to be made visible and audible in the gathered assembly as well, for the deacon has a liturgical role. We cannot, of course, cite history for one final or definitive pattern to express this liturgical-ethical unity today. We have from the early church some working models born out of the practice pastoral life of the churches. The Reformation period certainly assists us with its profound recovery of the "priesthood of all believers." African American churches have developed indigenous forms of lay ministries as well. No single pattern is best for all. The key point is that such charisms for servanthood must become more evident in the prayer of the church than they are at present in most communities.

I have been deeply impressed with those congregations where persons who are engaged in particular ministries such as hospital calling, service projects such as house building, caregiving, and the ongoing work of justice are themselves called upon to lead prayer in the gathered community. The ministry of interceding also can be heard in the music offered, and in the offertory rites. Music is often most empowering when its prophetic and sacramental character combine: this is evident in many late twentieth-century hymn texts as in "All Who Love and Serve Your City":

> All who love and serve your city,
> all who bear its daily stress,
> all who cry for peace and justice,
> all who curse and all who bless:
>
> In your day of loss and sorrow,
> in your day of helpless strife,
> honor, peace, and love retreating,
> seek the Lord, who is your life. . . .
>
> Risen Lord, shall yet the city
> be the city of despair?
> Come today, our Judge, our Glory,
> be its name, "The Lord is there!"[12]

It is no accident that this prophetic hymn, expressing such a clear Christian ethic, ends on such a resolute note of eschatological hope. The liturgy as gathered assembly can be profoundly affected by the presence of persons embodying our work in the world. We have lacked liturgical imagination and boldness here. But already, with the inclusion of more laity in reading, serving, leading in prayer, and the like, we are moving in a helpful direction. When our work and our moral struggles become more evident in our prayer and praise, the liturgy comes alive. The mutuality of liturgy and ethics is given room, and the church has a chance to become a community of moral discourse.

Authentic and faithful liturgy trains us for the reign of God yet to come in a society dying for lack of justice and peace. The mystery hidden from the plain view of social assumptions may yet be unveiled to ordinary believers. The ordering of our common life of worship and its renewal must therefore go hand in hand with the risk of a common life of service. This requires persons of deep biblical memory to be engaged in ministry to those who suffer and to those who hope. The task before us is to translate these experiences into the ongoing prayer and praise of the church, and to liberate the tradition's prophetic and priestly power for this work.

Fruits of the Spirit: Eschatological Being and Doing

It is important to make a contrast between *being* and *active* agency in the Christian life. But we also need a contrast between the prayerful life and a life without common prayer. These are not conflicting, but complementary contrasts. The pervasiveness of prayer is to be construed as a mark of Christian moral maturity only insofar as it expresses a wholehearted orientation of life to the person and work of Christ. We are thus led, as early Christian tradition has done, to extend the concept of prayer and worship from specific acts as a gathered community to the whole of one's life—of our being and our doing. As early patristic theologians were fond of observing, the whole life of the "saint" is one continuous prayer. We begin by praying in the ordinary sense of specific acts of worship, but now find ourselves drawn to prayerfulness which encompasses all of our feeling, knowing, and doing. Again Irenaeus, "the glory of God is the living human being."

This is the fundamental truth we explored in an earlier chapter on *doxa* and *dogma* in chapter 2.

Christian prayer in all of its modes shows a double focus of glorification of God and the sanctification of all that is creaturely. This is why we cannot finally *oppose* the joy of contemplating heavenly things and the enjoyment of the divine moral excellency of God (as we see in the next chapter) to the courage of active mission and ministry to the world. Both contain a joy that flows forth from having one's affections fixed upon the creating and redeeming self-giving of God. This has yet to be fully seen and heard. But this is what leads Barth and von Balthasar and others to see how the prayer of the church is congruent with the human character of divine revelation. The divine self-communication does not destroy the world in coming to it. Likewise the Word and grace of God does not destroy or reduce our humanity in being received. This is why the giving of ourselves to God in true worship is intimately linked with prayer as works of mercy. The whole of human life is to be offered and the whole of God's self-giving is to be the orienting vision of the moral life.

The fruits of the Spirit are always embodied in particular intention-action patterns. Thus they can never be adequately understood as private consolations in God. The deep affections of thanksgiving, joy, gratitude, and even sorrow over the world's heartbreak, constitute the Christian community's continuing prayer over time. These are necessary for our humanity in dialogue with God. To worship God and to love God entails social embodiment. The gifts of the Spirit are bestowed as capacities to know and to recognize God everywhere, even God's hidden glory in the groaning of creation for its liberation from sin and death.

But the secret hidden from the eyes of the world that animates the moral life and our being in the world lies more deeply still. Prayer responds to the world of suffering and dense ambiguity. Its animating principle is hidden from those of us untutored in suffering and compassion. Neither is it contained in the highest religious ecstasy. The Word and Spirit of God comes in forms compatible with our being human moral agents. But this is always in the process of transformation, sanctification and, finally glorification by the God to whom all things are returning. Both our being and our doing are "eschatological"—future-oriented—when the fruits of the Spirit take root in our life together.

In the end we must admit that it is misleading to speak of *the* relation between liturgy and ethics as though there were only one essential linkage. There are a multitude of connections between liturgy as enactment of the story of faith and the lived narratives of our lives. There are many relationships descriptively available. We cannot explore in detail here the political dimensions of authentic liturgy. But in our world, so full of the hermeneutics of suspicion, we also must admit that the liturgy has been used ideologically and politically by those in power to prevent the gospel from taking hold. The long history of abuses of prayer and liturgy in the name of God is worthy of deep lamentation. It must be noted, and a prophetic critique of the cultus must be engaged. But such a critique must itself have grasped the intrinsic connection between the fruits of the Spirit and the prophetic and priestly character of the community called out to worship God. A true critique is finally from the standpoint of an adequate eschatology.

The mutually critical correlation of liturgy and ethics is part of the critical reciprocity between the *lex orandi* (pattern of prayer) and the *lex credendi* (pattern of belief). But these issue in the *lex agendi* (pattern of intention-action) of the church. Hence we may say that true doxology issues in fitting orthodoxy as reflective faith, and both in orthopraxy of the church's servanthood in the social order in which it is placed. I have sought to trace the reciprocity of liturgy and the moral life through affections and virtues formed and ritually enacted ("rehearsed") in various modes of liturgical prayer. By reflecting on the ethics of character rather than into theories of obligation, we are in a better position to connect the ethical force of authentic Christian liturgy to notions of sanctification. This is not to suggest that there is one true doctrine of sanctification that follows. Various Christian traditions will have different accents to sound in this matter. But it does imply that the classical definition of liturgy as the glorification of God and the sanctification of all that is human—to which I would add, "all that is creaturely"—has more bearing upon ethics than most theologians have seen.

187

Human beings are formed in myriad ways. But in the Christian life, the mystery of redemption in the death and resurrection of Christ is the generative source of personal formation. The orientation and process of maturing into this mystery is therefore never merely a matter of adopting right behavior patterns or of conformity to *a priori* systems of rules for action. The qualities of formed character and the exercise of the virtues require the ongoing intentional rehearsal of the good in the communal rites, the bodily practices of remembrance and enactment. I have tried to suggest in this chapter how we might begin to think of ethical formation in the liturgical assembly.

There are questions more difficult and far-reaching we have not raised here. Some constitute the practical agenda for the church facing the actual ethical issues of our time and place. Others are basic to all times and places; for example, in the face of the inhuman and demonic powers, can the liturgical order of language and action still animate moral imagination and ethical judgment? What specific traditions and ecumenically emerging patterns of worship are most conducive to moral maturity and social wisdom? These questions, I contend, draw attention to the eschatological dimension of all Christian prayer and worship. There is no doubt in my mind, however, that the rediscovery of the primary symbols of faith and the critical enlivening of liturgical structures and style born of historical research and the twentieth-century theological construal of eschatology as a way of thinking have set a new framework in which to answer these questions. Then too, the critical appreciation of the eschatological character of the sacraments is part of the answer. Taken together with the explicitly ethical and political concerns of feminist and liberation theological critique of alienating power in particular traditions and practices, these open up a new way of looking at the anthropological and theological dimensions of liturgy.

Final Irreducibility

When Christian liturgy is regarded primarily as a means to moral exhortation or to advancing a particular political ideology, it loses its essential character as praise and thanksgiving to God.

The anamnetic and epicletic energies give way to social/cultural expression and didacticism. Instrumentalist definitions of liturgy, whether Protestant or Roman Catholic or "New Age," founder upon this rock. As it has been observed, when the Church marries the spirit of the age, she may be left a widow in the next generation.

Surely the church's worship of God in forms calling forth obedience to the gospel, and which open ears and hearts to the prophetic Word of God is desperately needed in our present circumstance. Worship is not merely *cultus*—it cannot be and remain faithful to its source and summit. In the New Testament it is clear that all of Christian existence is a rendering of service unto God. The sacrifice of praise and thanksgiving is already part of the formation of moral dispositions. The very notion of "sacrifice" in the biblical tradition is both cultic and ethical. The tensive unity of *leitourgia* and *diakonia* cannot be reduced. Worship of God is both in the assembly of praise and in the works of mercy. Both are held together in the narrative recital of God's covenant, and the history of the divine intention for the world. The focal point of this tensive unity remains God's free and gracious turning toward humankind and the created order.

Certainly the liturgical life of the Christian community cannot be reduced to the ethical implications or consequences of the cultus. Liturgy is the nonutilitarian enactment of the drama of the divine-human encounter, made flesh in the way of Jesus Christ. At the heart of this is our acknowledgment and our response to the divine initiative. The life of worship is drawn into the divine goodness. As James Gustafson has observed, "When one's being is rightly tending toward or intending God, when one's love is rightly directed, there will also be a right intention and direction of specific projects. Thus, what one is by virtue of God's creation, . . . can become realized to some extent in the moral life as one has the right objects of love."[13] How the life of worship and prayer helps to give direction toward the good and toward those right ends has been, in part, the burden of this book.

Within the historical ebb and flow of ecclesial life we cannot, nor should we, do away with the contingent relationships between liturgy and the realization of the good by Christians. The gap between our praise of God and our works of justice, mercy, and love is so great at times that Amos's voice must ring out again and again, "I despise your festivals, and I take no delight in your solemn assemblies. . . . Take away from me the noise of your songs; I will not listen to the melody of your harps. But let justice roll down like waters, and righteousness like an everflowing stream" (Amos 5:21-24).

This prophetic relativizing of liturgy is contained within the very narrative we must hear in the assembly itself. The "gap" is the evidence of an "already" if we but hear and see; and at the same time, it is evidence of the "not yet," if we understand what we have not yet seen and heard and done.

This tension is inevitable. It is, strangely and gracefully, also part of the beauty and holiness we encounter in the art of Christian liturgy. How this is so is the burden of the final chapter.

CHAPTER
12

MYSTERY, SUFFERING, AND THE ASSEMBLY'S ART

In the form of the crucified, humiliated and problematic, yet eternally worthy of worship, lies a judgment, but at the same time also a justification, for all human attempts at creating form.[1]

There is no authentic worship in spirit and in truth that does not engage the mystery of living, suffering, dying, and envisioning the good. This is because Christian liturgy itself takes its pattern, content, and dynamism from the self-giving of God in Jesus Christ. The power of authentic liturgy to form human beings in the deep emotions and intentions we sketched in the last chapter depends, in part, on the imaginative range of the forms employed. All the symbolic languages discussed in chapter 9 work at various levels to engage the whole range of our being; at the same time it is the central mystery of the divine self-communication—the miracle of grace in human form—which differentiates what is offered to the Christian community from art, generally conceived. The divine self-revelation *is* human form and thus generative of all creative subsequent significant form.

Among the requisites for participation in the form, content, and dynamism of Christian worship, two are central: a sense of wonderment and awe at the mystery of God's becoming flesh, and an awareness of suffering and the interdependency of all things. By this I do not mean that all pain and suffering leads to worship. Nor do I wish to imply that a more general sense of the holy in Rudolph Otto's classical interpretation is ruled out.[2] The sense of mystery and awareness of suffering is given specific focus and meaning in the whole sweep of the scriptural witness to God. Furthermore, while a general religious or even philosophical sense of wonderment at being may be brought to the forms of Christian liturgy, the central fact is that the texts, symbols, and ritual actions with ordinary elements of the earth reconfigure our general awareness. And the central broken symbol of Christ, crucified, humiliated, and problematic draws into itself the suffering of the world.

Another way of approaching this matter is to observe that when the Christian assembly worships *without* awareness of human suffering and death, or without any sense of the injustice and pathos of the world, it is extremely difficult to "read" the texts and the patterns of God. Likewise, *without* an awakened capacity for wonder at the created order or a reverence for what sustains each particular being in his or her life, the liturgy will remain a strange world of languages we cannot speak.

Of course, not all faithful worship involves the explicit memory of *our* pain or suffering, nor can all experience of the liturgical assembly be summed up by the phrase, "sense of mystery." But without the congruency of these features *in* the rites with these features of our humanity, the symbols cannot symbolize, nor can the texts "pray," nor the music offered sing our lives to God. What renders the art of Christian liturgy so difficult in much of our current cultural context in comfortable North American churches is that we are neither accustomed to awe and wonder, nor do we permit ourselves the vulnerability of reflecting very long on the suffering world. In a culture of amnesia, the *anamnesis* (remembering) of God's self-giving in Israel and in Jesus Christ is problematic.

To call something a "mystery" in American culture is to invite misunderstanding from the outset. Quite apart from the phenomena of "mystery novels" and films that are about the occult and the weird, there is a widespread ambivalence about the term "mysterious." On the one hand it is reduced to entertainment and fascination; on the other, to a puzzle to be solved, or merely to the irrational. Yet the Christian biblical tradition speaks of the divine in terms of mystery: both the being of God and the very name of God. Moreover, the Christian faith regards the will and concrete acts of God also in this light. This is why the central term for the holy meal is called the "Paschal mystery." By this the church has intended to focus on the paradox of God's disclosure and hidden-ness in Christ and, likewise, the hiddenness of human lives with Christ in God. "For you have died, and your life is hidden with Christ in God. When Christ who is your life is revealed, then you also will be revealed with him in glory" (Col. 3:3-4).

The Paschal mystery celebrated in the form of a simple meal, permeated with the words and Spirit of Jesus, thus brings together human suffering into Jesus' suffering. At the same time, this is the saving power of God become present to the assembly. Here is mystery that requires form: word and act patterned after the witness to what Jesus said and did. The mystery is not a puzzle to be solved, but a liberating power of life to be received. This is precisely what our study of some early eucharistic texts and ritual acts made clear. At the heart of the Word and Eucharist pattern of the Sunday assembly, then, is the vulnerability of God in Christ—the *kenosis* (self-emptying) of God on behalf of the creatures and the whole creation. This is expressed in the Philippians hymn: "And being found in human form, he humbled himself and became obedient to the point of death—even death on a cross. Therefore God highly exalted him and gave him the name that is above every name" (Phil. 2:7b-9).

In this strange manner, the pattern of praising, listening for God's voice in the memories of the church, breaking bread, and sharing a cup from Jesus' hand places us in a new relation to awe, wonderment, and to solidarity with human suffering. This pattern of assembly not only commemorates how Jesus' words and deeds recapitulate the whole history of God, from the beginning of the world until its ending, but renders us participants in the redemp-tive power of God's continuing advent. Here the vulnerability of God, which is the power of God's self-giving mercy and love, comprehends our vulnerability. This is the secret of the Eucharist's inexhaustible relevance to every particular human context of suffering.

And yet, the forms employed and the style of celebrating Christian liturgy may *subvert* the very saving mystery that resides in the incarnate action of God waiting to be realized in particular Christian assemblies. Here, too, as in the case of presumptive memory, we must listen to the critique from liberation and feminist voices who lament the history of Christian worship that systematically ignores its own injustice and patriarchy.[3] Here is where we must reconsider what is meant by the "art" and the "aesthetics" of the liturgy.

Imagination and the Assembly's Art

Whether self-consciously or not, religious communities gathering to worship God use forms and images that engage human perception and imagination. The question is not: should Christian worship use forms or not? There is a misplaced debate among traditions that haunts much of the "liturgical"/"nonliturgical" discussion. But the issue is not "forms" versus "freedom," but what kinds of significant forms (patterns, symbolic languages, and so on) invite and permit what kinds of freedoms in the assembly? Those who criticize liturgical traditions for placing too much emphasis on "aesthetics" fail to see that they, too, employ artistic means in worshiping God, no matter how simply. Likewise, traditions having powerful investments in a "classical" Western sacred music and related architectural and linguistic aesthetic tend to criticize other Christian traditions for having an underdeveloped aesthetic sense. But this is often a disguised cultural imperialism. Sorting these issues out cannot be done in these pages. The point is simply to examine carefully the actual aesthetic employed in specific cultural contexts of celebration. Then we can ask: what counts, in this tradition and in this community of worship, as "adequacy" to the Paschal mystery and to the Word of God to be received?

Training in religious affections and dispositions toward God and the neighbor, as we have explored in Part 2, always takes place in the environment of art forms: speaking, acting, gesturing, singing, moving, seeing, and hearing. The formation of faith in the ancient catechumenate depended upon the rhetorical art of the teachers, and hence the eliciting of imaginative entry into the scriptures.[4] In every age and culture, the process of evangelization into faith is, at the same time, a process of being formed in a certain aesthetic—that is into certain patterned forms of perception. We shall examine the more specific concept of the "beautiful" in the next chapter.

From the simplest prayer at mealtime, through the learning of hymns and chants, to ways of hearing preaching, to the most elaborate or most austere ceremonial gestures, this process of forming an assembly in the art of worship takes place. This means that human beings are formed religiously, liturgically, and aesthetically at the same time. Thus, any expression of religious faith in the gathering for praise of God requires a form of artistic embodiment, even if the plainest sort. Again, we must not equate the aesthetic dimension of the assembly's forms of communication and receptivity with one particular cultural "aesthetic canon." Here class differences and the clash between "high" and "low" (often equated with "popular") cultural tastes, makes a discussion of this matter quite difficult.

At the same time, we find ourselves making judgments about the adequacy of the forms—whether musical, kinetic, visual, or otherwise, to the reality celebrated. This reality, I contend, must involve the sense of mystery, with its attendant awe and wonder, and the awareness of human suffering, with its attendant anger, sorrow, and humility. Some patterns and styles of worship simply never engage the assembly in these matters. To put it bluntly, God is not adequately praised and adored with the showy, the pompous, the self-serving, the mawkish, the cleverly casual, or the thoughtlessly comfortable forms of art.

No judgment about the aesthetics of liturgy can be made on *purely* musical or artistic grounds alone. Liturgy is not a recital, or for aesthetic enjoyment. It involves the art of self-presentation, and hence the character of faithfulness counts as part of the "aesthetic" of the action. God regards the sincere gestures of the faithful, no matter how humble and how less culturally elaborate the form: here the widow's mite and the dance of David are not rejected. But the lowliness of the origins of the music or art offered cannot be made into a rule against continuing to find forms that best serve to articulate the deeper mysteries of God and the human condition before God. Here we must make judgments about the range of hymns, the kinds of homiletical "stories" told, and the environment of hospitality and human interaction permeating the celebration of the sacraments.

While it would be a mistake to think that the heightened imagination is the most essential part of religious life and worship, it is true that being God's people at worship cannot be fully exercised except in and through the heightened speech of scripture (the poetry of the prophets and the wisdom literature, and the unique literary form of the Gospels in the New Testament).

This the actual Christian assembly knows: the Word of God cannot be fully received and celebrated until it is spoken and sung in human language and manifest in the lives of the worshipers. Here is the clue, then: the "theology" articulated and expressed in living liturgy is concerned with the arts and with the life of human beauty indigenous to the communication of faith itself in the rites. These cannot be and should not be divorced from the moral practices of a holy life—for these have their own excellence and beauty. The *doxa* of God (and the glory God wishes to confer and renew in us) comes to human means of expression, not so much in "works of art," but in the artistic dimensions of faithful liturgical assembly. One contemporary theologian has put the point this way:

> Christ is for us merely extant, rather than existent, until we give him out to the world in Michelangelo's *Pieta* or in "Jesu, Joy of Man's Desiring," and in every other significant form which the spirit sees fit to release into the world. It is not enough that he should be the eternally extant word: he must also be the living idiom.[5]

The liturgical action of the assembly gathered in the name of Jesus to praise God is such a "giving out" to the world. It is, as van der Leeuw reminds us, a supreme form of art. And it is, as we shall see in the following chapter, both more and less than a human "aesthetic object" or work of art.

In gathering to worship God in the name of Jesus and by invoking the Spirit, we enact a mystery under human words and signs. We do not create the mystery, but receive it. It is revealed. Living liturgy teaches us that it is *given,* the mystery is revealed, not constructed. Yet the human imagination is thoroughly involved and required. So the assembly's art is primary.

Liturgy as Revelatory Art

The mystery of revelation is described by Karl Barth as: "the ground on which we stand, the horizon by which we are bounded, the atmosphere in which we breathe."[6] Precisely because it is more real than our projections, it remains concealed. Our thought has no initiating control. Yet, when our language, music, and ritual actions are directed toward the mystery, the enactment *becomes* the receptivity—the radical openness to God. The mystery of God's self-giving in Christ always comes as something we cannot control. But in this case, its presence and reality is conceivable only to our deepest images of life.

The transformative power of liturgy finally rests on the mystery of grace. Part 2 of this book explored liturgy as prayer precisely because it is in the act of prayer that the divine mystery is received. Prayer is the way God enables the created being to know because it is the creature's vulnerability to "being known" by God. Here again we may refer to Karl Barth: "On the basis of the freedom of God. . . . God is conditioned by the prayer of faith." Again: "God is and wills to be known as the One who will and does listen to the prayers of faith."[7]

This is the freedom of God and the freedom of the creatures who, in responding to God, show forth the mystery in the very act of gathering about the book of memory, the font of identity, and the table of sustenance and future hope.

There is an extraordinary passage in the mid-second century document, *Acts of St. John,* which captures much of what I have been saying about the art of the assembly. The passage describes a hymn that Jesus and his disciples sang after concluding the upper room meal before going to Mount Olivet. The text reads in part:

197

So (Jesus) told us to form a circle, holding one another's hands, and himself stood in the middle and said, "Answer Amen to me." So he began to sing the hymn and to say, "Glory be to thee, Father." And we circled around him and answered him, "Amen."

The account goes on, depicting the hymn and the circling dance of figures, building to a responsorial ending:

Grace dances.
"I will pipe,
Dance, all of you."—
"Amen."
"I will mourn,
[Lament, all of you.']'—"Amen."
"(The) one . . . sings
praises with us."—
"Amen."

"The twelfth number
dances on high."—"Amen."
"To the Universe
belongs the dancer."—"Amen."
[Whoever] does not dance
does not know what happens."—"Amen."[8]

Despite its gnostic elements, this image is revelatory of the art of authentic liturgy in the name of Jesus. In the whole "canon" of Christian worship, the song and the dance are not simply our doing. All our imagination and energy are concentrated on the One who stands in our midst and bids us to respond. So, in praise, lament, and joyful movement, we hymn the world back to God. We join Christ in his liturgy, and the Holy Spirit configures and transforms our art into a living icon of what has come and yet is to come.

The art of which we have been speaking is not simply "sacred art"—something to be admired as it portrays deeply religious subject matter. Rather the art of true liturgy is congruent with the self-giving of God in our humanity at full stretch. This baptism, Eucharist, and all Scripture are present to us in the figures of the Paschal mystery. To be known by the God who has come to us in this humility is greater than our imaginative powers can comprehend. Yet this is the power of freedom for God, and of liberation from every captivity.

We speak of this quality as "holy." Rudolf Otto defines the holy as "the emotion of a creature, abased and overwhelmed by its own nothingness in contrast to that which is supreme above all creatures . . . "[9] [The "holy" is experienced as present. The human response to that presence is adoration, awe, wonder, humility and reverence.] But the revelatory character of the Word of God also brings a prophetic and liberating power to the assembly. We are not left in "fear and trembling." Rather, we are empowered to stand before God. So the liturgy declaims: "You have counted us worthy to stand and praise you." In this sense the holiness of God cannot be confined to our ecstatic experience, though in large measure most worship in our churches lack, the supremely doxological as the encounter with the numinous. The art of the liturgical assembly must also receive the daily and the ordinary as holy gifts.

If the art of liturgical assembly is to be revelatory, it must seek the whole emotional range: from the ecstatic praise to the depths of lamentation, and the ordinary, daily struggle to be human. From the otherness and the incomprehensibility of the glory of God to the intimacy of the Spirit's interior strengthening of love, mercy, and justice—this is the emotional range the liturgy offers us over time. The art is diminished when we allow our worship to limp badly between either false intimacy (chumminess) with God or an artificial formalism that substitutes propriety for a genuine encounter with the "living God." Yet even the most cursory glance at the language, symbols, gestures, and ritual acts in the most ordinary assembly reveals that the potential is always there for the larger range of emotional openness to the divine disclosure.

A twentieth-century hymn by Fred Pratt Green expresses the mystery of how the art of the assembly becomes a metaphor for the graced vocation of the whole creation:

> When in our music God is glorified,
> And adoration leaves no room for pride,
> It is as though the whole creation cried
> Alleluia![10]

It is in and through the whole music of the liturgy offered to God in the whole range of our humanity that everything in creation—the commonplace and the extraordinary—is liberated to be what it is: a creature of God's own.

In his study of the trinitarian heart of Christian liturgy, Jean Corbon speaks of the "iconography of culture" as rooted in the fundamental vocation of human beings to praise God.[11] The drama of human culture itself is "the drama of human beings as created creators, as nature rooted in the cosmos but called to bear fruit in communion with God."[12]

Art is therefore not innocent. On the one hand it is a gift from God, on the other hand, it is entangled in the world of human moral ambiguity. This is what leads Corbon to observe, "If beauty is to save the world it must first cleanse the world. If the work of artisan or artist is to reveal the glory resident in beauty and bring it to fulfillment, it must first have passed through the fire in which creation is restored to its integrity."[13] I take this "fire" to be the crucible of human suffering. That is, the human imagination, which is capable of birthing the demonic and the monstrous, must itself undergo transfiguration. This is, in part, what the revelatory power of authentic liturgy can do. The goodness of creation is affirmed, but ambiguity, suffering, and death are named and confronted in the figure of the humiliated one whose arms stretch out to embrace all. The very act of bringing something to significant form and expression, whether in music, poetry, or in the long art of a life well lived, traces the pattern of God in the incarnation.

The revelatory character of Christian liturgy is finally dependent on the transforming energy of the Holy Spirit. This is both the promise to the gathered community of chastened biblical memory in the name of Jesus, and it resides hidden in the world that opens to the transformative energies of God.

This is precisely the central point of the dance and song of every liturgical gathering. So Corbon can claim:

> If our gaze is to liberate the beauty hidden in all things, it must first be bathed with light in [God] whose gaze sends beauty streaming out. If our words are to express the symphony of the Word, they must first be immersed in the silence and harmony of the Word. If our hands are to fashion the icon of creation, we must allow ourselves to be fashioned by him who unites our flesh to the splendor of the Father.[14]

These thematics belong, of course, to the liturgical theology of Orthodoxy we find in Schmemann, Staniloe, and others. But they are indigenous to all authentic liturgy where continual *epiclesis* (invocation) pervades a radical openness to God.

But all our discourse about art and the aesthetics of worship may obscure the fact that nonartistic people who suffer the world profoundly may know more about the sustaining power of God than anyone else. The Russian peasant women, who through the deepest times of political suppression and severe suffering, kept on praying with the orthodox liturgy, or the African American women of slavery who, under the extremities of hatred, violence, and racism, kept on praying and singing—these are the witnesses to the more profound art. It is no accident that these women kept a sense of holiness alive, though in vastly different ecclesial and cultural contexts, because their lives, mirroring the incarnate love of God in the midst of human enmity, were brought fully to prayer and song. They lived out the deepest art—they struggled to embody the images of God. Their praise—whether "off key" or in full harmony—liberated by keeping the hope of God alive.[15]

Let us sum up these first reflections on liturgy as an eschatological art. To speak and sing in such language that we mean far more than can be said; to break bread together and feast on more than we can know; to wash and be washed, body and feet, and thus belong to far more than the living empirical world; to sing and sound more than the ear can fully take in of the glory of creation; to bring all of life (the mundane, the frightening, the joyful and a hope for the world) to a place where it is held in the light of One who knows us; to bring joy and heartbreak to a place of ordered Word and sacramental action only to receive healing and a greater hope than we could imagine: *this* is the transformative art of the assembly. This is to learn the true advent of God, ever-fresh. Such revelatory art is not mere utopian projection. It is the *parousia* made accessible in human form.[16]

Yet even as authentic liturgy figures God's future coming toward us, it remains uncontrolled by our devices of power and presumption. For the tension between the already and the not yet—the glory of God stretched between cross and empty tomb, between creation and final fulfillment—remains. But the liberating power is in the meeting. Setting the prophet Isaiah's images to sound in Epiphany, the church may sing this twentieth-century hymn: "Arise, shine out, your light has come, unfolding city of our dreams. On distant hills a glory gleams: the new creation has begun." But the tension remains: "The sounds of violence" we struggle with now, "shall cease as dwellings of salvation rise . . . from avenues of praise and peace."[17] Where there is no lamentation in the art there will be no vision of what this text sings.

But the art includes all for whom it prays, individually and collectively. So, too, in Charles Wesley's hymn, "Love Divine" the church is invited to witness the saving art of Christ:

> Finish, then, thy new creation;
> pure and spotless let us be.
> Let us see thy great salvation
> perfectly restored in thee;
> changed from glory into glory,
> till in heaven we take our place,
> till we cast our crowns before thee,
> lost in wonder, love, and praise.[18]

CHAPTER

13

THE BEAUTIFUL
AND THE HOLY

Heaven is revealed upon the earth both in the cup of cold water which is given to the poor . . . and in Michelangelo's *David*; in both the dance of a child and a melody of Mozart.[1]

We began our explorations by concentrating on the pathos of our human condition that is brought to the ethos of God in word and sacrament. Or, to that "among" in the Augsburg Confession, which describes the church as, "the assembly of all believers among whom the Gospel is preached in its purity and the holy sacraments are administered according to the Gospel."[2] Without heresy we might add: where the arts are brought to be transfigured and transformed by the same grace that is God's self-communication.

In chapter 2, I assembled some reminders about *doxa* and what we believe. Without the primary orientation of liturgy and life to the glory of God, our doctrines are diminished to cognitive human systems. Without doxology, our doctrines become dogmatic in the negative sense. The glory of God cannot be contained as sheer transcendence in the immanent Trinity, but must lavish itself on the whole creation—heaven and earth—and be manifest in history. This comes to expression in the liturgy because God's glory has shone in human flesh in Jesus. The paradoxical glory of the cross also *receives* our violence and brokenness in word and sacramental action. How our worship, both as cultic ritual (liturgy), and as public action (ethics), proclaims and shows forth these matters has led us to questions of liturgy and culture. Here too, further linkages between aesthetics and ethics will be illumined.

Christian liturgy speaks within its particular culture, always using a range of the available cultural languages. But the truth-claims made and explored therein are not founded upon the culture. In this sense the "world" does not know why the church says what it says, though it shares the modes of communication: music, language, symbol, ritual, and gesture. Joseph Sittler concludes the address we referred to in chapter 2 in this way:

> The impact of the reality of the faith, as that comes to expression in worship, has always been . . . most effective beyond the cult when the making of an impact is not a primary intention. That impact is most productive, its forces most free when its own order, content and passion is true to its interior substances. . . . (The church) discloses best what the culture needs when she speaks out of her own integrity.[3]

This echoes Dean William Inge's observation that the church that marries the spirit of the age is a widow in the next generation. Can public worship both employ the cultural languages with integrity and avoid becoming captive to the spirit of the age?

Beauty and Holiness Revisited

Out of the complexities of cultural issues, I wish to focus attention on that pair of terms so necessary, yet so obscured by our practices: beauty and holiness. These terms have been used in a wide variety of ways, and inevitably when we speak of something in the liturgy, or the whole liturgy itself as beautiful, differences in aesthetic judgment surface. When a small all-white country church refers to the singing of "In the Garden" as beautiful, it seems vastly different from a Palestrina Mass setting led by a paid choir in an urban cathedral. And yet, something is being recognized by connecting the beautiful with the worship of God. This alerts us immediately to the complex relationship between "beauty" and "holiness" in the context of living liturgy, whether simple or elaborate.

In a dense but discerning work, *Beauty Revisited*, Mary Mothersill argues that beauty is a necessary concept in human life. It is not simply an abstract and disputed term belonging to philosophy of art. What is perceived as "beautiful" may, of course, be inconsequential in some instances and settings, while possessing spiritual range and power in others. "Some things," she claims:

> . . . like a pebble or a clear and cloudless sky, have simple souls. They please in virtue of their aesthetic properties, but those properties once noted and appreciated, do not invite prolonged critical analysis. Decorative formal designs, . . . may be elegant, intricate, admirable, and yet, once understood, easily forgotten. All persons and some works of art—those to which we pay homage—have souls that are complex, multilayered, and partly hidden. They are not to be taken in at a glance, and long study leaves room for fresh discoveries.[4]

Let us paraphrase this to apply to liturgical rites and their celebration: Some aspects of our worship, even whole liturgies enacted, please in virtue of their aesthetic properties, but they cannot withstand prolonged spiritual analysis. Some artistic "enhancements" in worship may be elegant, but are easily forgotten. But liturgical celebrations that have "deep souls" always yield new discoveries. They continue to be luminous, even revelatory. These are occasions where the doxa of God is at the center, and the pathos of human beings is truly prayed and sung. Perhaps we could use the term "holy" to characterize liturgical celebrations with deep souls. Encountering the holiness of God fills the forms we employ with what cannot be manufactured.

Aesthetic experience as such is not the primary aim of the public worship of God.[5] The praise, the glorification of God, and the transformation toward the Holy is. Yet such glorification and sanctification require human modes of communication, and must "touch down" into the whole range of human experience. Thus, at times liturgy takes us "out of ourselves" into the sublime, as in Oliver Messiaen's harmonic and rhythmic vocabulary. But at other times, the encounter of "ordinary time" in the liturgical year offers another less intensive expression. There is the beauty of the "Service of Lessons and Carols" at King's College Chapel, Cambridge, England, and there is the beauty of a small gathering of faithful in a plain meetinghouse somewhere in Appalachia singing, "I Wonder as I Wander" accompanied on a dulcimer.

There is an art to all this. Insofar as liturgy brings all that is human to the holiness of God, and makes real a future that only God can confer, it is an eschatological art. It requires all that art requires: form, material, discipline, imagination, and pain. As Bobby McFarrin's song goes: "No discipline is pleasant at the time, but painful." One of the first practical principles here is that the Holy Spirit has never yet rejected good and faithful planning.

In exploring the various "languages" of liturgical celebration in chapter 9, we noted how images, symbols, gesture, sight, sound, and communal ritual actions worked together. The creative imagination that seeks to order the various aesthetic dimensions of these languages must be schooled in public ritual as an art. Unlike the context of the concert hall or of other forms of entertainment that may employ "religious" art and music, Christian liturgy has its eye and ear on the holiness of God. If no wonder is aroused, and no sense of awe before the mystery of the divine presence and absence, then the liturgical imaginative power of the assembly cannot discern the holiness of God, or the holiness to which our lives as worshipers are called.

But with creative imagination there is a crucial element: seeking God. While liturgy is not solely an art form, it requires gathering about the book, the font, the table, and the ordering of matter and form. As Gerardus van der Leeuw admonishes, "Look at the liturgy: among the forms of Christian art, it is the transcendent and dominant one; the Spirit of God itself formed it, in order to have pleasure in it."[6] But the beauty inherent in liturgy that he speaks of is only received and enacted when the worshipers seek God and God's kingdom. Otherwise, he observes, "the liturgy becomes a spectacle and a sin." Here van der Leeuw reminds us of the permanent tension between the holy and the beautiful articulated by the biblical prophets. So Amos must be heard: "Take away from me the noise of your songs; I will not listen to the melody of your harps. But let justice roll down like waters" (Amos 5:23-24).

Certainly the art of liturgy can indeed form us and give expression to our deepest desires and our hopes and fears. Texts and music that do not reach into these places of the human psyche and body do not serve the holiness of God and the sanctification of what is human very well. So the art must be "artless." The critique of "beautiful worship" that lacks reality and the practices of justice in the lives of the worshipers is, in part, an aesthetic/cultural concern. There is a mutually critical tension between the sanctity and the beauty of holiness. Perhaps we may begin to see the series of permanent tensions built into the fact that true Christian liturgy is eschatological and a symbolic art.

If the primary intention of liturgical celebration is participation in the mystery of God's holiness and the divine self-communication, then the beautiful is always at the service of the holy. This is part of what Aidan Kavanagh mentioned in claiming, "The liturgy thus is said to 'use' symbols and art only to the extent that it is itself artful symbol in the first instance."[7] In this sense 'beauty' does have to do with what is intrinsic to the various cultural forms employed, but always as viewed in light of their teleology in the divine beauty.

The Church as Eschatologically Gifted

I recall reading John Meagher's *The Gathering of the Ungifted*.[8] It was, in part, a prophetic critique of the church's forms of dishonesty about itself. The tensions exist not only between the holiness of God and the beautiful within the liturgy, but within the lives of those who gather to worship, between those "gifted" with faith and those who are not. At the same time, we cannot deny the eschatology implied when, as Paul speaks of the church in the Corinthian letters, we are empowered and graced *in* the gathering. We may not discern the gifts in any one standard manner. In fact, the gifts may be systematically abused and suppressed. But at the heart of gathering for the worship of God is the mystery of baptism; of having been called together by the presence of holiness, however obscurely, which is not the sum of our piety. In the very act of gathering to sing, to listen, to pray, and to eat and drink, the assembly must be gifted. This is the point of invoking the Holy

Spirit. So when singers, preachers, servers, celebrants, givers of hospitality, and others engage in prompting the assembly, there is openness to the gifts of God. These are gifts that differ, now brought together in this particular event, never yet enacted with just these particular contextual dynamics. Each gathering is marked by the cry, "Veni, Creator Spiritus," even if no one knows Latin. And the assembly, though it be the same "ungifted" people, are not the same as when they have gathered before: not only have their lives shifted, however imperceptibly, but each gathering in the name of Jesus is a new opening to God.

We must speak of the art of celebration as both engendering and requiring the gifts of God's people brought together. This is why we keep praying that next Sunday's liturgy will bring expectancy that the texts, the symbols, and the ritual actions will speak to us. The promise of the art of liturgy over time is that, in singing a new song to the Lord, God will reveal some new aspect of our lives in light of God's future for the world. Fred Pratt Green, the British Methodist hymn writer, says this eloquently: "How often, making music, we have found a new dimension in the world of sound, as worship moved us to a more profound Alleluia!"[9]

So, despite ourselves, the gathering opens us to the possibility anew of authentic adoration, however mixed our motives may be. "Many members, one body; many gifts, one spirit" is a reminder especially to those of us tempted in the face of indifference, to become technicians of the sacred or presumptive keepers of holiness.

Though there are specific leadership roles necessary in celebrating word and sacrament, the primary minister is the assembly—this very unlikely "ungifted" group when seen from a human point of view. We thus recognize that there is an art of celebration that may open us to, and also require of us, the gifts (charisms) given by the Holy Spirit. At the heart of liturgical worship are corporately shared symbolic forms into which we are invited, and by means of which we are formed and give expression to adoration, praise, truth-telling (whether lament or confession), supplication, and thanksgiving. As Godfrey Diekmann reminds us in chapter 2, "holiness is not something we get that leaks out of us during the week."[10] Rather, holiness is that power of perception and life for the world, of our relationship to neighbor and to God.

Our means of participation in doxology to God is not by abstract rules but embodied cultural forms that open up levels of reality they do not "contain" in themselves. The very means of singing, praying, and ritual enactment confer something beyond a sum of the various component parts of liturgy. There are rules as well, but these are part of the discipline enabling the arts to become "artless" in the Christian assembly. The early church knew about this. St. Basil, in preaching on the Psalms, refers to them as, "a bond of unity harmoniously drawing people to the symphony of one choir."[11] And St. John Chrysostom reports:

> The psalms which occurred just now in the office blended all voices together, and caused one single full harmonious chant to arise; young and old, rich and poor, women and men, slaves and free, all sang one single melody.... Together we make up a single choir in perfect equality of rights and of expression whereby earth imitates heaven.[12]

Centuries later we discover a text like this and reflect—so this is what we are meant for when we gather! Various graced capacities are given to those who lead and all who participate in the assembly. But these are for the enlivening of the whole body. Words, holy things, signs, actions with light and water: these remain waiting for a community to continually rediscover their eschatological lure and art. Of course, not all "harmonies" are the same—the question of cultural particularity and cultural "difference" still must be faced, as we discussed in Part 3.

All the arts employed in liturgy find their best being when they respond to the grace inherent in what God loves so much about heaven and earth—its created and creative otherness. Authentic liturgy constitutes these into ever fresh unities. When the *doxa* of God is sought, the primary languages of our humanity are released, not as individual virtuosity, but as a consort of praise, thanksgiving, and intercession for the world. Christian liturgy in this sense can supply our common morphology—the shape of our common humanity when attracted to the glory and holiness of God. This is another way to speak of the future orientation of liturgy and to discern the theological import of its inherent eschatology.

Gathering to acknowledge the mystery of the Holy One, to confess truthfully, to listen for and to remember, and take to heart what God says and does in Jesus, goes beyond our cognitive assent to certain beliefs. Liturgy is not simply doctrine well dressed and ornamented. The truth revealed in such a gathering is truth in the form of music heard deeply enough to make us the music; stories told so well that we become part of the story—indeed, actors; prayers prayed with such integrity that we become prayerful; and meals celebrated so graciously that we are nourished and become ourselves bread for others. This is the supremely transforming art. It is the holiness of God that lures us, delights us, and, in time, transfigures the world before us. But like the Transfiguration Feast Day, it remains partly veiled, with difficult life in history still ahead down the mountain.

But the transforming power involves concrete work in the medium. There is space, sound, silence, the visual, the kinetic, and the concretely experiential perception of our worship. We must be discerners of those times in which the forms no longer work or are empty or fossilized. Thus, a new century gives us new realities to sing, and some older hymns turn out to have less sustaining power than a previous generation had judged. I recall a small rural church that had always sung, "Blessed Assurance, Jesus Is Mine" as their opening hymn. They knew it by heart. The day they first sang it in the communion rite, the phrase, "O what a foretaste of glory divine," became a moment of insight and connection with the meal. So the art of ever-new juxtaposition is ongoing, even in the humblest circumstances.

There is need for beauty in the concretely experimental dimensions of worship, but this cannot be judged solely on artistic grounds. This is because of the three levels of participation I mentioned previously: at the level of the rites, with the people *as* church, and in the saving reality of the Paschal mystery itself. These are interrelated levels: the aesthetic phenomena of the rites, in and through the rites as the "people of God," and in union with the grace and mercy of God through Christ in the Spirit. It is, once again, the beauty of divine holiness, regarded eschatologically, that is at the heart of authentic liturgical participation. Every song, every prayer, every act of washing, eating, and drinking together, is eschatological—that is, God intends it to point toward completion in the fullness of time.

All this takes time and discipline. The German phrase has it: *Gabe und Aufgabe*—task as well as gift. The task and the gift of every liturgical assembly is to become an artful symbol of the church in communion and dialogue with God. Here all the various arts find their origin and their true end in the love and glory of God.

The Aesthetics of the Holy

Christian liturgy in its whole range—from rites of initiation, the Eucharist, daily offices, the rites of passage and pastoral offices, and the cycles of time (temporal and sanctoral)—possesses formative and expressive power for human imagination, emotion, thought, and volition. This power is for good or for ill. When liturgy is thoughtlessly performed, without affection and life-connection, it will far less awaken us to the realities of biblical faith much less to the holy things signified. At its worst, Christian liturgy has formed communities in deep hatred, as against the Jews, or has created and sustained social indifference and privatization of faith. But this is not inherent in the aesthetics of liturgical celebration. Respect for the aesthetic power and cultural embeddedness of language can liberate the multiple ranges of meaning accumulated in the primary symbols, sign-actions, and the texts. Rediscovery of the deep humanity of the sacraments in our own time of reform and renewal requires attentiveness to the permanent tension of which we have spoken. We can discern when liturgies violate the glory of God. Here the new "literalisms" born of various ideologies simply cannot serve as our framework of interpretation for the polysemantic character of liturgical action. The library called the Holy Bible presents us with too much richness for literalist reduction to help us. Attending to this very richness and to the complexity of symbol in relation to suffering and hope can inform a liberating style of celebration. The continual juxtaposition of the readings with song, variable prayers, and the fixed and variable structures of symbol and sacramental action is generative of ever-fresh insight.

Classical definitions of liturgy speak of the glorification of God and the sanctification of our humanity. This may be best understood as a simultaneous ongoing process. For only when the art of liturgy simultaneously takes us into the mystery of God's own being and action *and* into the depths of our humanity will its holiness be revealed. If Jesus Christ is by virtue of the animating power of God's Holy Spirit, at the center of our assemblies, then the image of the humanity of God "at full stretch" is always before us. Healing, reconciling, feeding, in prophetic cries, in weeping over Jerusalem or Lazarus, or in arms outstretched in blessing and forgiveness, this offer of grace is extended. At the heart of God's mercy, justice, and love is the free offer to us of our own true humanity. This is what St. Irenaeus meant in claiming that the glory of God is the living human being.

Such a range of images and passion returns us again to the Psalms. They are the artless songs of faith stretching toward the God who is enthroned upon the praises of Israel. They cry out again and again with our pathos, our longings, our laments, our angers, our anxieties, our joys, and our hopes. They are acoustic metaphors, if you will, for the formative and expressive power of Christian liturgy. Thus when our songs are reduced to the pleasant, the comfortable, the domesticated, or the pompously self-serving, the emotional reach of the liturgy is diminished and the aesthetic range dulled. When the words we preach and pray are dull or unctious, and the style of presiding or the modes of participation are perfunctory, then the power of the liturgy to awaken us to awe, wonder, and joy is diminished. Why do we settle for so little when so much has been promised in the eschatological art? When the texts we sing and pray, the style of common participation in ritual actions, and the primary symbols are resonant with the mystery proclaimed and signified, then the power of liturgy to reach our depths and transform lives will become clear once again.

The art of it all may be summed up: Christian liturgy is symbolic, parabolic, and metaphoric. It is an epiphany of the divine self-communication in and through the created order's sensible signs. Thus the arts that serve, the art of common prayer, and ritual action must lead to sharing what theology cannot finally explain in rational categories. It is for liturgy to allow us to apprehend in wonder, gratitude, and adoration what theology tries to say is holy. St. Augustine reminded us long ago that when we receive the Eucharist, it is our own mystery we receive.

Like Jesus' own parables, good liturgy disturbs, breaks open, and discloses a new world. The aesthetic—that is, the perceptual power—of liturgy pulls together, even "throws together" (*symbolein*) words, signs, and acts to reveal. Liturgy is metaphoric—it carries us across the border of our own consciousness, across the border of our ordinary common-sense world of cause and effect. It is epiphanic: a shining-forth of what the eye does not yet see. In these ways liturgy has aesthetic range, and this has to do with the well-formed, the beautiful, and the sensate activities of how we come to know God through the created order. All of these artful features of liturgical celebration led Roman Guardini to define Christian liturgy as "Holy Play"—a wondrous set of improvisations on the *cantus firmus:* the song of creation, incarnation, resurrection, and consummation. This is hidden in every "Glory to God in the highest," and is made explicit in "Maranatha." Advent discerns the end and thus becomes an ever-new beginning: "Come, O Come, Emmanuel."

Beauty and Holiness: A Permanent Tension

The symbolic value and the beauty of various elements of Christian liturgy derive from the mystery of the events celebrated in, with, and through Jesus Christ. These claims are based on the faith that God has created all things and called them good, and has become incarnate in Jesus Christ, gathering a historical community that is always culturally specific for worship, and service in the world of human history. Speaking theologically, the art of liturgy is thus grounded in the doctrines of creation, incarnation, and redemption. All things are rendered holy by virtue of the creative and the redemptive work of God. All things are to be referred to God, and thus brought to expression in sight, sound, gesture, and word. Here liturgical worship respects the difference between Creator and creature, employing the things of earth to refer to and to invoke the glory of God. But we will miss all this unless a fundamental sensibility oriented to the divine source of all created things is taught and sustained.

But there is also a permanent tension involved in the use of material forms and objects, and in the domain of the human senses. This is behind the suspicion of human imaginative power and of human art expressed in fear of idolatry. Are human beings in full harmony with the created order? Is any human community or culture congruent with a fully transformed world? These questions remind us of why all liturgical celebrations remain "east of Eden" and captive to the limits of human cultural codes and perception. Whatever significant form is realized in liturgical celebration, we still "see through a glass darkly." Ultimately all expressive forms negotiate between the symbol-breaking iconoclasm of the cross and the symbol-enriching glory of creation and resurrection. The art of liturgy must therefore always point to an eschatological self-critique of its own forms and energies.

The question of liturgical style is not only a matter of human technique. God knows we sometimes attempt this by producing "effects" by the manipulation of lighting, more tremulo or sound on the organ, and the volume on the guitar or voice. But the dynamism of authentic liturgical celebration is just the opposite of such manipulation of human response—of such magic. It is the opening up of the interrelations between the holy and the human, the rendering vulnerable toward God of our self-protective (or self-destructive) energies. This opening is itself a matter of attentiveness to form and matter and to the whole environment of the assembly's worship. Each unit and subrite invites a specific quality appropriate to the nature of the whole and its human contexts. Together with integrity of materials and the aesthetic range and power of the forms, such dispositions are integral to the artful symbolism itself. Leaders and the assembly share mutual responsibility and accountability for the art of liturgy well prayed.

The aesthetics of liturgy faces us with another tension. For if what I have said is true, we must attend to the specifics of cultural ethos in the community. So new emphasis is rightly placed on the modes of expression indigenous to the social/cultural milieu of the people gathered. If liturgy is to be divine/human interaction, the modes of appropriating and sharing the mystery in and through language, symbol, and song must be the people's. The aesthetics of liturgy demand that we know and respect differences between ethnic backgrounds and cultural histories. At the same time, the symbolic action of liturgy points to realities in tension with all inherited cultural assumptions and patterns of perception. The permanent tension is between the necessity of local cultural modes of communication and interpretation and what is common to Christian faith and life. Only by maintaining these tensions can we also assert the particularity of Christian faith and life against the assumptions of modern or "post-modern" or technological culture. There may be a matter of celebration that stems from the particular truth of the Paschal mystery itself. Is there such a way of enacting the word and sacrament that is ultimately the human reception of what God has done in creation and in Jesus Christ? Joseph Gelineau and others have spoken of the "paschal human in Christ"—a manner or style always enacted in particular cultural languages that nonetheless evidences, "both reserve and openness, respect and simplicity, confident joy... and true spontaneity."[13]

Liturgy belongs to the created world and thus is a human art, for the created order has its freedom as God's handiwork. The art of authentic liturgy concerns the intrinsic means, not simply the external decoration or ceremonial elaboration of the rites. Without such aesthetic considerations as we have named—quality of materials, appropriateness, proportionality, and integrity of performance within the liturgy—the whole may be lessened in symbolic power. Yet, lest we take delight only in the beautiful forms in the liturgy, and not discern the empowering grace of God to shape a community of faith engaged in the world, the final word must be eschatological. All artistic effort in service of worship is itself proleptic as well as participatory in God's creativity. The mystery of God in Christ celebrated is never exhausted or fully contained in any act of worship.

From time to time we are given to experience the vision of God's holiness and of the vision of creation fully restored. Some feasts are dedicated to this, but all—whether in a great Easter Vigil or in ordinary time—partake of it. The vision of a created order transformed and reconciled to the life of God should thus animate all our art. Where all that is creaturely will be permeated with light, dance, and song, there is the splendor of God's glory, there is Dante's *Paradiso*, the time/place of which John the Seer speaks: "a new heaven and a new earth." Insofar as we experience the prefigurement of that reality in particular times and places, the art of liturgical celebration becomes congruent with the holiness of God, and is lured by the beauty of the triune life of God, at once incarnate in human history, yet transcendent in glory beyond all created beings.[14]

Yet a final question remains: how does the beauty of God's holiness and righteousness turn us toward the world of our present history? Can the liturgical order of things in the communities of worship and service we know prepare us for the shape of things to come? Clues may be found in returning to Advent whose juxtapositions bring ending and beginning together.

C H A P T E R
14
ADVENT AND ESCHATON

"I am the Alpha and the Omega," says the Lord God, who is and who was and who is to come, the Almighty. . . . "See, I am making all things new." (Rev. 1:8; 21:5)

Christians mark the beginning of liturgical time by recalling the end of time. But beginning by remembering means that something has gone before: a witness, an intersection of images, a promise. The tensions we have uncovered and traced throughout these investigations are all prefigured in the Advent paradox of beginning with the ending, though not all see and hear this. Some churches obscure this by neglect or fear of being "liturgical." Others obscure Advent by allowing Christmas to smother it in sentiment. Many outside the church find other ways to spend time, skeptical of any such promises.

We gather about the book, the font, and the table to praise the Holy One of all creation and history by preparing for an advent yet to come. The yearning for a new advent of God in this terrifying and expectantly beautiful world is itself the fruit of having lived with God's earlier advent. Only because we have seen and heard what Christmas, Epiphany, and Easter/Pentecost celebrate, through the eyes and ears of earlier witnesses, do we have such a hope. Only because of the revealed vulnerability and power of God in the cross and empty tomb is there anything to recognize in the birth of a child and in human flesh bearing the glory of God. So we begin to mark time by remembering forward and backward.

The familiar tensions of Advent are not to be taken lightly, especially in our North American context where nearly everything Advent announces is against the grain. This "against the grain" is not simply because Christmas carols sound in our shopping malls from late November or before, nor is it simply because the churches feel the need to do something "dramatic" and different to be heard amidst the raucous selling voices and images. No, the tensions of Advent must be attended to because they sound and show the deepest human issues our culture hastens to avoid: suffering, the mystery of human existence itself, and the destiny of the world. Chief among these is the significance of time. For us all, inside and outside the churches, the matter of the quality of our lifetimes, and the haunting of all human projects by death, finitude, and social-political enmities persist.

Alerted now by what we have said about pathos and ethos, the modes of prayer, and the field of forces in which all Christian rites are celebrated, let us now turn to the prayers, readings, and songs of Advent. I want to hear and see, as if for the first time, what may be opened up for Christian liturgy and common life by the double advent of God.

The Prayers and Readings of Advent

How does Advent pray? What are its soundings? What, if anything, can it disclose to our age? We begin with some examples of the ancient form of seasonal collects—brief opening prayers at the beginning of the liturgy of the Word that contain central images from Scripture.[1] These images, as we shall see, are already juxtaposing the old and the new. More immediately in the actual liturgical context, they are juxtaposed with readings, hymns, and a range of nonverbal symbols. In turn, they await our "reading" of human concerns and hopes both "from" and "into" them.

But first, the texts. We begin with the contemporary rendition of the four collects from the *Book of Common Prayer.*[2] On the first Sunday of Advent, following the singing of an Advent hymn (often in procession) and the invoking of the trinitarian name of God, the community is led to pray:

> Almighty God, give us grace to cast away the works of darkness, and put on the armor of light, now in the time of this mortal life in which your Son Jesus Christ came to visit us in great humility; that in the last day, when he shall come again in his glorious majesty to judge both the living and the dead, we may rise to the life immortal; through him who lives and reigns with you and the Holy Spirit, one God, now and forever. Amen.[3]

The immediate petition for grace is placed in the context of human mortality. Drawn from the Pauline texts, the prayer reminds the assembly of Jesus' coming in humility. But the consequence of this petition—that which we intend as the result of divine grace—comes with an eschatological turn: that "in the last day" when judgment is brought to the dead and living, we will be raised to eternal life through Christ. Already, then, on the *first* Sunday we ask to be prepared by God for the *last day* by putting off works of destruction and putting on the "armor of light" in order to struggle with the forces of evil here and now. The wider import of the collect is not perceived until the assembly hears the readings, especially the reading from Romans 13:11-14 which exhorts, "let us put on the armor of light."

This is made even more explicit in the proper preface of the eucharistic prayer for Advent, which asks God to extend the faithfulness of the promise in Christ, or redemption from sin and death, that "when he shall come again in power and great triumph to judge the world, we may without shame or fear rejoice to behold his appearing."[4] This chain of texts is taken into the action of eating and drinking in Christ's holy meal. This way the juxtaposition of verbal image, symbol, and ritual act generate a new sense of the old words—for it is now *this* assembly, with all its own yearnings and hopes, which is being interpreted by the words.

The second Sunday's collect begins with the prophetic heralds of Christ's coming:

> Merciful God, who sent your messengers the prophets to preach repentance and prepare the way for our salvation; Give us grace to heed their warnings and forsake our sins, that we may greet with joy the coming of Jesus Christ our Redeemer; who lives and reigns with you and the Holy Spirit, one God, now and for ever. Amen.[5]

There is a studied ambiguity as to which "coming of Jesus Christ" we may be referring. The lectionary readings appointed for the second Sunday are from three prophetic scriptures. First, there is the prophecy of Isaiah 11 in year A, with Matthew's account of John the Baptist in chapter 3. Then there is the prophecy of Isaiah 40 in year B, with John the Baptist's appearance at the beginning of Mark's Gospel. And finally, from Baruch 5 or the prophecy of Malachi 3, there is the sending of the messenger to prepare the way in year C, or the account of John in Luke 3:1-6. To heed the warnings of the prophets reminds us that Jesus, who preached the kingdom of God, was preceded by the Baptist's warnings.

Are we to ponder the coming of Jesus in Bethlehem, or are we to look for his final victory over sin and death? The answer is yes to *both* questions. Thus the affection of joy at the heart of the consequence is found in greeting the Christ Child and in being greeted by Christ as redeemer and judge of all human history. Here the Advent preface in the eucharistic prayer pulls us forward and keeps the tension of "already" and "not yet" in the ritual action itself.

The third Sunday's collect begins starkly with the petition:

Stir up your power, O Lord, and with great might come among us; and, because we are sorely hindered by our sins, let your bountiful grace and mercy speedily help and deliver us; through Jesus Christ our Lord, to whom, with you and the Holy Spirit, be honor and glory, now and for ever. Amen.[6]

Here we pray that God will come into our midst and deliver us from the sins that imprison and hinder our acknowledgment of God. Here again we hear from the prophets. Isaiah in years A and B, and Zephaniah in year C. There is a special urgency in this collect, and yet there already opens here a vision of what God will bring out. The images from the first reading of Year A, Isaiah 35:1-10, are unmistakably of promise fulfilled:

The wilderness and the dry land shall be glad,
    the desert shall rejoice and blossom. . .
Then the eyes of the blind shall be opened,
    and the ears of the deaf unstopped;
then the lame shall leap like a deer,

and the tongue of the speechless sing for joy.
For waters shall break forth in the wilderness,
    and streams in the desert. . . .
And the ransomed of the LORD shall return,
    and come to Zion with singing;
      everlasting joy shall be upon their heads;
they shall obtain joy and gladness,
    and sorrow and sighing shall flee away. (Isa. 35: 1*a*, 5-6, 10)

The collect also anticipates the epistle reading from James 5: 8, which admonishes, "Strengthen your hearts, for the coming of the Lord is near."

On the fourth Sunday, the relation between the present and the future is once again in the foreground of the prayer:

Purify our conscience, Almighty God, by your daily visitation, that your Son Jesus Christ, at his coming, may find in us a mansion prepared for himself; who lives and reigns with you, in the unity of the Holy Spirit, one God, now and for ever. Amen. [7]

This links in varying ways with the readings; but especially noteworthy is the connection with the Gospel reading from Luke 1:26-28 in year B that depicts the angel visiting Mary. She prepares a home for the one to come.

In fact, Mary is the dominant figure in this Sunday's readings all three years: as she made room for the Word made flesh, so we too must prepare our hearts for his coming. This is a remarkable inversion of the farewell discourse of Jesus in which he gives the eschatological assurance of a home he is preparing: "In my Father's house there are many dwelling places" (John 14:2*a*). The "daily visit of God" is in our moral conscience, placed next to the future "at his coming we may be prepared." We are to make room for this Christ of whom the prophets speak: Isaiah, Micah, and 2 Samuel.

This is but a touchstone to the powerfully condensed theology that Advent prays and sings. Though the result of reflection on the web of prophecy placed in light of Jesus of Nazareth, these collects become "primary theology" in their being prayed and in the enactment of these images in the eucharistic meal. A complete reading, backward and forward, of all the lections appointed for the four Sundays of Advent would reveal, in rich variety, the tensive character of the double advent of God.

The Songs of Advent

If all we had in the "art" of Advent liturgy were the prayers, the readings, and the Holy Meal, we would have more than enough to discern how Christian liturgy utters with boldness and reticence the eschaton—the new heaven and earth of God. But the music of Advent carries us even further, for in its texts and musical forms, the hymns, psalms, and antiphons cause us to "pray twice" the wonder of the advent of God. A brief exploration of a few hymns will illustrate this.

We begin with Martin Luther's, "Savior of the Nations, Come." In Lutheran churches this is traditionally sung on the first Sunday in Advent, often preceded by J. S. Bach's chorale prelude on the same tune. The text is a plea, a variant on *Maranatha!*

> Savior of the nations, come;
> Virgin's Son, here make thy home!
> Marvel now, O heaven and earth,
> that the Lord chose such a birth.[8]

Immediately we sing of a universal Savior whose coming in the form of a vulnerable child is cause for wonderment. The plaintive melodic line, especially as harmonized by J. S. Bach, brings out the yearning and the marvel of the text. The second stanza echoes the Johannine theology of the Word made flesh:

> Not by human flesh and blood;
> by the Spirit of our God was the Word of God made flesh,
> woman's offspring, pure and fresh.

Two other classical Advent hymns deserve special mention, Charles Wesley's, "Come, Thou Long-Expected Jesus," and the ninth-century tune VENI EMMANUEL, "O Come, O Come, Emmanuel."

Wesley's text of 1744 summarizes the hopes of the prophets and the paradox of the double advent: "born a child and yet a King."

Here, too, is the echo of the eschatological cry of the *Maranatha*. The Christian assembly prays that the long-expected one should "from our fears and sins release us." And in the marvelous scope of God's liberating power, the messianic hope is to include "Israel's strength and consolation" as well as every nation and "all the earth" as well as the longing heart. Here is eschatology that comprehends the cosmos and each individual: "By thine own eternal spirit rule in all our hearts alone;/ by thine all sufficient merit, raise us to thy glorious throne." The traditional Welsh tune, HYFRYDOL, articulates these images with a wonderful triple rhythm and a fitting confident musical melodic and harmonic setting.

"O Come, O Come, Emmanuel" is based on a series of messianic names that are also images drawn from the prophets: Emmanuel, Wisdom, Adonai ("great Lord of might"), Root of Jesse, Key of David, Dayspring, and King of the Gentiles ("desire of nations"). The origins of the hymn text are found in eighth- and ninth-century antiphons sung at vespers during the Advent season. Thus not only is there a juxtaposition of names for God's messianic advent, but all of these call forth the entire range of prophetic contexts. Each stanza is musically set to a plainsong melody, followed by a refrain: "Rejoice! Rejoice! Emmanuel *shall* come to thee, O Israel." I emphasize the future fulfillment that is juxtaposed with the plaintive musical prayer of the church on behalf of the whole world. It is as if, in the ritual context of prayers, readings, and the messianic meal, this hymn permeates the whole, and sings the whole world's yearning.

These ancient images, already having accumulated the yearning of God's people through centuries of exile, suffering, and the rise and fall of political hopes, come to living utterance in every generation and in every cultural circumstance. That is, the "O Antiphons" sound out the ancient and ever-painfully fresh cry to God. Come to save your people, come to fulfill the ancient divine promises! The images themselves will be heard and construed in varying ways, and not all cultural contexts will find them equally compelling. Yet any community of faith that wishes to bring forward the message of the Law and the prophets focused in the narrative of Jesus Christ will recognize the reality these images articulate. This is the perennial cry of the earth to heaven. This is the utterly real art of those caught in the truth of absence and presence of God in the world.

While singing this hymn and hearing the echo of the primordial antiphons of Israel-Church-World requires having read and heard the prophets and the New Testament witness, this does not limit them to any single cultural interpretation. This brings to light once again a basic point undergirding this whole inquiry: we must live in a language received in order to speak a new word and to hear a new word from God. This was the burden of chapter 10.

One recent Catalonian hymn draws these themes out in a contemporary idiom, "Toda la tierra espera al Salvador. . . . " A lilting simple folk song sings out, "All earth is waiting to see the Promised One, / and open the furrows, the sowing of the Lord. / All the world, bound and struggling, seeks true liberty; / it cries out for justice and searches for the truth."[9] In yet another distinctive "aesthetic," this hymn goes on to sing of Isaiah's prophecy (40:3-5) about the virgin mother whose child should be "our brother" and "with him hope will blossom once more within our hearts." Here are the distinctive accents of liberation theology in the mode of sung prayer.

The Eschaton: Judgment and Hope

Only by dwelling with the living symbols of the biblical and Christian tradition can critical theological thought (secondary theology) arise. We should not be surprised that narratives of God seek, in every age and culture, a gathered community to actualize them. Stories are for *telling*. But these particular stories of prophecy and fulfillment cannot be fully alive until the actualities of human oppression, poverty, and all manner of human suffering are brought to them. For that was their original context in human pathos. This suggests how Advent can *fail*—indeed, how Christian liturgy can and has failed humanity. It fails when the Word is left without the sacramental action that manifests the fulfillment of hope, or sacraments "done" without a Word of prophecy, *and* both Word and sacrament without lamentation and real encounter with those whom the church is called to remember and serve before God.

To speak of the end of history is to go beyond the limits of language. While the larger biblical and Christian tradition has received and created a wide range of apocalyptic images for this, we finally confess that we do not know the day or the hour. This is what Advent speaks: "You do not know the hour or the day." That is, human beings cannot fathom the eschaton. And yet the image of an end to human history and to the physical world as we know it exercises a deep influence on our way of "reading" the world and human history. This is especially so in an age that has conceived its own self-destruction.

As when we consider our individual death or the death of the world, we are forced to read backward and forward, both the biblical stories and our lives. An awakened sense of *arche* (primordial origin) and *telos* (the future aims of our world) is indispensable to the worship of God, as we noted in chapter 12. In this sense the grammar of Advent is necessary for making any sense out of eschatological hope. This, in turn, is necessary to make any sense out of God's reign, already begun in Christ and yet to come.

Our discourse about the eschaton is like discourse about the resurrection. This is why Advent must live in the paradox of our temporality and our finite location in space and the whole created order. If we regard the resurrection as the manner in which Jesus is available to the fullness of God in the power of the Spirit, then this same mode of availability pertains to the gathered assembly of the church, and also to the ongoing historical world. Christ's liberating, transforming presence has a *bodily* availability, but no longer constituted by natural physicality. In short, the resurrected Christ is present as eschatological body. That is why the Advent prayers and some of its hymns plead that we may "rise with him." Invoking the presence of God is forever reoriented in light of the resurrection.

Advent signals the church's proclamation and sacramental enactment of the availability of God in Christ. The multiple ways in which Christ is present are acknowledged by the communal assembly. The eschaton is not metaphysical news from nowhere about a science-fiction event to come; instead it is the state of being caught up in what God has revealed of the glory of human-ity, and in the "city" promised to be. Advent then is as much about the resurrected presence of the crucified Jesus as it is about running to Bethlehem with the shepherds.

Yet paradoxically, Advent's texts, images, sounds, and ritual enactments cause us to see more significance in the birth of Mary's child than we could possibly have imagined with only the birth narratives, or only the life-story of Jesus of Nazareth.[10]

The great Lutheran chorale, forged in the music of J. S. Bach speaks this eloquently in Johann Rist's seventeenth-century text:

> This child, now weak in infancy,
> our confidence and joy shall be,
> the power of Satan breaking,
> our peace eternal making.[11]

If the central thesis of this book is true, that Christian liturgy, both as prayer and as rite, is eschatological, then we may say that Advent is a metaphor for the whole temporal cycle. Christian celebration, in all of its cultural variety, does not presume (that is, *theologically cannot presume*) upon the presence of God. Yet each gathering is an invoking, a confident remembering by giving thanks and praise, and a continuing pleading for the sake of the world that God's promises are so. Christ, raised from the dead, dies no more, and is made available to us by the power of God, through the Holy Spirit. Every gathering is oriented toward the *adventus* of God.[12]

We can hear this sounded in the great African American spiri-tuals such as, "My Lord, What a Morning" which sings of the trumpet sound, the sinner's moan, the Christian shout to all to, "wake the nations underground . . . when the stars begin to fall."[13] The unmistakable song from earth's pathos, from the particular context of slavery's oppression is here. But so is something more, something for every nation, for every context—especially neces-sary for the powerful and proud to hear: God is not mocked by the injustices of history. No one may grasp what existence is about until the limits of history and of all human power is viewed from the future of God's promises coming to fulfillment. This does not settle the question of whether this is to be fully realized in a social-political "thousand years." Our century has taught suspicion about too easy an identification of the reign of God with any one political realm. Yet, if Christ's double advent shatters all our images, it also works to protest against all unjust, dehumanizing political and social arrangements. It reminds us all, high or low, that God remains sovereign. Even in the desperation of our experience of the divine absence, the memory is pregnant with hope.

A Final Song of Advent's Art

In the Western churches, both Roman Catholic and Protestant, another great chorale is sung in advent: "Wake, Awake, for Night Is Flying." Written in the midst of the terrible plague of 1599 in Westphalia by Philipp Nicolai, himself tending the dying, it takes up the image of the coming bridegroom from Matthew 25:1-13. It juxtaposes this eschatological parable with the watchmen on the walls in Isaiah 52, and the enormous images from the Apocalypse of St. John.

> Wake, awake, for night is flying;
> the watchmen on the heights are crying:
> Awake, Jerusalem, at last!
> Midnight hears the welcome voices and at the thrilling cry rejoices;
> come forth, ye virgins, night is past.[14]

The shouts of "alleluia!" are sung by those who go to the marriage feast, the messianic banquet. The art of this text releases the full, polyvalent symbolism of the Eucharist as eschaton present in the meal. Thus the second stanza is Zion's rejoicing in *hearing* the watchmen's song, and in *seeing* that "Her Star is risen; her Light is come."

In the final stanza we hear what this study dimly points toward:

> Nor eye hath seen, nor ear hath yet attained to hear
> What there is ours; but we rejoice and
> Sing to thee our hymn of joy eternally.

This is where the song of heaven and the cry of earth, the saints' and angels' prayers for our sharp pain and the songs of the church conjoin. Here is where heaven and earth meet in the choir immortal. The images of lamentation and the reality of human injustice, all our kingdoms of death, sounded earlier in the apocalypse of St. John, now are foregathered. The great unashamed nuptial *eros* is fully present, reminding the church of the allegorical reading of the love poetry of the Song of Solomon that flows between the people of God and the messiah.

There is after all, the permanent tension and paradox of Christian liturgy that we neglect to our peril, a "fittingness." The incarnate divine life in human flesh is God's supreme art. It fits the human condition because God's power is hidden in vulnerable flesh. Only such an eschatological art can make us, in all our confusion and forgetfulness, *present* to God.

Christian doctrinal theology seeks to fix the meaning and truth of all that Advent activates. So theologians speak of God's having acted once and for all in Jesus Christ, and then must find some theoretical way to account for how the present church can appropriate such a saving truth. Some theologies have focused on the authority of the church and the power of the sacraments to preserve and to communicate what Christ said and did. Other traditions, principally Protestant, have focused on the power of the preached Word of God to present and effect the saving reality of Christ, while Pentecostals stress the power of the Holy Spirit in present experience.

Whatever their strengths, these approaches suffer three difficulties. First, if what Jesus said and did is the basis for our access to his presence, then we must begin with the interaction of Word *and* sacrament in the Spirit—the interanimation of narrative and bodily action. It is the whole person and work of Christ that is presented by the liturgy, and therefore the texts of prayers, creeds, hymns, readings, and sermons, when conjoined fully with the continuation of his initial eating and drinking, his forgiving and healing, Christ's inviting and anointing us and breathing Holy Spirit, are crucial. The performative force of the narrative of what he said and did is conjoined with the bodily reception of his life under ordinary signs of earth—wine, bread, water, and oil.

The second difficulty is the too simple account of time: past, present, and future. Discursive theology of Christian doctrine tends to speak of the meaning of "past" events as being discontinuous with the present appropriation of them, and of the future as inaccessible. But the celebration of Advent renders such a literalist, chronological account of time improbable. Rather, we must think *from* the future toward the present in light of the past. But the simultaneity of Christ's becoming present as infant Redeemer who is the world's Judge breaks open our chronology. The babe whose cradle, cross, and tomb are forever fused in his resurrection body reverses and shatters our timekeeping.

This Advent paradox speaks as though the crisis of a future-depicted eschaton were already here. The present action of God is now. If salvation is truly drawing close, and we are to prepare, then we are to prepare for the double advent. Rather, the advent of God is both *from* the past, gathering up all the Law and the prophets and the nativity and the death, and from the future, coming to us *from* certainty of God's promised reign over the whole of the created order, both heaven and earth. This is both narrative (story) and body (sacramental act) in one supreme presence: the resurrected Jesus Christ. But as another hymn of the more recent Advent/Christmas/Epiphany cycle sings: "Our God, heaven cannot hold him, nor earth sustain; heaven and earth shall flee away when he comes to reign."[15]

Yet the eschaton, while always pictured in human dramatic social images, such as we have seen in Revelation and earlier in the prophet's "Day of the Lord," cannot be fathomed except as a completion of what we have prayed for in, with, and through Jesus Christ.

The third difficulty is the misconstrual of the eschaton simply as a latter-day pyrotechnical display of God's power. Such an ending to human life and history—indeed to the whole created order—seems more calculated to satisfy *our* need for vengeance or retribution, than to do honor to what we know of God in the resurrection story. The church's liturgy, in some way is always Advent, is always *"Maranatha!,"* hovering between "Come, Lord!" and "The Lord is come!" This points toward that which is yet to be, but which must be continuous with what we know of God's self-giving.

Judgment is part of that self-giving vulnerability of God at the heart of the water bath and the holy meal we know called baptism and Eucharist. The judgment is the permanent crisis ushered by the Word of God made flesh. The judgment is for us who do *not* see and hear what of God is present under the signs of Christ: the narrative, the sign-actions, and the human beings with whom he most clearly identified—God's little ones. So abide these three: Word, Sacrament, and suffering human beings. And all three are Jesus Christ—the unity of his person and work. But no discernment is possible unless the Spirit he gives also conjoins with the uncreated Spirit of God permeating the created order. And these, the liturgy shows us, by invocation of the same, are one.

Advent, as we have noted, does not stand simply on its own. It is already a prophetic rereading of incarnation-death-resurrection. Advent is a kind of double helix that forces us, every liturgical year to consider the full mystery of God's self-communication backward and forward from the present. This is only possible because the resurrected one is made accessible to us by the God of promise, whose creative Spirit still hovers, illuminates, and empowers. We can still pray out of the world's terror and beauty, with Jesus, "Because the Holy Ghost over the bent/World broods with warm breast and with ah! bright wings."[16]

In the eschatological art faithfully celebrated, in every time and place and culture, human ears hear things that speak what no ear has yet heard, human eyes see things that manifest that which no eye has yet seen. But such seeing and hearing is faithful when what is prayed becomes a way of justice and mercy. The foretaste of glory divine nurtures the fruits of the Spirit in human history. God's promises hold the future, calling us to taste and see, to work and pray.

NOTES

Introduction

1. Schmemann, *Introduction to Liturgical Theology* (New York: St. Vladimir's Seminary Press, 1966).

2. Geoffrey Wainwright, *Doxology: The Praise of God in Worship, Doctrine, and Life* (New York: Oxford University Press, 1980).

3. David W. Fagerberg, *What Is Liturgical Theology?: A Study in Methodology* (Collegeville, Minn.; The Liturgical Press, A Pueblo Book, 1992).

4. An illuminating instance of this contrast between "primary" and "secondary" *liturgical* theology is found in Gordon W. Lathrop, *Holy Things: A Liturgical Theology* (Minneapolis: Fortress Press, 1992), Parts 1 and 2.

Part One: Liturgy and Theology
1. Human Pathos and Divine Ethos

1. Annie Dillard, *Holy the Firm* (New York: Harper & Row, 1984), p. 4.

2. Annie Dillard, *Teaching a Stone to Talk* (New York: Harper & Row, 1985), p. 40.

3. Ibid.

4. Theological interpretation of the sacraments, especially the Eucharist, as personal encounters with God-in-Christ emerged among Dutch theologians in the 1950s and 1960s and remains widely influential in sacramental and liturgical theology today. See Edward Schillebeeckx, *Christ the Sacrament of the Encounter with God* (New York: Sheed and Ward, 1963); "Transubstantiation, Transfinalization, Transignification," *Worship* 40 (1966): 324-38; and Piet Schoonenberg, "Presence and the Eucharistic Presence," *Cross Currents*, 17 (1967); 39-54. For a treatment of these two theologians' work, and that of others not available in English, see Joseph M. Powers, *Eucharistic Theology* (New York: The Seabury Press, 1967), pp. 111-79.

5. Jacques Ellul, *Hope in Time of Abandonment*, trans. C. Edward Hopkin (New York: The Seabury Press, 1973), p. 3.

6. Ibid., p. 8

7. Cited by Ellul, p. 191.

8. Ibid.

9. Gerard Manley Hopkins, "God's Grandeur" in *Poems of Gerard Manley Hopkins*, 3rd ed. (New York and London: Oxford University Press, 1948) p. 70.

10. Like many engaged in recent liturgical studies, I have been deeply influenced by developments in ritual theory and analysis. The best starting point may be found in Ronald L. Grimes, *Beginnings in Ritual Studies* (Washington, D.C.: University Press of America, 1982). The "performative" character of living liturgy is essential to any subsequent theological work on the basis of liturgy.

11. The contributions of feminist and liberation theologies to a rethinking of what is remembered and how the process of remembering takes place are critical here. The notion of retrieving forgotten or suppressed memories in the tradition, both biblical and liturgical, is restoring crucial dimensions of *anamnesis*.

12. Joseph Gelineau, *The Liturgy Today and Tomorrow* (New York: Paulist Press, 1978).

13. We will return to a detailed discussion of this in Part 3 of the book in the chapter 13 on beauty.

14. T. S. Eliot, "Choruses From *The Rock*" in *Complete Poems and Plays* (New York: Harcourt Brace Jovanovich, 1957), p. 96. Used by permission of Harcourt Brace Jovanovich and Faber & Faber Ltd.

15. See also Henri J. M. Nouwen, *The Living Reminder: Service and Prayer in Memory of Jesus Christ* (New York: The Seabury Press, 1977).

16. The lengthy Prayer of Thanksgiving (*anaphora*) praises God for all of creation proceeding from one image to another drawn from Genesis and the creation psalms, "set out heavens as a vault"; "appointed the sun in heaven to begin the day and the moon to begin the night"; "made water for drinking and cleansing, life-giving air for breathing in and out"; "fire for comfort and darkness"; "divided the ocean from the land"; "filled it with creatures small and great, tame and wild"; "you wove it a crown of varied plants and herbs, you beautified it with flowers and enriched it with seeds." The praise and thanksgiving continues through the Creation and the Fall of humankind as well as a recital of Old Testament history before arriving at the people's acclamation. See *Prayers of the Eucharist: Early and Reformed*. R. C. D. Jasper and G. J. Cuming, 2nd ed. (New York: Oxford University Press, 1980), pp. 70-79.

17. This is my conflation of the style and some themes in the Jewish *berakah* formula, a pattern of prayer that lies behind much of the early Christian prayers of thanksgiving.

18. *Didache*, chapter 9, 1-4, *The Eucharist of the Early Christians*, by Willy Rordorf et al., trans. Matthew J. O'Connell (New York: Pueblo Publishing, 1978), p. 2.

19. Johannes Metz with Karl Rahner, *The Courage to Pray* (New York: Crossroad, 1981), p. 18.

20. See especially Roberta Bondi, *To Love As God Loves: Conversations with the Early Church* (Philadelphia: Fortress Press, 1987).

21. Huub Oosterhuis, *Your Word Is Near*, trans. by N. D. Smith (Paramus, N.J.: Paulist-Newman, 1973).

22. The meaning of *anamnesis* ("remembrance" or "memory") in the Pauline and Lukan accounts of the Last Supper has been an ongoing inquiry and debate,

sparked especially by the controversial theses of Joachim Jeremias. See his, *Eucharistic Words of Jesus* (Philadelphia: Fortress Press, 1966), pp. 237-55; Louis Bouyer, *Eucharist: Theology and Spirituality of the Eucharistic Prayer* (Notre Dame, Ind.: University of Notre Dame Press, 1968), pp. 103-5; Xavier Léon-Dufour, *Sharing the Eucharistic Bread: The Witness of the New Testament* (Paramus, N.J.: Paulist Press, 1987), pp. 102-16; and William R. Crockett, *Eucharist: Symbol of Transformation* (New York: Pueblo Publishing, 1989), pp. 21-28.

23. "Liturgy of St. James," from *Prayers of the Eucharist: Early and Reformed*, 2nd ed., R. C. D. Jasper and G. J. Cuming (London: Collins, 1975), p. 60.

24. Godfrey Diekmann, *Personal Prayer and the Liturgy* (London: Geoffrey Chapman, 1971), p. 62.

25. For further reflection on consumerism's impact upon liturgy, see James L. Empereur and Christopher G. Kiesling, *The Liturgy That Does Justice* (Collegeville, Minn.: Michael Glazier, 1990), pp. 231-46.

26. This is drawn from interviews conducted by the Georgetown Center for Liturgical Study of fifteen Roman Catholic parishes in the United States in the late 1980s. See *The Awakening Church*, ed. Lawrence Madden, S.J. (Collegeville, Minn.: The Liturgical Press, 1991).

2. Dogma and Doxa

1. I heard this question over twenty years ago at a Lutheran worship conference held in Minneapolis under the title, "Good News in Action." The theologian-prophet, Joseph Sittler, of blessed memory, delivered a keynote address entitled "Dogma and Doxa." This address, along with other lectures was later published in *Worship: Good News in Action*, ed. Mandus A. Egge (Minneapolis: Augsburg, 1973).

2. Joseph Sittler, "Dogma and Doxa," in *Worship: Good News in Action*, ed. Mandus A. Egge (Minneapolis: Augsburg Publishers, 1973), p. 23.

3. He goes on to criticize the tendency, both Protestant and Roman Catholic, to substitute right belief or right teaching for right worship as a loss of the proper ontological condition for theology. See *On Liturgical Theology* (New York: Pueblo Publishing Company, 1984), p. 82.

4. Prayer and liturgy (doxology) play a crucial role in Catherine Mowry LaCugna's effort to retrieve and revitalize the doctrine of the trinity for Western theology. See her *God For Us: The Trinity and Christian Life* (San Francisco: Harper Collins Publishers, 1991), especially chapters 4, 7, and 8. For a concise and reliable presentation of John Damascene's theory of *perichoresis* that includes attention to Syrian liturgy, see Yves Congar, *I Believe in the Holy Spirit*, vol. 3 (New York: The Seabury Press, 1983), pp. 36-43.

5. Systematic theologians are recovering the Hebrew concept of the *shekinah*— God's compassionate "dwelling" with the lost and suffering—in their efforts to reflect upon how God is present to humanity. See Jürgen Moltmann, *The Spirit of Life: A Universal Affirmation* (Minneapolis: Fortress Press, 1992), pp. 47-51; and Elizabeth A. Johnson, *She Who Is: The Mystery of God in Feminist Theological Discourse* (New York: Crossroad, 1992), pp. 85-86.

6. *The Elegies and the Songs and Sonnets of John Donne*, ed. Helen Gardner (Oxford: The Clarendon Press, 1965), p. 83.

7. Edward Schillebeeckx provides an illuminating presentation of the concept of "glory" in the Gospel of John that includes attention to the Spirit, baptism, and catechesis in *Christ: The Experience of Jesus as Lord* (New York: Crossroad, 1981), pp. 409-27.

8. Johannes Metz, *Courage to Pray* (New York: Crossroad, 1981), p. 24.

9. This is the reason for some form of practical sanctoral cycle.

10. Gerard Manley Hopkins, "As Kingfishers Catch Fire," in *Poems of Gerard Manley Hopkins*, 3rd ed. (New York and London: Oxford University Press, 1948), p. 95.

11. Julian of Norwich's famous line quoted four lines from the end of T. S. Eliot's "Four Quartets." In *Complete Poems and Plays* (New York: Harcourt, Brace, 1957).

3. The Eschatological Character of Worship

1. Geoffrey Wainwright, *Eucharist and Eschatology* (London: Epworth Press, 1971), p. 70.

2. The comparison of Eastern and Western liturgies is far more complex than this. See Alexander Schmemann, *Introduction to Liturgical Theology* (New York: St. Vladimir's Seminary Press, 1966), chapters 1-2.

3. See Wainwright, *Eucharist and Eschatology* (London: Epworth Press, 1971), note 258, p. 183.

4. Justin Martyr's "First Apology," trans. in Jasper and Cuming, *Prayers of the Eucharist* (London: Collins Publishers, 1975), p. 17.

5. *Epistle of Barnabas*, XV, 8-9, trans. in Kirsopp Lake, *Apostolic Fathers* (Cambridge: Harvard University Press, 1965), pp. 395-96. We note also the association of Sunday with the ascension of Jesus. Thus the concept of an octave between Sunday and Sunday gathers into itself a rhythm of death/resurrection/ascension moving from Sunday to Sunday.

6. A protracted debate known as the Quartodeciman controversy was resolved in the fourth century by declaring, "Never on any day other than the Lord's Day should the mystery of the Lord's resurrection from the dead be celebrated." (Eusebius, *The History of the Church*, v. 23.) A minority had argued that the Christian Pascha (Easter) should be celebrated according to the Jewish calendar, thus falling on different days in different years.

7. Wainwright, *Eucharist and Eschatology*, p. 77.

8. Kirsopp Lake, *The Apostolic Fathers*, p. 331.

9. Augustine, *Letters*, trans. Wilfrid Parson (New York: Fathers of the Church, 1951), p. 283.

10. John Chrysostom, trans. from "Opera Omnia" (Paris: Gume, 1834), I, p. 608, cited in James F. White, *Documents of Christian Worship* (Louisville: John Knox/Westminster Press, 1992), p. 30.

11. Considerable debate has raged over this point, beginning with Dom Gregory Dix's assertion that the fourth century saw an end to the original eschatological fervor of the church, and replaced it with an attempt at "historicizing" worship. See his *Shape of the Liturgy* (London: Dacre Press, 1945).

12. Justin Martyr, "First Apology," cited in White, p. 147.

13. Clement of Alexandria, "The Teacher," I, vi, 26; and J. F. White, *Documents of Christian Worship*, p. 148.

14. See the work of Hugh M. Riley, *Christian Initiation* (Washington, D.C.: Catholic University of America Press, 1974); and Edward Yarnold, *The Awe-inspiring Rites of Initiation*.

15. This is a Roman Catholic post-conciliar development. The Second Vatican Council called for a revised rite for baptism of adults that would restore the process and successive rites of the catechumenate. See *Rites of Christian Initiation of Adults*, Study Edition (Washington, D.C.: U.S. Catholic Conference, 1988).

16. Hans Schwarz, *On the Way to the Future* (Minneapolis: Augsburg, 1972), p. 166.

17. *A troparion* is a short sung prayer in verse found in Greek Orthodox liturgical offices like evening prayers related to a specific feast day.

18. The work on this service began in the mid-1970s , in light of significant ecumenical sharing with Lutherans, Episcopalians, Presbyterians, and Roman Catholic reforms. A trial liturgy appeared in 1978 and was soon widely distributed among United Methodist local churches. It is this liturgy, which became part of the official ritual of the denomination when approved by the General Conference of 1988 that adapted its incorporation into *The United Methodist Hymnal* (1989) and subsequently in the *Book of Worship* (1992).

19. A Service of Death and Resurrection, in *The United Methodist Book of Worship* (Nashville: The United Methodist Publishing House, 1992), p. 141.

20. Ibid., p. 142.

21. Ibid., p. 151. This passage from Ephesians 3 is used in the dismissal with blessing in the United Methodist Service of Death and Resurrection.

22. See especially Karl Barth's *Evangelical Theology: An Introduction*, trans. Grover Foley (New York: Holt, Rinehart & Winston, 1963), chapter 14.

4. Liturgy and Theology: Conversation with Barth

1. Alexander Schmemann , "Liturgy and Theology," *Greek Orthodox Theological Review*, vol. 17, no. 1 (Spring, 1972), p. 100. This remark by the Orthodox theologian Alexander Schmemann, of blessed memory, sets the stage for a conversation with Barth. While Barth does not make use of the ancient *lex orandi, lex credendi* as does Schmemann, I contend that the relation between prayer and theology that emerges is compatible with it.

2. G. E. Bromiley, *Introduction to the Theology of Karl Barth* (Grand Rapids: Wm. B. Eerdmans, 1979), p. 249.

3. For a fresh reading of Barth compatible with these pages, see George Huntsinger's *How to Read Karl Barth* (New York and London: Oxford University Press, 1992).

4. See Hans Urs von Balthasar's appreciation and critique in *The Theology of Karl Barth* (Garden City, N.Y.: Doubleday-Anchor, 1972).

5. Eberhard Busch, *Karl Barth*, trans. John Bowden (Philadelphia: Fortress Press, 1976), p. 235.

6. Ibid.

7. C. S. Lewis, *Letters to Malcolm: Chiefly on Prayer* (San Diego, New York, and London: Harcourt, Brace, Jovanovich, 1964), p. 5.

8. Karl Barth, *The Humanity of God* (Richmond: John Knox Press, 1960), p. 90.

9. Karl Barth, *Church Dogmatics* (Edinburgh: T. & T. Clark, 1936-39), I/1, pass.

10. Clear evidences of this are seen in his lectures on ethics and permeate the whole of the *Church Dogmatics*, surfacing explicitly in the Anselm book and especially again in the *Evangelical Theology: An Introduction*.

11. Karl Barth, *Evangelical Theology: An Introduction*, trans. G. Foley (New York: Holt, Rinehart, & Winston, 1963), p. 160.

12. Ibid., p. 163.

13. Ibid.

14. Ibid., p. 164.

15. See George Lindbeck's account of doctrine in *The Nature of Christian Doctrine* (Philadelphia: Westminster, 1984) for a proposal about how the doctrine may be so construed.

16. Karl Barth, *Church Dogmatics*, III/3, p. 268. John Berntsen first called these passages to my attention.

17. Ibid., p. 269.

18. Karl Barth, *Church Dogmatics*, IV/3, p. 93.

19. Karl Barth, *Church Dogmatics*, I/1, p. 244.

20. Karl Barth, *The Christian Life: Church Dogmatics*, 1 v. 14 "Lecture Fragments," trans. G. W. Bromiley (Grand Rapids: William B. Eerdmans, 1981), p. 86.

21. Ibid., p. 106.

22. Barth, *Church Dogmatics*, I/1, p. 23.

23. Barth, *Church Dogmatics*, IV/1, p. 758.

24. Barth, *The Christian Life*, p. 32.

25. Ibid., p. 102.

26. Karl Barth, *Prayer*, 2nd. ed. Ed. Don E. Saliers, from trans. of Sara F. Terrien (Philadelphia: Westminster Press, 1985), p. 33.

27. Karl Barth, *Ethics*, ed. Dietrich Braun, from trans. of Geoffrey W. Bromiley (New York: Seabury Press, 1981), p. 472.

28. Barth, Karl, *Church Dogmatics*, IV/3/2, p. 883.

29. Barth, *Ethics*, pp. 472-73.

30. Barth, *The Christian Life*, p. 269.

31. Marianne H. Micks, *The Future Present: The Phenomenon of Christian Worship* (New York: Seabury Press, 1970).

32. I am indebted to the Rev. Dr. John Berntsen, whose Ph.D. thesis at Emory focused on liturgical themes in Barth, for the shape of certain ideas and phrases in this section.

Part Two: Liturgy as Prayer
5. Praising, Thanking, Blessing

1. The notion of "canonized" memories displays a systemic ambiguity. On the one hand, religious tradition requires a determinate set of core remembrance. On the other hand, this is precisely what leads to suppression and distortion of memory. Here feminist, womanist, and a range of liberation theologies have called into question the way in which Christian liturgical tradition has been deaf to what is *not* heard in the texts scriptural and liturgical (prayers, hymns, etc.); and has been blind to what is *not* seen in the actual manner of celebration. See especially Marjorie Procter-Smith's *In Her Own Rite: Constructing Feminist Litur-*

gical Tradition (Nashville: Abingdon Press, 1990). For a more systematic historical study, see Elisabeth Schüssler Fiorenza's *In Memory of Her: A Feminist Theological Reconstruction of Christian Origins* (New York: Crossroad, 1983), which has become a foundational book. Elizabeth Johnson's *She Who Is: The Mystery of God in Feminist Theological Discourse* (New York: Crossroad, 1992) explores the systematic theological issues of reconstructing trinitarian doctrine of God.

2. See especially Aidan Kavanagh, *On Liturgical Theology* (New York: Pueblo Publishing Company, 1983) and Gordon Lathrop, *Holy Things: A Liturgical Theology* (Philadelphia: Fortress Press, 1993).

3. Geoffrey Wainwright, *Doxology: The Praise of God in Worship, Doctrine, and Life* (New York: Oxford University Press, 1980), p. 422.

4. David Steindl-Rast, *Gratefulness, The Heart of Prayer* (Paramus, N.J.: Paulist Press, 1984), p. 40.

5. Romano Guardini, *Prayer in Practice*, trans. Prince Leopold of Lowenstein-Wertheim (New York: Pantheon Books, 1957), p. 96.

6. A consistent theme over the years in the writings of Bernard Cooke has been the way in which sacramental liturgies provide the vision and values necessary for a development of human maturity that is salvific—the experience of grace—in the lives of Christians. See his *Sacraments and Sacramentality* (Mystic, Conn.: Twenty-Third Publications, 1983), and *Reconciled Sinners: Healing Human Brokenness* (Twenty-Third Publications, 1986), but also his early book, *Christian Sacraments and Christian Personality* (New York: Holt, Rinehart, & Winston, 1965), pp. 22-23.

7. Guardini, *Prayer in Practice*, p. 98.

8. This point is often overlooked by those who treat the New Testament as a "rule-book" for worship. The liturgical assembly itself generated the literature over time. Doxological fragments and formulae throughout the Pauline letters, for example, and the literary pattern of the Apocalypse of St. John are cases in point. A recent study that makes this point clearly is *Theology as Thanksgiving: From Israel's Psalms to the Church's Eucharist*, by Harvey H. Guthrie, Jr. (New York: Seabury, 1981).

9. See Acts 2:4 ff. which sets forth a brief, schematic account of the early Jerusalem community, perhaps somewhat idealized in recollection.

10. *Didache,* chapter 9, 1-4. Trans. in *The Eucharist of the Early Christians,* Willy Rordorf et al. trans. Matthew J. O'Connell (New York: Pueblo Publishing Company, 1978), p. 2.

11. Ibid., p. 3.

12. See, for example, H. J. Gibbins, "The Problems of the Liturgical Section of the *Didache,*" *Journal of Theological Studies,* 36 (1935) pp. 383-86. A recent article of crucial import for a more technical understanding of the *Didache* is Thomas J. Talley's, "The Eucharist Prayer of the Ancient Church According to Recent Research: Results and Reflections," *Studia Liturgica* 11 (1976) pp. 138-57.

13. *Eucharistic Prayer of Hippolytus* (Washington: International Commission on English in the Liturgy, 1983). A few minor changes were made in this liturgical version published in *Holy Communion* (Nashville: Abingdon Press, 1987), p. 11. In the citations which follow, I am using this restored text now used on certain occasions in some United Methodist churches and in some ecumenical gatherings.

14. Ibid.

15. Augustine, Sermon 272.

16. See pp. 90-91.

17. Johannes Metz and Karl Rahner, *The Courage to Pray* (New York: Crossroad, 1981), p. 18.

18. Ibid., p. 20.

19. C. S. Lewis, *Reflections on the Psalms* (New York: Harcourt, Brace and Company 1958), p. 94.

20. Ibid., p. 95.

21. On the basis of his exhaustive analysis of the New Testament, Edward Schillebeeckx provides a synthesis of the concept of grace. See his *Christ: The Experience of Jesus as Lord*, pp. 463-538. Particularly helpful is his introductory treatment of the Hebrew concepts of *hesed* and *hanan*, and his presentation of sixteen principal, recurrent ways in which New Testament authors elaborate upon the fundamental grace of redemption. For a detailed study of grace (*charis*) in relation to the Spirit in the Letters of Paul, see James D. G. Dunn, *Jesus and the Spirit: A Study of the Religious and Charismatic Experience of Jesus and the First Christians as Reflected in the New Testament* (Philadelphia: Westminster Press, 1975), pp. 199-258.

22. Karl Barth, *Church Dogmatics,* IV/1 (Edinburgh: T. and T. Clark, 1956), p. 41.

23. Karl Barth, *Church Dogmatics,* II/1 (Edinburgh: T. and T. Clark, 1957), p. 655.

24. See Jonathan Edwards, *Treatise on the Religious Affections,* ed. John E. Smith, (New Haven: Yale University Press, 1968).

25. C. S. Lewis, *Reflections on the Psalms*, p. 96.

26. Gerard Manley Hopkins, "Pied Beauty" in *Poems of Gerard Manley Hopkins,* 3rd ed. (New York and London: Oxford University Press, 1948), p. 74.

27. See his *Gratefulness, The Heart of Prayer.*

28. Metz and Rahner, p. 24.

6. Invoking and Beseeching

1. From *The Art of Prayer: An Orthodox Anthology,* trans. E. Kadloubovsky and E. M. Palmer (London: Faber & Faber, 1951), p. 208.

2. Theodore W. Jennings, Jr., *Life as Worship: Prayer and Praise in Jesus' Name* (Grand Rapids: Wm. B. Eerdmans, 1982), p. 17. Jennings has in mind the thoughtless prayers that are disguised announcements or sermons, or with so much public praying that is simply addressed to ourselves. His point is to refocus on praying addressed to God. I am indebted to the vigor of his theological discussion in the following paragraphs.

3. See Ann Ulanov and Barry Ulanov, *Prayer As Primary Speech* (Atlanta: John Knox Press, 1982). Their approach is primarily psychological and psychoanalytical; yet it is informed with significant theological concerns. Especially important is their discussion of how all the unconscious desires may be part of the speech of prayer that nevertheless meet the "otherness" of the divine.

4. Jennings, *Life as Worship*, p. 26.

5. Ibid.

6. Ibid., p. 27.

7. See *The Confessions of St. Augustine.*

8. For a powerful discussion of the prayer of Jesus from the cross, see Jürgen Moltmann's *The Crucified God* (New York and San Francisco: Harper & Row, 1974), esp. 145-58.

9. Perhaps the most definitive Protestant work on Christian liturgy that begins with the distinctive character of prayer in Jesus' name is Peter Brunner's *Worship in the Name of Jesus*, by M. H. Bertram (Saint Louis and London: Concordia Publishing House, 1968). The more proximate parallel to my thinking in this section is found in Theodore Jennings' *Life as Worship.*

10. Jennings, *Life as Worship*, p. 35.

11. Walter Brueggemann, *Israel's Praise: Doxology Against Idolatry and Ideology* (Philadelphia: Fortress Press, 1987). See especially pages 39-53 and 123-9.

12. Brunner, *Worship in the Name of Jesus*, p. 200.

13. Ibid. p. 201. He also makes a strong eschatological case, fully congruent with my exposition in chapter 3, in the following paragraph: "It is especially our recognition of the end-time crisis, ushered in for us by the Word and the Lord's Supper, that compels our prayer. To be sure, God grants us his incarnation-presence in the words of the gospel and in Holy Communion; but we pray that this may become a gracious presence for us too. We pray that we may accept Him and His gifts in faith, and that we do not reject them impenitently. [Whoever] recognizes the critical aspect of the salvation-event in the proclamation of the Word and in Holy Communion is aware why he is praying and for what he is praying in this event" (p. 201).

14. R. C. D. Jasper and G. J. Cuming, *Prayers of the Eucharist: Early and Reformed*, 3rd ed. (New York: Pueblo Publishing Company, 1987), p. 23.

15. Ibid., p. 35.

16. Ibid., p. 71.

17. Hippolytus, *The Apostolic Tradition*, trans. Geoffrey J. Cuming, cited in James F. White, *Documents of Christian Worship: Descriptive and Interpretive Sources* (Louisville: Westminster/John Knox Press, 1992), p. 187.

18. Cyril of Jerusalem, *Mystagogical Catechesis*, trans. R. W. Church, cited in James F. White, *Documents*, p. 191. Here we notice a more detailed concentration on the elements and their transformation. This will eventually lead in time, with the diminished sense of the epicletic nature of the whole prayer-action, to preoccupation with the "consecratory moment." This is an extremely important question in the history of sacramental theology. For now my point is to show the invocatory force of the epiclesis.

19. Justin Martyr, *First Apology*, trans. Edward Rochie Hardy, cited in James F. White, *Documents of Christian Worship*, p. 147.

20. A fascinating, if not humorous note, occurs in the baptismal passage from Justin Martyr just cited: "Those who lead to the washing of the one who is to be washed call on [God by] this term only. For no one may give a proper name to the ineffable God, and if anyone should dare to say that there is one, he is hopelessly insane." Cited in James F. White, *Documents*, p. 147. Here we see again the remarkable combination of boldness and reticence!

21. The relative emphasis of the words of institution (*Verba*) in the Roman rites in contrast to the emphasis on the Spirit-invocation (*epiclesis*) in the orthodox churches is a complicated story. Suffice it to say at this point that, because of the gradual loss of pneumatology in the "primary theology" of the liturgy in the

medieval West, most Protestant traditions began with a diminished trinitarian understanding of the sacraments. However, every major liturgical reform of baptism and Eucharist among major Protestant bodies in the twentieth century has attempted to recover not only an "epiclesis" section of the eucharistic and baptismal prayers, but also a deepened appreciation for the Holy Spirit as the basis of the Christian assembly at prayer, proclamation, and sacramental celebration.

7. Lamenting and Confessing: Truthful Prayer

1. Miguel De Unamuno, *The Tragic Sense of Life*, trans. J. E. Crawford Flitch (New York: Dover Publications, 1954), p. 193.

2. Claus Westermann, *The Living Psalms*, trans. J. R. Porter (Grand Rapids: Wm. B. Eerdmans, 1989), p. 22.

3. Ibid., p. 23.

4. Claus Westermann, *Praise and Lament in the Psalms* (Atlanta: John Knox Press, 1981), p. 267.

5. This is found in 4 Esdras 3:20-36 at the end of his song. See Westermann, *Praise and Lament in the Psalms*, pp. 270-71.

6. David N. Power, *Worship: Culture and Theology* (Washington, D.C.: The Pastoral Press, 1990), p. 160. His chapter "When to Worship Is to Lament" has helped shape my approach to status and the possibility of lament in Christian worship.

7. Ibid., p. 165.

8. Ibid., pp. 166-70.

9. There are both traditional Elizabethan and contemporary versions of this. This version is found in *The United Methodist Book of Worship* (Nashville: The United Methodist Publishing House, 1992), p. 33.

8. Interceding: Remembering the World to God

1. *Liturgy of St. James* from *Prayers of the Eucharist: Early and Reformed*, R. C. D. Jasper and G. J. Cuming 3rd ed. (New York: Pueblo Publishing Company, 1987), p. 95.

2. Justin Martyr, "First Apology," cited in James F. White, *Documents of Christian Worship: Descriptive and Interpretive Sources* (Louisville: Westminster/John Knox Press, 1992), p. 148.

3. For the texts of these intercessions internal to the anaphorae of these rites, see R. C. D. Jasper and G. J. Cuming, *Prayers of the Eucharist: Early and Reformed*, 3rd ed. (Collegeville, Minn.: The Liturgical Press, 1987), esp. pp. 88-99, 114-23, and 129-34.

4. Leonel Mitchell, *Praying Shapes Believing* (Minneapolis: The Winston Press, A Seabury Book, 1985), p. 171.

5. See *The United Methodist Book of Worship*, (Nashville: The United Methodist Publishing House, 1992), p. 446.

6. *Book of Common Prayer* (New York: The Church Hymnal Corporation, 1979), p. 102. A study of the form and pattern of the suffrages in morning and evening

prayer yields more detailed confirmation of the line of reasoning I have taken in this chapter. They are rhetorically condensed because they are dialogical, either between the leader and the congregation, or done antiphonally between sections of the assembly. See *Book of Common Prayer*, pp. 97-98 and 121-22. Increasingly in the past twenty years, other Protestant traditions, including many "free church" congregations, have been gradually rediscovering these forms of intercessory prayer.

7. This was characteristic of the early treatises on the Lord's Prayer. See especially Tertullian's, Cyprian's, and Origen's works on prayer. I refer to these in my introduction to the second edition of Karl Barth's *Prayer* (Philadelphia: Westminster Press, 1984).

8. Karl Barth, *Evangelical Theology: An Introduction*, trans. G. Foley (New York: Holt, Rinehart, & Winston, 1963), p. 38.

Part Three: Liturgy in Context
9. Beyond the Text: The Symbolic Languages of Liturgy

1. Joseph Gelineau, *The Liturgy Today and Tomorrow*, trans. Dinah Livingstone (Paramus, N.J.: Paulist Press, 1978), pp. 98-99.

2. Lawrence A. Hoffman, *Beyond the Text: A Holistic Approach to Liturgy* (Bloomington: Indiana University Press, 1989), p. 8. In clarifying how liturgical studies have moved from its original concentration on philological and form-critical methods to the recent multi-disciplinary treatment of social/cultural and performative character, he explores a wide range of Jewish liturgical prayers and thematics. His concept of studying a "liturgical field" is closely related to my use of the phrase "field of force."

3. Ibid., p. 182.

4. See the "Constitution on the Sacred Liturgy" *Sacrosanctum Concilium* in *Documents on the Liturgy 1963-1979: Conciliar, Papal, and Curial Texts* (Collegeville, Minn.: The Liturgical Press, 1982), p. 8.

5. Two significant Roman Catholic studies are: "The Notre Dame Study of Roman Catholic Parishes" and the Georgetown Study of fifteen parishes reported in *The Awakening Church: Twenty-five Years of Liturgical Renewal*, ed. Lawrence J. Madden, S.J. (Collegeville, Minn.: The Liturgical Press, 1992.) The first section of this chapter includes data from my own research, taken from my essay in this volume. See pp. 69-82. My own recently concluded study of thirteen United Methodist churches also reveals important factors among Protestant congregations concerning participation and symbol.

6. "Constitution on the Sacred Liturgy," par. 14.

7. Mary Collins, *Worship: Renewal to Practice* (Washington, D.C.: The Pastoral Press, 1987), pp. 61-62.

8. Victor Turner, *The Forest of Symbols* (Ithaca: Cornell University Press, 1967), especially pp. 1-47; and "Forms of Symbolic Action: "Introduction," in *Forms of Symbolic Action*, ed. Robert F. Spender; *Proceedings of the 1969 Annual Meeting of the American Ethnological Society* (Seattle: University of Washington Press, 1969), pp. 3-25.

9. For an illuminating account of how we may approach the "things" of Christian liturgy, see Gordon W. Lathrop's *Holy Things: A Liturgical Theology* (Philadelphia: Fortress Press, 1933), especially pp. 87-138.

10. Gelineau, *Liturgy Today and Tommorrow*, p. 96.

11. The term *archaeology* is borrowed from the work of Paul Ricoeur, who has shown how religious symbols are layered with accumulated meanings through time. Yet living symbols also exhibit a "teleology" of meaning—opening toward new insight and future experience. See especially Paul Ricoeur, *The Symbolism of Evil*, trans. Emerson Buchanan (Boston: Beacon Press, 1967).

12. See Aidan Kavanagh, *Elements of Rite: A Handbook of Liturgical Style* (New York: Pueblo Publishing, 1982), esp. p. 44: "Not every prayer is liturgical, but rite always includes prayer without being reducible to this form of discourse alone."

13. A good example of the use of human sciences to analyze aspects of contemporary culture that renders liturgical participation difficult is found in Frank Senn's *Christian Worship and Its Cultural Setting* (Philadelphia: Fortress Press, 1982).

14. Lathrop, *Holy Things: A Liturgical Theology*.

15. Here I am indebted to the use of this concept in the pages of Ludwig Wittgenstein's *Philosophical Investigations*, trans. G. E. M. Anscombe (Oxford: Basil Blackwell, 1963) and elsewhere in his writings. While much more contemporary work on language and human culture has ensued, Wittgenstein's work remains a singularly illuminating source for the interpretation of liturgical discourses. See my essay, "Religious Affections and the Grammar of Prayer" in *The Grammar of the Heart*, ed. Richard H. Bell. (San Francisco: Harper & Row, 1988), pp. 188-205. Part I of that volume shows other uses of Wittgenstein.

10. The Liturgical "Canon" in Context

1. Paul W. Hoon, *The Integrity of Worship: Ecumenical and Pastoral Studies in Liturgical Theology* (Nashville: Abingdon Press, 1971).

2. Here I am indebted to the use of this phrase in the pages of Ludwig Wittgenstein's *Philosophical Investigations*, trans. G. E. M. Anscombe (Oxford: Basil Blackwell, 1963) and elsewhere in his thinking about language as itself embedded in cultural forms and the web of human activity.

3. The literature relevant to the so-called anthropology of Christian worship is vast. Among the most important works that have influenced my approach are: Mary Douglas, *Natural Symbols: Explorations in Cosmology* (New York: Pantheon Books, 1973); Louis Bouyer, *Rite and Man: Natural Sacredness and Christian Sacraments* (Notre Dame: University of Notre Dame Press, 1963); David N. Power, *Unsearchable Riches: The Symbolic Nature of Liturgy* (New York: Pueblo Publishing, 1984); *Made, Not Born*, The Murphy Center for Liturgical Research (Notre Dame: The University of Notre Dame Press, 1976); Victor Turner, *The Ritual Process* (New York: Cornell University Press, 1969); Anscar Chupungco, *Cultural Adaptation of the Liturgy* (Paramus, N.J.: Paulist Press, 1982); and Frank Senn, *Christian Worship and Its Cultural Setting* (Philadelphia: Fortress Press, 1983).

4. The terminology of "sign" has arisen in semiotics and in theories of signification used by many in liturgical studies today. See, for example, Emil J.

Lengeling, "Word, Image and Symbol in Liturgy," *Liturgisches Jahrbuch*, 30 (1980):4.

5. Justin Martyr, "Apology," trans. Bard Thompson in *Liturgies of the Western Church* (New York: Meridian Books, 1961), p. 9.

6. See for example *Environment and Art in Catholic Worship*. Bishop's Committee on the Liturgy (Washington: U.S. Catholic Conference Publications, 1978). An especially helpful book that employs the best insights from the past twenty-five years in church architecture is *Church Architecture: Building and Renovating for Christian Worship* by James F. White and Susan J. White (Nashville: Abingdon Press, 1988). This book contains a useful working bibliography on pp. 166-70.

7. See my essay, "The Integrity of Sung Prayer" in *Worship* 55, no. 4 (July, 1981): 290-303.

8. Adrien Nocent, "Gestures, Symbols, and Words in Present-Day Liturgy," in *Concilium* 132 no. 2 (1980).

9. See James F. White, *Introduction to Christian Worship*, 2nd ed. (Nashville: Abingdon Press, 1992).

10. Gordon W. Lathrop, *Holy Things: A Liturgical Theology* (Minneapolis: Fortress Press, 1993); see especially pp. 33-83.

11. Ibid., p. 33.

12. Ibid., p. 50.

13. Ibid., p. 52.

14. Ibid., p. 60.

15. Ibid., p. 222.

16. It is interesting to compare this approach with Robert J. Schreiter's mention of liturgy in *Constructing Local Theologies* (New York: Orbis Books, 1985); see especially pp. 26-27 and 112.

11. For the Sake of the World: Liturgy and Ethics

1. Dom Gregory Dix, *The Shape of the Liturgy* (London: Dacre Press, 1945), p. 741.

2. A classical treatment of this point is found in Max Kadushin's *Worship and Ethics*. For a vigorous exposition of the resources within biblical tradition of praise for the critique of idolatry, see Walter Bruggemann, *Israel's Praise: Doxology Against Idolatry and Ideology* (Philadelphia: Fortress Press, 1987).

3. In chapter 4 we saw the intrinsic connection between liturgy and ethics suggested in our reading of Karl Barth's approach to prayer and theology. What he does not pursue because of a suspicion of emphasizing human "religious" agency, our chapters on the modes of liturgical prayer did pursue. The line of reasoning followed in this chapter is, in this respect, not a characteristically Barthian line.

4. Here I continue to learn from Dietrich Bonhoeffer's *Life Together* (New York and Evanston: Harper and Bros., 1954) despite its own cultural limitations. Without the daily practices linking the disciplines of prayer, reading, listening, and mutual accountability, the Christian community suffers both loss of interior strength and social-ethical relevance.

5. Stanley Hauerwas, *Character and the Christian Life: A Study in Theological Ethics* (San Antonio: Trinity University Press, 1975), p. 210.

6. Ibid., p. 233.

7. Anthony Bloom, *Living Prayer* (Springfield, Ill.: Templegate Publishers, 1966), p. 123.

8. See Urban T. Holmes, III, "A Taxonomy of Contemporary Spirituality," in *Christians at Prayer*, ed. John Gallen, S. J. (Notre Dame : University of Notre Dame Press, 1977), pp. 26-45.

9. See especially Jonathan Edwards, *Treatise Concerning the Religious Affections*, ed. John E. Smith (New Haven: Yale University Press, 1959), esp. pp. 98-111.

10. See Hippolytus, *The Apostolic Tradition*, trans. Geoffrey J. Cuming.

11. Ironically, some of the so-called free churches, which began in protest of excessive hierarchy and the clerical domination of liturgy, have, especially in American religious culture, been dominated by the preacher's "personality" or charistmatic leadership, often to the suppression of the variety of gifts for worship and service in the community.

12. Text by Erik Routley, composed in 1966, found in several new hymnals, quoted from *The United Methodist Hymnal* (Nashville: The United Methodist Publishing House, 1989), p. 433.

13. James Gustafson, *Can Ethics Be Christian?* (Chicago : University of Chicago Press, 1975), p. 75.

12. Mystery, Suffering, and the Assembly's Art

1. Gerardus van der Leeuw, *Sacred and Profane Beauty: The Holy in Art*, trans. David E. Green (New York: Holt, Rinehart& Winston, 1963), p. 327.

2. See Rudolf Otto, *The Idea of the Holy*, trans. by John W. Harvey (London: Oxford University Press, 1926), pp. 1-41.

3. See especially Marjorie Procter-Smith, *In Her Own Rite: Constructing Feminist Liturgical Tradition* (Nashville: Abingdon Press, 1990) and Mary Collins, *Women At Prayer* (Paramus, N.J.: Paulist Press, 1987), alongside Elisabeth Schüssler-Fiorenza, *In Memory of Her: A Feminist Theological Reconstruction of Christian Origins* (New York: Crossroad, 1983).

4. An illuminating account of this process, linking the art of rhetoric to the formation of affections in the catechumens by Cyril of Jerusalem is found in "Affections and the Catechumenate," by John A. Berntsen, in *Worship* vol. 52, no. 3 (May 1978), pp. 194-210.

5. Julian N. Hartt, *A Christian Critique of American Culture* (New York: Scribner's , 1967), p. 353.

6. Karl Barth, *Church Dogmatics*, II/2, (Edinburgh: T. and T. Clark), p. 777.

7. Ibid., pp. 510-11.

8. Edgar Hennecke, *New Testament Apocrypha 2* (Louisville: Westminster Press, 1965), pp. 227-29.

9. Rudolf Otto, *Idea of the Holy*, p. 10.

10. Fred Pratt Green, "When in Our Music God Is Glorified," in *The United Methodist Hymnal*, (Nashville: The United Methodist Publishing House, 1989), p. 68.

11. Jean Corbon, *The Wellspring of Worship*, trans. Matthew J. O'Connell (Paramus, N.J.: Paulist Press, 1988).

12. Ibid., p. 161.

13. Ibid.

14. Ibid., p. 162.

15. See especially Walter F. Pitts' remarkable study of the power of African American worship patterns in slavery and beyond in *Old Ship of Zion: The Afro-Baptist Ritual in the African Diaspora* (New York: Oxford University Press, 1993), pp. 59-90. For a moving account of Russian Orthodox liturgical piety under the repressions of the former Soviet Union, see Anthony Ugolnik, *The Illuminating Icon* (Grand Rapids: Wm. B. Eerdmans Publishing, 1989), especially pp. 84-85.

16. Here Jürgen Moltmann's distinction between *Zukunft* (the "future") and *Adventus* (the coming of God toward us) makes sense. See *The Future of Creation* (Philadelphia: Fortress Press, 1979), p. 29.

17. "Arise, Shine Out, Your Light Has Come" by Brian Wren, in *The United Methodist Hymnal*, p. 725.

18. Charles Wesley, "Love Divine, All Loves Excelling" in The *United Methodist Hymnal*, p. 384.

13. The Beautiful and the Holy

1. Gerardus van der Leeuw, *Sacred and Profane Beauty: The Holy in Art*, trans. David E. Green (New York: Holt, Rinehart & Winston, 1963), p. 253.

2. Augsburg Confession, paragraph 7. Translation by Gordon Lathrop, Gordon W. Lathrop, *Holy Things: A Liturgical Theology* (Minneapolis: Fortress Press, 1993), p. 183.

3. Joseph Sittler, "Dogma and Doxa," in *Worship: Good News in Action*, ed. Mandus A. Egge (Minneapolis: Augsburg Publishers, 1973), p. 23.

4. Mary Mothersill, *Beauty Restored* (Oxford: The Clarendon Press, 1984), p. 423.

5. Several recent pastoral/liturgical studies have addressed this issue, focusing on the idea of the assembly as a "performing audience." Among them are Patrick W. Collins' two books, *More Than Meets the Eye* (Paramus, N.J.: Paulist Press, 1983) and *Bodying Forth: Aesthetic Liturgy* (New York, 1992). Janet R. Walton, *A Vital Connection* (Collegeville, Minn.: Michael Glazier, 1988). Her work highlights ways in which the graphic arts in particular serve the worship of God, encouraging a contemporary dialogue.

6. van der Leeuw, *Sacred and Profane Beauty:* The Holy in Art, p. 110.

7. Aidan Kavanagh, "The Politics of Symbol and Art," in *Symbol and Art in Worship*, ed. Luis Maldonado and David Power. *Concilium: Religion in the Eighties*, No. 132. (Edinburgh: T. and T. Clark; New York: The Seabury Press, 1980), p. 38.

8. John Meagher, *The Gathering of the Ungifted* (Paramus, N.J.: Paulist Press, 1972).

9. Fred Pratt Green "When In Our Music God is Glorified" found in *The United Methodist Hymnal* (Nashville: The United Methodist Publishing House, 1989), p. 68.

10. Godfrey Diekmann, *Personal Prayer and the Liturgy* (London: Geoffrey Chapman, 1971).

11. St. Basil, *Homilia in psalmum*, 1.2, *Patrologia Graeca*, vol. 29, p. 212.

12. St. John Chrysostom, *Homilia*, 5.2, in *Patrologia Graeca*, Vol. 63, 486-87, from Joseph Gelineau, *Voices and Instruments in Christian Worship: Principles, Laws,*

Applications, trans. Clifford Howell (Collegeville, Minn.: The Liturgical Press, 1978), p. 82.

13. Joseph Gelineau, *The Liturgy Today and Tomorrow,* trans. Dinah Livingstone (New York/Paramus: Paulist Press, 1978), p. 113.

14. See parallel material in my article "Liturgical Aesthetics" in *A Dictionary of Sacramental Theology,* ed. Peter Fink, S.J. (Collegeville, Minn.: Michael Glazier, 1990), pp. 30-39.

14. Advent and Eschaton

1. The term *collect* derives from the Latin *collecta,* designating a brief prayer form. It originally referred to the collecting of the petitions of the assembly into one short prayer. Collects occur at the conclusion of the intercessions in the classical rites, East and West, and also at the offertory. Here I restrict the discussion to the four Advent collects from the *Book of Common Prayer.* A close study of collects and "opening prayers" in other traditions for the Sundays of Advent yield different theological accents; however, the *theological point* of such prayers remains the same.

2. In some traditions, the collect is read by the entire congregation, especially in United Methodist and Presbyterian practice, while it is customary for a representative minister in the Episcopal, Lutheran, and Roman traditions to pray these collects on behalf of the whole assembly, which is standing.

3. *The Book of Common Prayer* (New York: The Church Hymnal Corporation and Seabury Press, 1977), p. 211.

4. The "proper preface" is a short insertion into the opening section of the eucharistic prayer highlighting the specific theological theme of a particular feast or season of the church year. In the *Book of Common Prayer* two of the four prayers (namely, canons A and B) are structured to receive a proper preface, while C and D are through-composed, belonging to another historical type of eucharistic prayer. Both types of prayers are found in nearly all Protestant twentieth-century reformed rites.

5. *Book of Common Prayer,* p. 211.

6. Ibid., p. 212.

7. Ibid.

8. This text is from *The United Methodist Hymnal* (Nashville: The United Methodist Publishing House, 1989), p. 214.

9. The *United Methodist Hymnal,* p. 210.

10. See especially the monumental work of Raymond Brown, *The Birth of the Messiah,* for an account of what is presupposed and proclaimed in the Gospels' birth narratives.

11. *The United Methodist Hymnal,* p. 223.

12. My indebtedness to the pages of Jürgen Moltmann should be obvious here. Of special import is *The Church in the Power of the Spirit* (San Francisco: Harper/Collins, 1991). See especially pp. 189-96 and his discussion of worship, pp. 261-74: "Understood as a messianic feast, the Christian service of worship is entirely determined by the history of God and by what takes place in it. The assembled community perceives anew the complete history of Christ, his giving himself up to death for the salvation of creation, and his glorification in the life

of God for creation's future. The messianic feast renews the remembrance of Christ and awakens hope for his kingdom" (p. 261).

13. *United Methodist Hymnal,* no. 719.

14. *United Methodist Hymnal,* no. 720. This is the translation of Catherine Winkworth. A vigorous alternative translation is found in the *Lutheran Book of Worship* (1978) and in *The Hymnal 1982* (New York: The Church Pension Fund, 1982), translation by Carl P. Daw, Jr.

"Sleepers, wake!" A voice astounds us,
the shout of rampart-guards surrounds us:
"Awake, Jerusalem, arise!"
Midnight's peace their cry has broken,
their urgent summons clearly spoken:
"The time has come, O maidens wise!
Rise up, and give us light;
The Bridegroom is in sight. Alleluia!
Your lamps prepare and hasten there,
that you the wedding feast may share."

Zion hears the watchmen singing;
her heart with joyful hope is springing,
she wakes and hurries through the night.
Forth he comes, her Bridegroom glorious
in strength of grace, in truth victorious:
her star is risen, her light grows bright.
Now come, most worthy Lord,
God's Son, Incarnate Word, Alleluia!
We follow all and heed your call
to come into the banquet hall.

Lamb of God, the heavens adore you;
let saints and angels sing before you,
as harps and cymbals swell the sound.
Twelve great pearls, the city's portals:
through them we stream to join the immortals
as we with joy your throne surround.
No eye has known the sight,
no ear heard such delight: Alleluia!
Therefore we sing to greet our King;
forever let our praises ring.

15. "In the Bleak Midwinter," *United Methodist Hymnal,* no. 221.

16. "God's Grandeur," in Gerard Manley Hopkins, *Poems of Gerard Manley Hopkins,* 3rd ed. (New York and London: Oxford University Press, 1948), p. 70.

A Select Bibliography

Adam, Adolf. *The Liturgical Year*. New York: Pueblo Publishing Company, 1981.
Baldovin, John. *City, Church and Renewal*. Washington, D.C.: The Pastoral Press, 1991.
Barth, Karl. *Evangelical Theology: An Introduction*. Translated by Grover Foley. New York: Holt, Rinehart & Winston, 1963.
Bouyer, Louis. *Eucharist*. Notre Dame: University of Notre Dame Press, 1968.
———. *Rite and Man*. Notre Dame: University of Notre Dame Press, 1963.
Brueggemann, Walter. *Israel's Praise: Doxology Against Idolatry and Ideology*. Philadelphia: Fortress Press, 1987.
Brunner, Peter. *Worship in the Name of Jesus*. Translated by M. H. Bertram. St. Louis: Concordia Publishing House, 1968.
Casel, Odo. *The Mystery of Christian Worship and Other Writings*. Maryland: The Newman Press, 1962.
Childs, Brevard. *Memory and Tradition in Israel*. London: SCM Press, 1962.
Chupungco, Anscar. *Cultural Adaptation of the Liturgy*. New York: Paulist Press, 1982.
Collins, Mary. *Worship: Renewal to Practice*. Washington, D.C.: The Pastoral Press, 1987.
Collins, Patrick W. *Bodying Forth: Aesthetic Liturgy*. New York, Mawway, NJ: Paulist Press, 1992.
Cooke, Bernard. *Sacraments and Sacramentality*. Mystic, Conn.: Twenty-Third Publications, 1983.
Corbon, Jean. *The Wellspring of Worship*. New York: Paulist Press, 1988.
Crockett, William R. *Eucharist: Symbol of Transformation*. New York: Pueblo Publishing, 1989.
Cullmann, Oscar. *Early Christian Worship*. London: SCM Press Ltd., 1953.

Dix, Gregory. *The Shape of the Liturgy*. London: Dacre Press, 1945.

Douglas, Mary. *Natural Symbols*. New York: Random House, 1973.

Egge, Mandus A., ed. *Worship: Good News in Action*. Minneapolis: Augsburg, 1973.

Ellul, Jacques. *Hope in Time of Abandonment*. Translated by C. Edward Hopkin. New York: The Seabury Press, 1973.

Empereur, James L. and Christopher G. Kiesling. *The Liturgy That Does Justice*. Collegeville, Minn.: Michael Glazier, 1990.

Fagerberg, David W. *What Is Liturgical Theology? A Study in Methodology*. Collegeville, Minn.: A Pueblo Book, The Liturgical Press, 1992.

Fink, Peter, ed. *The New Dictionary of Sacramental Worship*. Collegeville, Minn.: A Michael Glazier Book, The Liturgical Press, 1990.

Gallen, John, ed. *Christians at Prayer*. Notre Dame: University of Notre Dame Press, 1977.

Gelineau, Joseph. *The Liturgy Today and Tomorrow*. Translated by Dinah Livingstone. New York/Paramus: Paulist Press, 1978.

Gelpi, Donald L. *Committed Worship: A Sacramental Theology for Converting Christians*, 2 vols. Collegeville, Minn.: Michael Glazier, 1993.

Grimes, Ronald L. *Beginnings in Ritual Studies*. Washington, D.C.: University Press of America, 1982.

Guthrie, Harvey H., Jr. *Theology as Thanksgiving: From Israel's Psalms to the Church's Eucharist*. New York: Seabury Press, 1981.

Hauerwas, Stanley. *Character and the Christian Life: A Study in Theological Ethics*. San Antonio: Trinity University Press, 1975.

Hoffman, Lawrence A. *Beyond the Text: A Holistic Approach to Liturgy*. Bloomington: Indiana University Press, 1978.

Hoon, Paul Waitman. *The Integrity of Worship: Ecumenical and Pastoral Studies in Liturgical Theology*. Nashville and New York: Abingdon Press, 1971.

Jasper, R. C. D., and Cuming, G. J. *Prayers of the Eucharist Early and Reformed*. London: Collins Publishers, 1975.

Jennings, Theodore W., Jr. *Life As Worship: Prayer and Praise in Jesus' Name*. Grand Rapids: William B. Eerdmans, 1982.

Johnson, Elizabeth A. *She Who Is: The Mystery of God in Feminist Theological Discourse*. New York: Crossroad, 1992.

Jones, Wainwright, and Yarnold, eds. *The Study of Liturgy*. New York: Oxford University Press, 1978.

Kavanagh, Aidan. *On Liturgical Theology*. New York: Pueblo Publishing Company, 1984.

———. *Elements of Rite: A Handbook of Liturgical Style*. New York: Pueblo Publishing Company, 1982.

———. "Response: Primary Theology and Liturgical Act," *Worship* 57 (1983): 321-24.

Keifer, Ralph A. "Liturgical Text as Primary Source for Eucharistic Theology." *Worship* 51 (1978): 186-196.

Kilmartin, Edward. *Christian Liturgy: Theology and Practice*. Kansas City: Sheed & Ward, 1988.

LaCuna, Mowry. *God For Us: The Trinity and Christian Life*. San Francisco: Harper Collins Publishers, 1991.

Lathrop, Gordon W. "A Rebirth of Images: On the Use of the Bible in Liturgy." *Worship* 58 (1984) 291-304.

————. *Holy Things: A Liturgical Theology*. Minneapolis: Fortress Press, 1993.

Madden, Lawrence J., S. J., ed. *The Awakening Church: Twenty-Five Years of Liturgical Renewal*. Collegeville, Minn.: The Liturgical Press, 1992. Martos, Joseph. *Doors to the Sacred*. New York: Image Books, 1982.

McDonnell, Kilian and George T. Montague. *Christian Initiation and Baptism in the Holy Spirit: Evidence from the First Eight Centuries*. Collegeville, Minn.: Michael Glazier, 1991.

Metz, Johannes and Karl Rahner. *The Courage to Pray*. New York: Crossroad, 1981.

Micks, Marianne H. *The Future Present: The Phenomenon of Christian Worship*. New York: The Seabury Press, 1970.

Mitchell, Leonel. *Praying Shapes Believing*. Minneapolis, Chicago, New York: The Winston Press, A Seabury Book, 1985.

The Murphy Center for Liturgical Research. *Made, Not Born*. Notre Dame: University of Notre Dame Press, 1976.

Pitts, Walter F. *Old Ship of Zion: The Afro-Baptist Ritual in the African Diaspora*. New York, Oxford: Oxford University Press, 1993.

Power, David N. *Unsearchable Riches: The Symbolic Nature of Liturgy*. New York: Pueblo Publishing Company, 1984.

————. *Worship: Culture and Theology*. Washington, D.C.: The Pastoral Press, 1990.

Power, David and Luis Maldonado, eds. *Liturgy and Human Passage*. New York: The Seabury Press, 1979.

Power, David and Herman Schmidt, eds. *Liturgical Experience of Faith*. New York: Herder & Herder, 1973.

Procter-Smith, Marjorie. *In Her Own Rite: Constructing Feminist Liturgical Tradition*. Nashville; Abingdon Press, 1990.

Rordorf, Willy. *The Eucharist of the Early Christians*. New York: Pueblo Publishing Company, 1978.

Saliers, Don E. *The Soul in Paraphrase*. New York: The Seabury Press, 1980. 2nd ed. Cleveland: OSL Publications, 1991.

————. "Prayer and the Doctrine of God in Contemporary Theology." *Interpretation* 30 (1980): 265-78.

————. *Worship and Spirituality*. Philadelphia: The Westminster Press, 1984.

Schillebeeckx, Edward. *Christ the Sacrament of the Encounter with God*. New York: Sheed & Ward, 1963.

Schmemann, Alexander. *For the Life of the World*. New York: St. Vladimir's Seminary Press, 1973.

————. *Introduction to Liturgical Theology*. New York: St. Vladimir's Seminary Press, 1966.

————. "Liturgy and Theology." *The Greek Orthodox Theological Review* 17 (1972): 86-100.

Schreiter, Robert J. *Constructing Local Theologies*. New York: Orbis Books, 1985.

Schwarz, Hans. *On the Way To the Future*. Minneapolis: Augsburg, 1972.

Searle, Mark, ed. *Sunday Morning: A Time for Worship*. Collegeville, Minn.: The Liturgical Press, 1982.

Seasoltz, R. Kevin, ed. *Living Bread, Saving Cup*. Collegeville, Minn.: The Liturgical Press, 1982.

Senn, Frank C. *Christian Worship and Its Cultural Setting*. Philadelphia: Fortress Press, 1983.

Shaughnessy, James D., ed. *The Roots of Ritual*. Grand Rapids: Eerdmans Publishing Company, 1973.

Taft, Robert, S.J. "Liturgy as Theology." *Worship* 56 (1982): 113-16.

———. *The Liturgy of the Hours in East and West: The Origins of the Divine Office and Its Meaning for Today*. Collegeville, Minn.: The Liturgical Press, 1986.

Talley, Thomas J. *The Origins of the Liturgical Year*. New York: Pueblo Publishing Company, 1986.

Thompson, Bard. *Liturgies of the Western Church*. Philadelphia: Fortress Press, 1961.

Turner, Victor, *The Ritual Process*. New York: Cornell University Press, 1969.

———. *The Forest of Symbols*. Ithaca: Cornell University Press, 1967.

Ugolnik, Anthony. *The Illuminating Icon*. Grand Rapids: William B. Eerdmans Publishing Company, 1989.

Ulanov, Ann and Barry. *Prayer As Primary Speech*. Atlanta: John Knox Press, 1982.

Vagaggini, Cyprian. *Theological Dimensions of the Liturgy*. Collegeville, Minn.: The Liturgical Press, 1976.

van der Leeuw, Gerardus. *Sacred and Profane Beauty: The Holy in Art*. Translated by David E. Green. New York: Holt, Rinehart & Winston, 1963.

von Allmen, J. J. *Worship: Its Theology and Practice*. New York: Oxford University Press, 1965.

Wainwright, Geoffrey. *Eucharist and Eschatology*. London: Epworth Press, 1971.

———. *Doxology: The Praise of God in Worship, Doctrine, and Life*. New York: Oxford University Press, 1980.

Westermann, Claus. *The Living Psalms*. Translated by J. R. Porter. Grand Rapids: William B. Eerdmans Publishing, 1982.

———. *Praise and Lamentation in the Psalms*. Atlanta: John Knox Press, 1981.

White, James F. *Introduction to Christian Worship*, rev. ed. Nashville: Abingdon Press, 1991.

———. *Sacraments as God's Self-Giving*. Nashville: Abingdon Press, 1983.

———. *Documents of Christian Worship: Descriptive and Interpretive Sources*. Louisville: Westminster/John Knox Press, 1992.

Willimon, William H. *The Service of God: How Worship and Ethics Are Related*. Nashville: Abingdon Press, 1983.

Wolterstorff, Nicholas. "Liturgy, Justice, and Holiness." *The Reformed Journal* 39, no. 12 (Dec. 1989): 12-20.

INDEX

AUTHORS

SUBJECTS

Printed in the United States
67513LVS00007B/67-69

9 780687 146932